RAGE COMICS

FFFFFFF
FFFFFFF
FFFFFF
FFFUU
UUUU
UUUU
UUUU
UUUU
UUUU

VOLOL. I

LE CONTENT

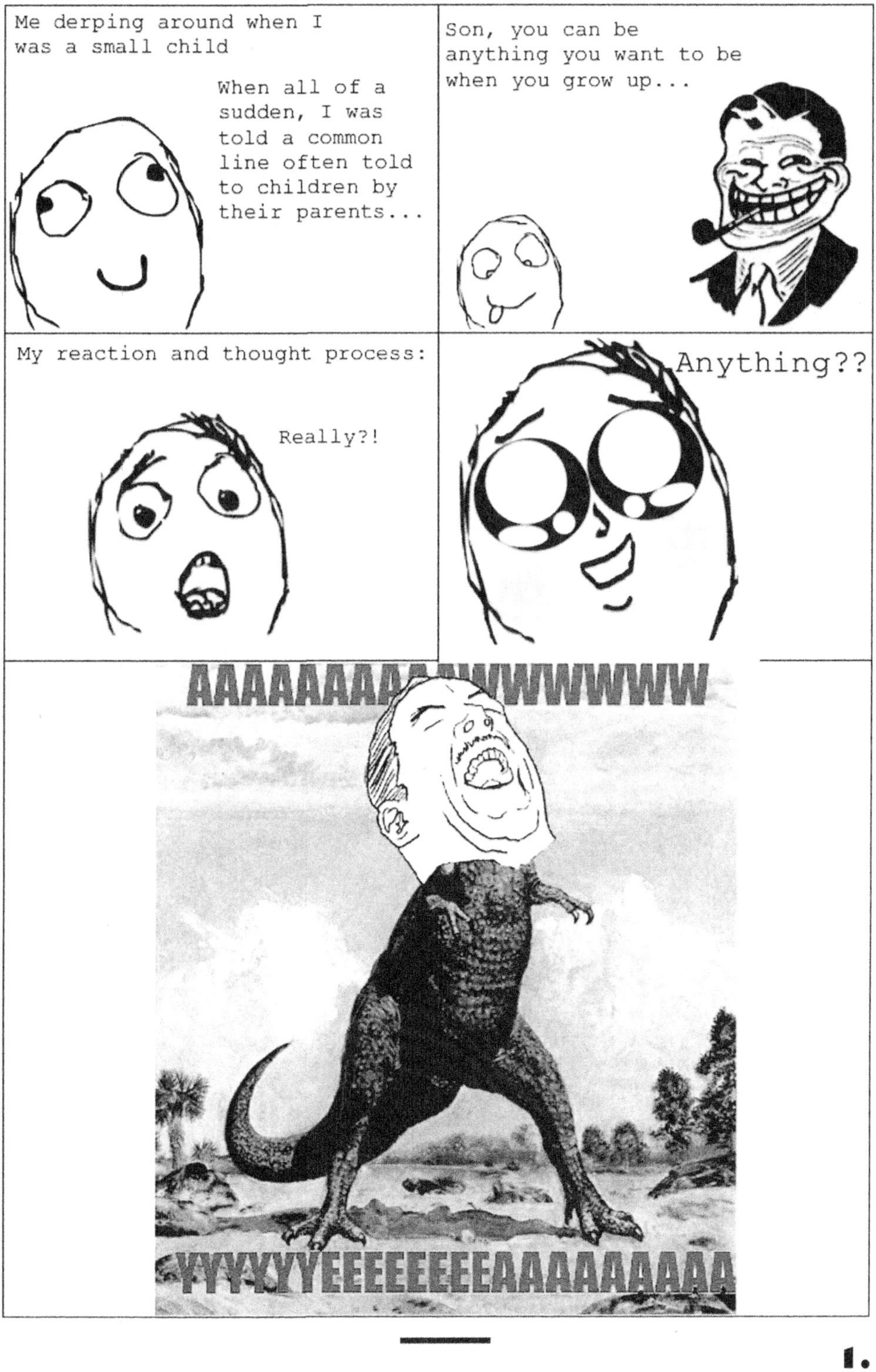
Me derping around when I was a small child
When all of a sudden, I was told a common line often told to children by their parents...
Son, you can be anything you want to be when you grow up...
My reaction and thought process:
Really?!
Anything??
AAAAAAAA
WWWWWW
YYYYYYEEEEEEEEAAAAAAAAA

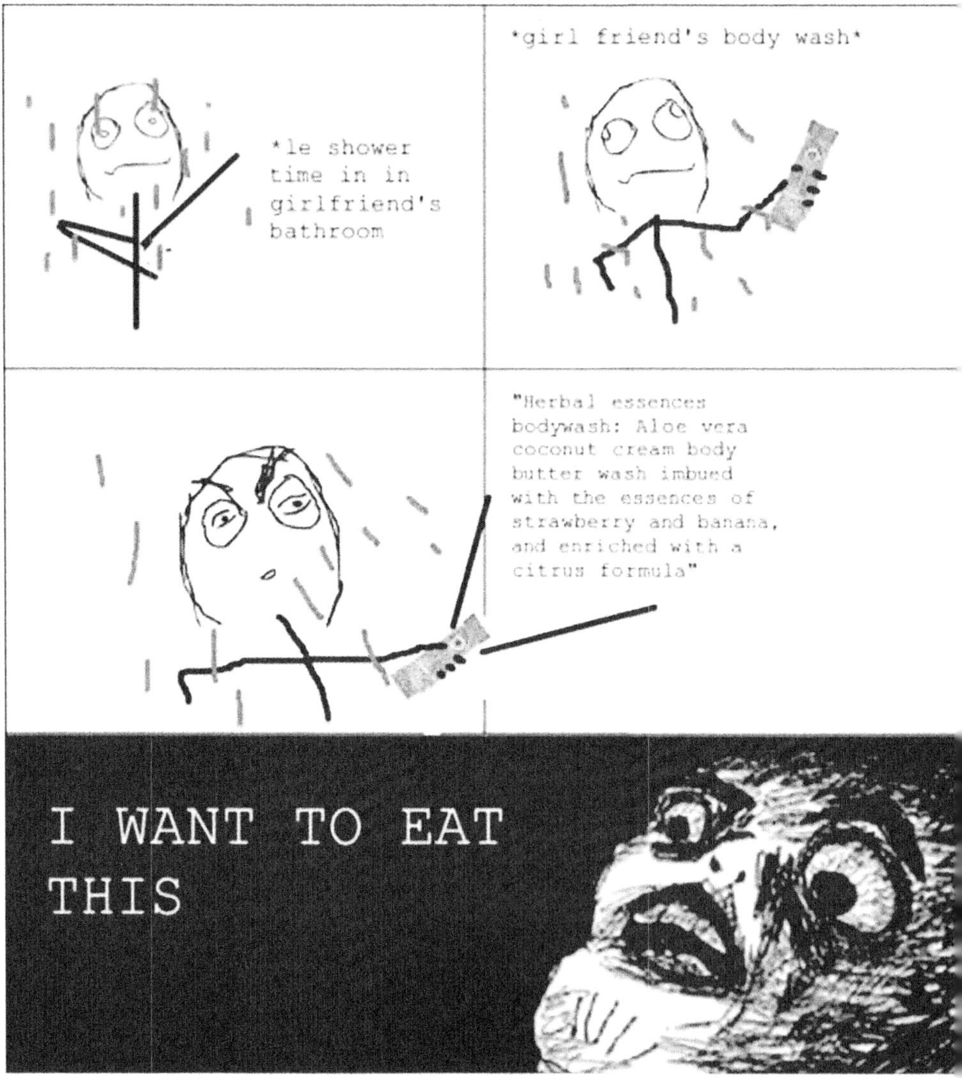
*le shower time in in girlfriend's bathroom
girl friend's body wash
"Herbal essences bodywash: Aloe vera coconut cream body butter wash imbued with the essences of strawberry and banana, and enriched with a citrus formula"
I WANT TO EAT THIS

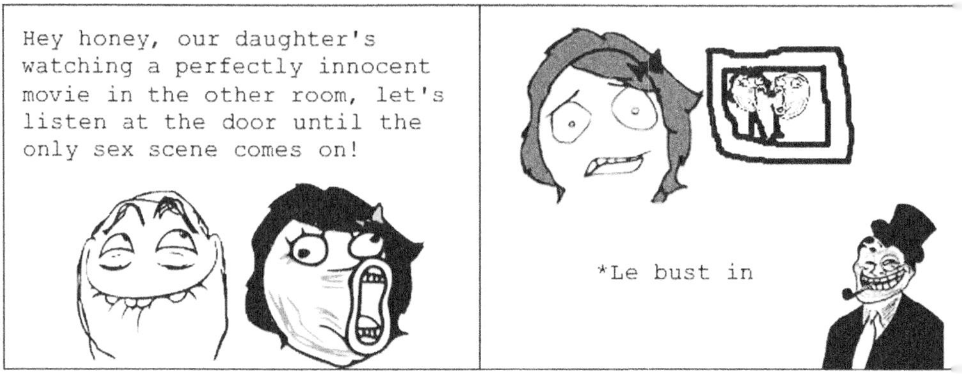
Hey honey, our daughter's watching a perfectly innocent movie in the other room, let's listen at the door until the only sex scene comes on!
*Le bust in

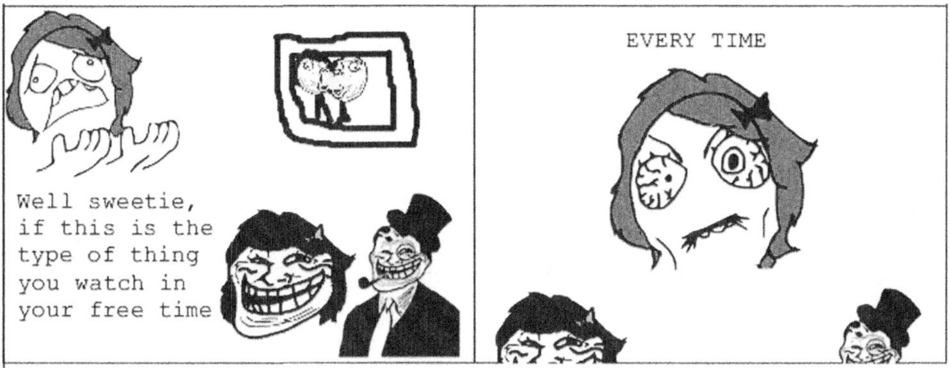

Well sweetie, if this is the type of thing you watch in your free time
EVERY TIME

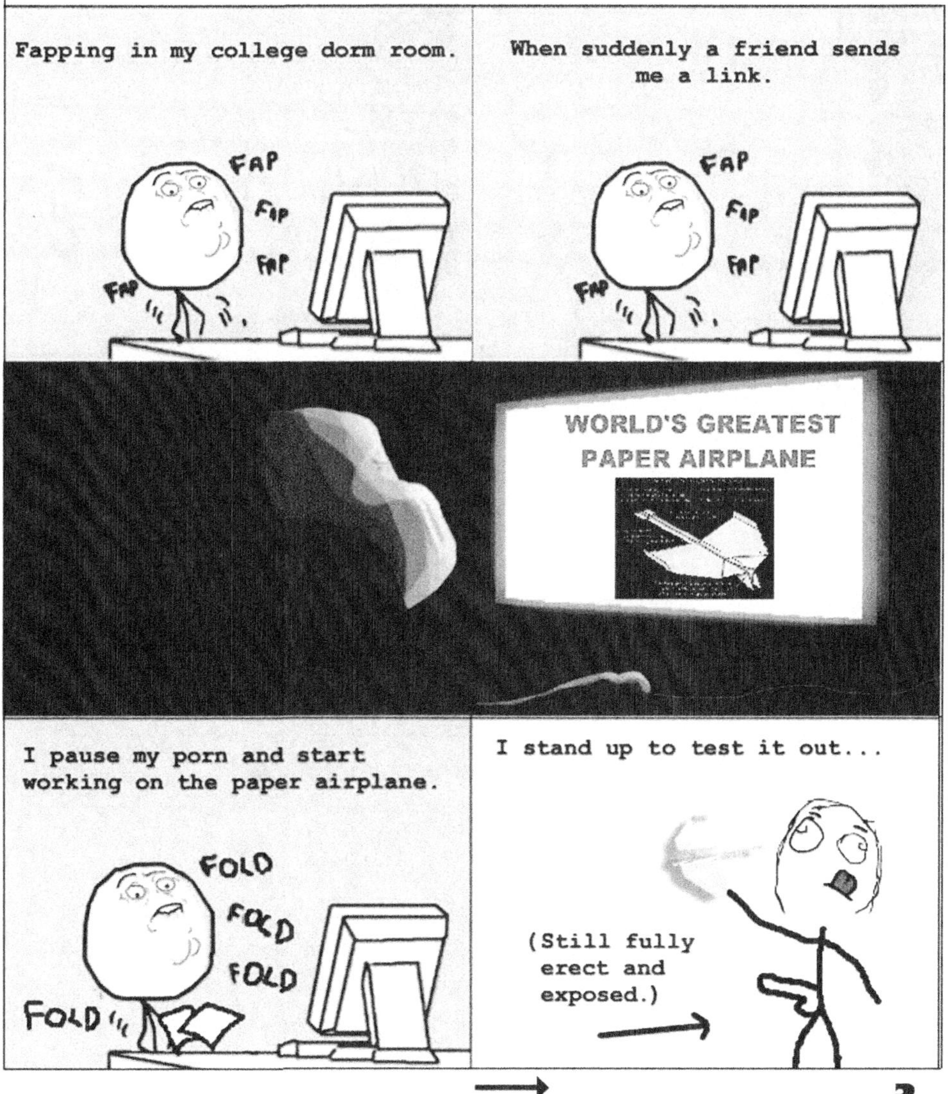

Fapping in my college dorm room.
FAP
FAP
FAP
FAP
When suddenly a friend sends me a link.
FAP
FAP
FAP
FAP
WORLD'S GREATEST PAPER AIRPLANE
I pause my porn and start working on the paper airplane.
FOLD
FOLD
FOLD
FOLD
I stand up to test it out...
(Still fully erect and exposed.)

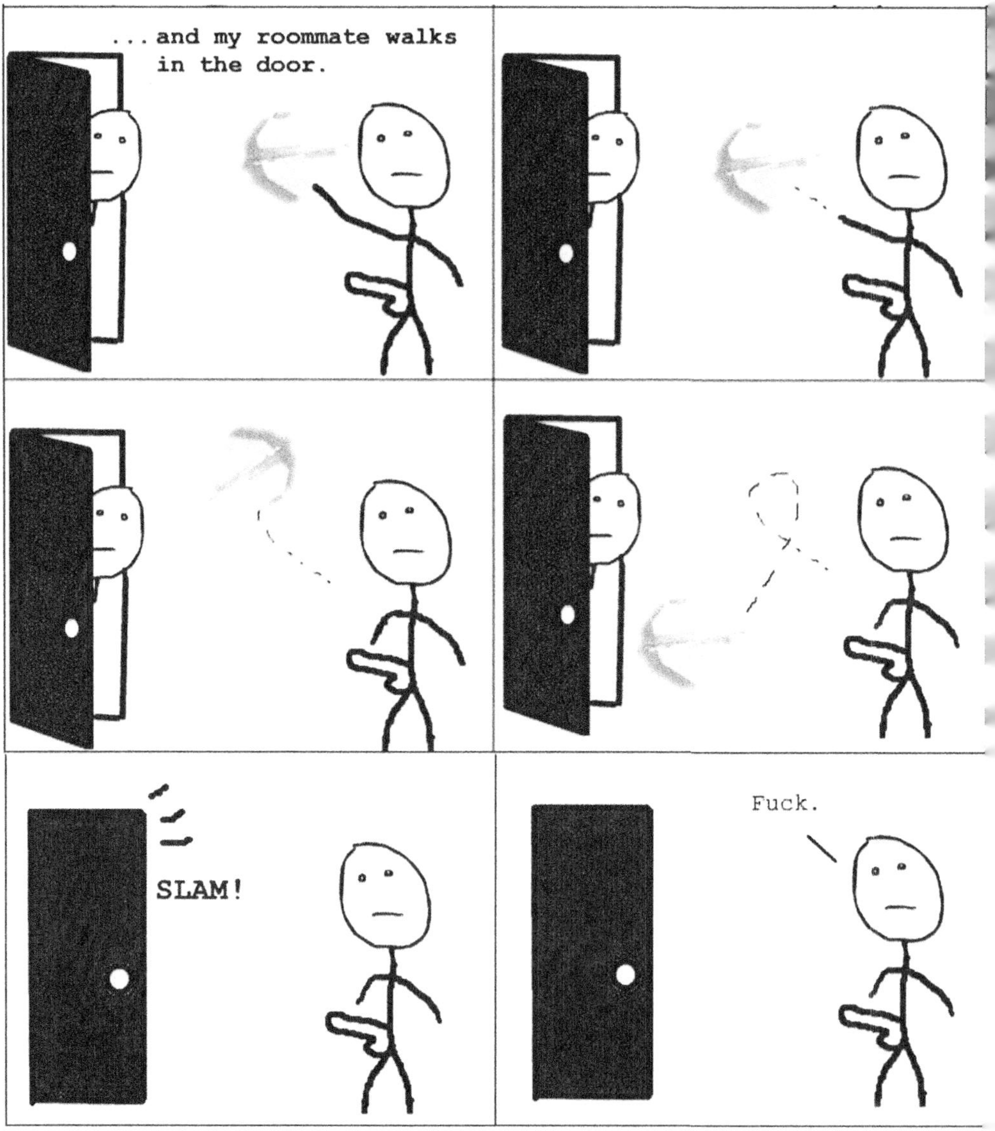
...and my roommate walks in the door.
SLAM!
Fuck.

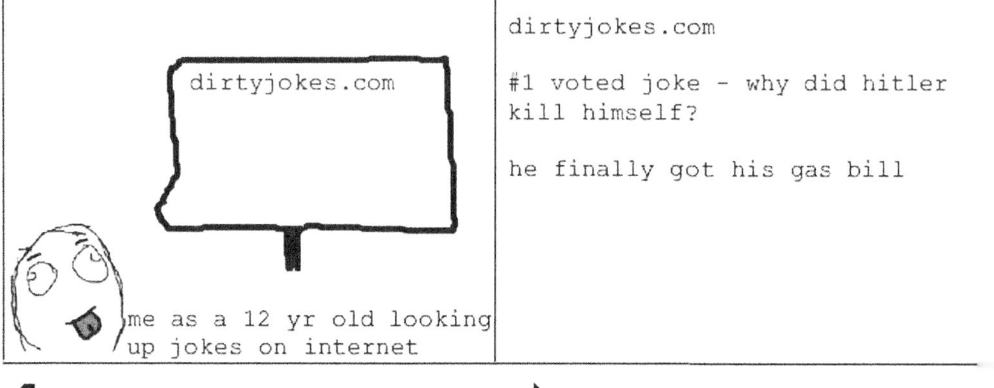
dirtyjokes.com
me as a 12 yr old looking up jokes on internet
dirtyjokes.com
#1 voted joke - why did hitler kill himself?
he finally got his gas bill

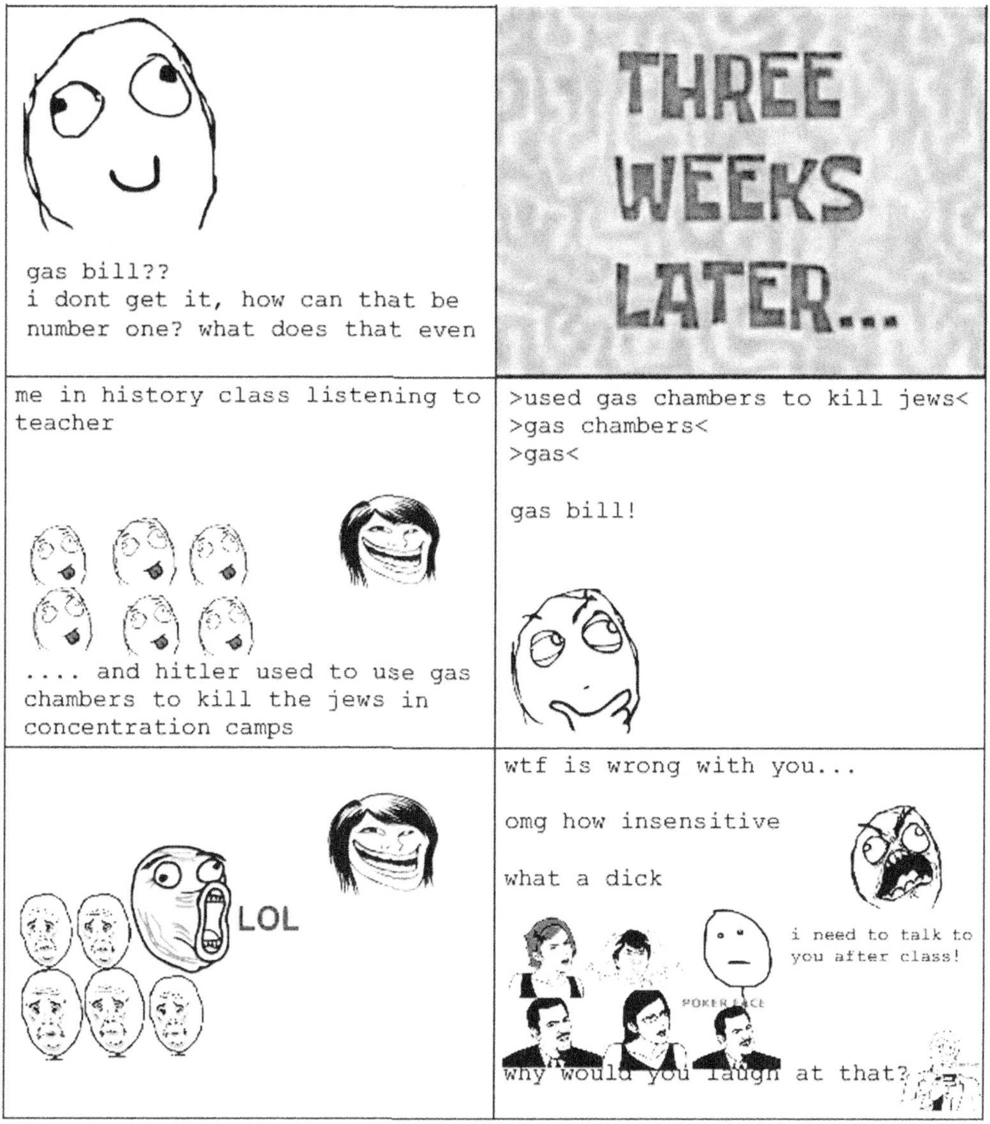
gas bill??
i dont get it, how can that be number one? what does that even
THREE WEEKS LATER...
me in history class listening to teacher
.... and hitler used to use gas chambers to kill the jews in concentration camps
>used gas chambers to kill jews<
>gas chambers<
>gas<
gas bill!
LOL
wtf is wrong with you...
omg how insensitive
what a dick
i need to talk to you after class!
why would you laugh at that?

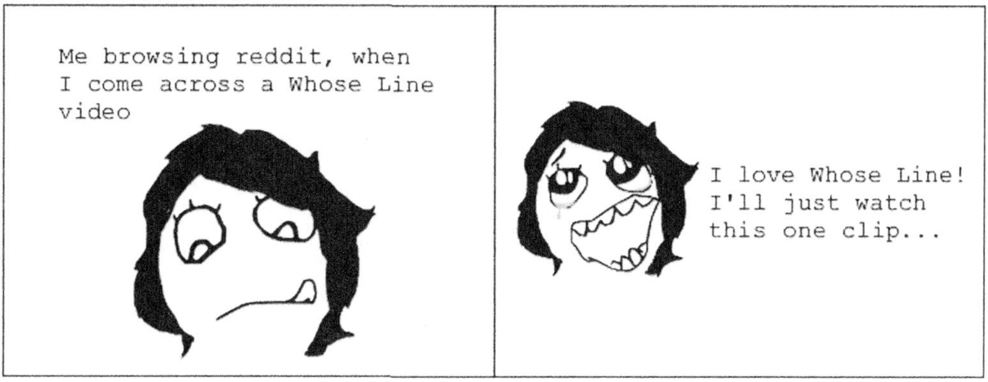
Me browsing reddit, when I come across a Whose Line video
I love Whose Line! I'll just watch this one clip...

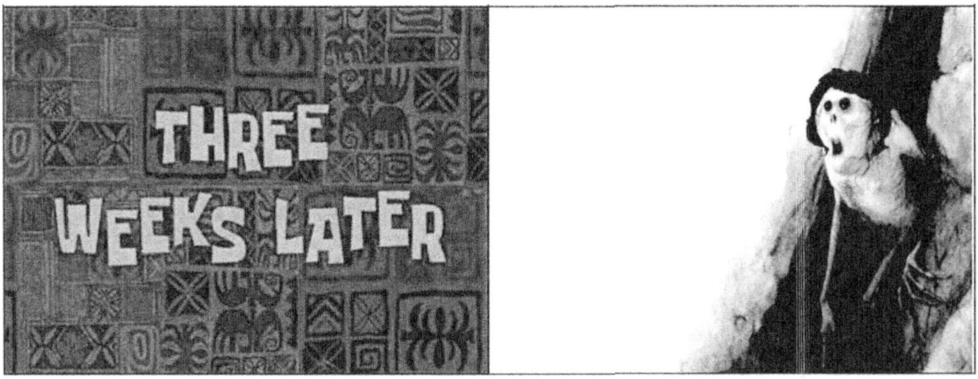
THREE
WEEKS LATER

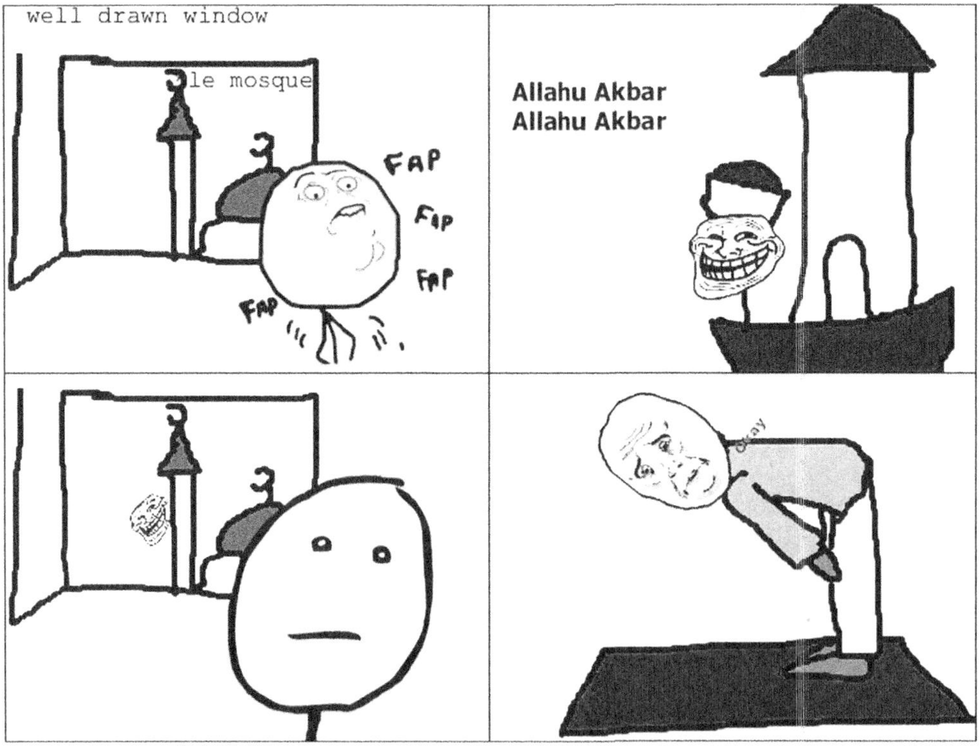
well drawn window
le mosque
FAP
FAP
FAP
FAP
Allahu Akbar
Allahu Akbar

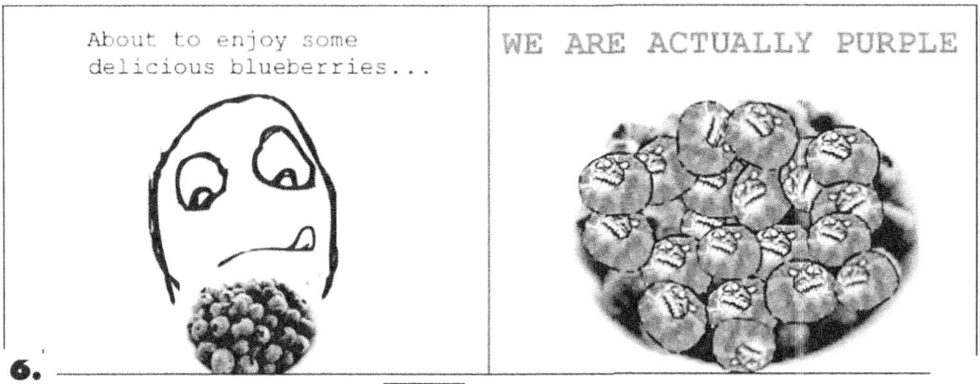
About to enjoy some
delicious blueberries...
WE ARE ACTUALLY PURPLE

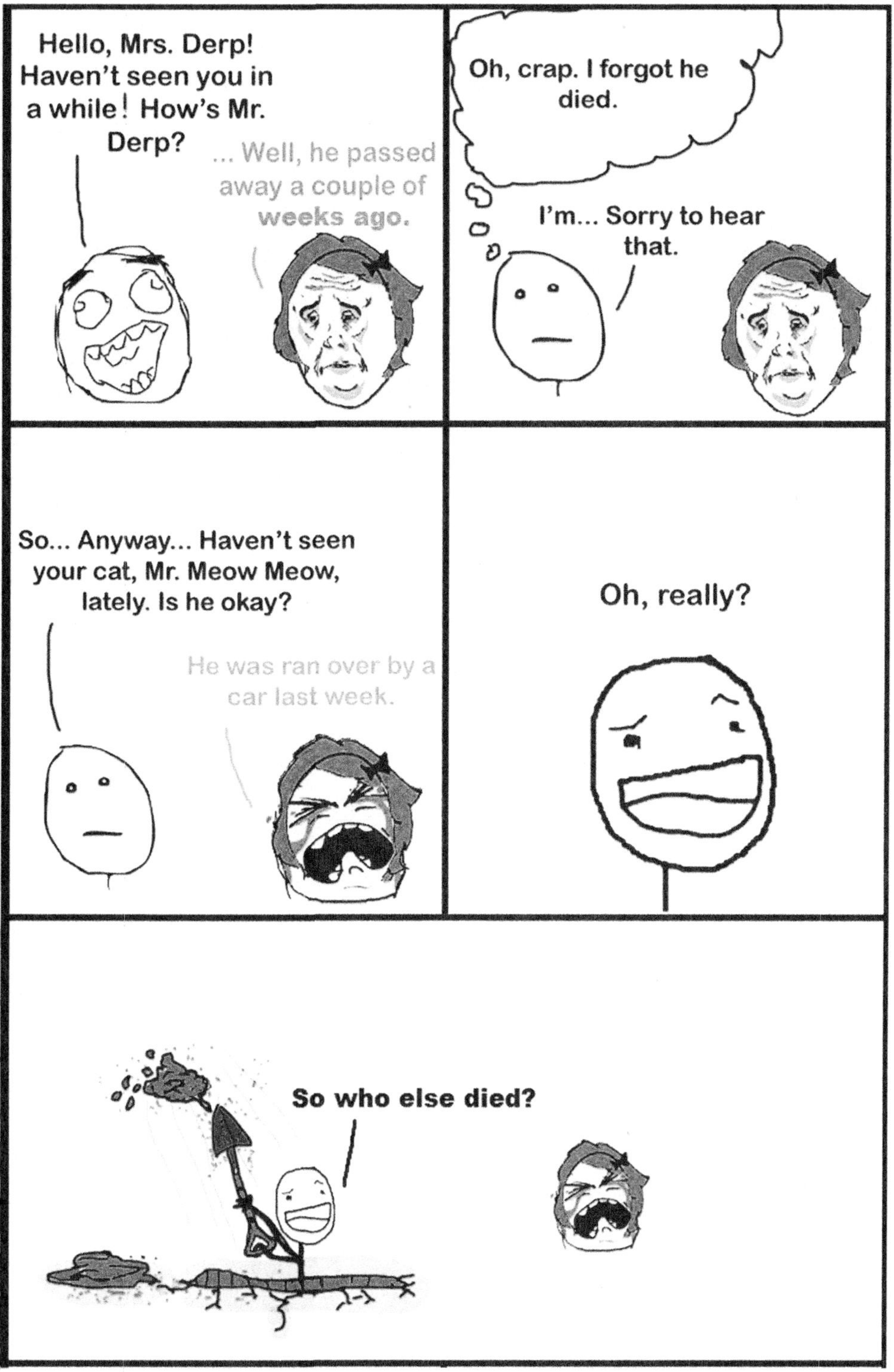
Hello, Mrs. Derp! Haven't seen you in a while! How's Mr. Derp?
... Well, he passed away a couple of weeks ago.
Oh, crap. I forgot he died.
I'm... Sorry to hear that.
So... Anyway... Haven't seen your cat, Mr. Meow Meow, lately. Is he okay?
He was ran over by a car last week.
Oh, really?
So who else died?

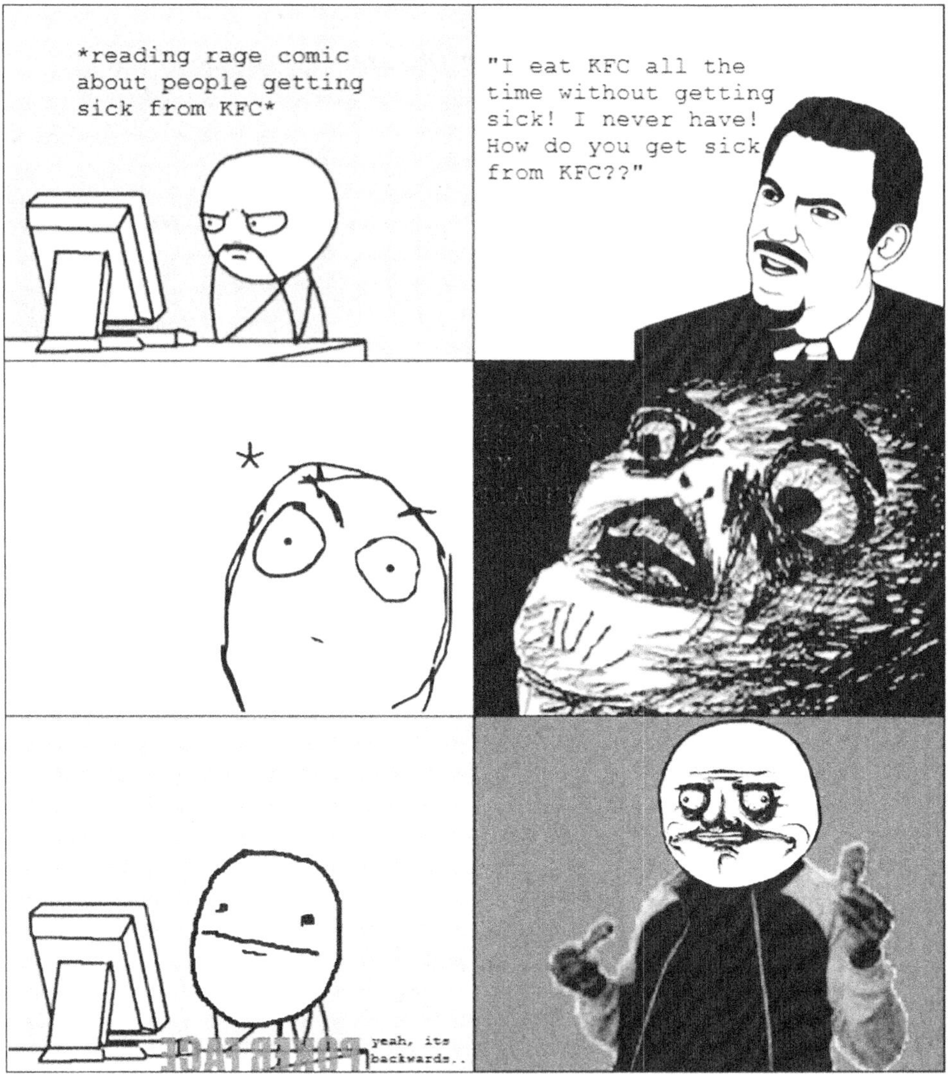
reading rage comic about people getting sick from KFC
"I eat KFC all the time without getting sick! I never have! How do you get sick from KFC??"
*
yeah, its backwards..

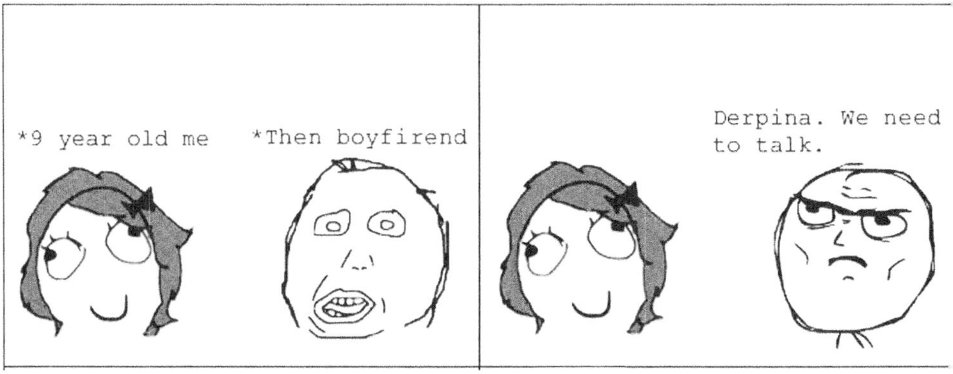
*9 year old me
*Then boyfirend
Derpina. We need to talk.

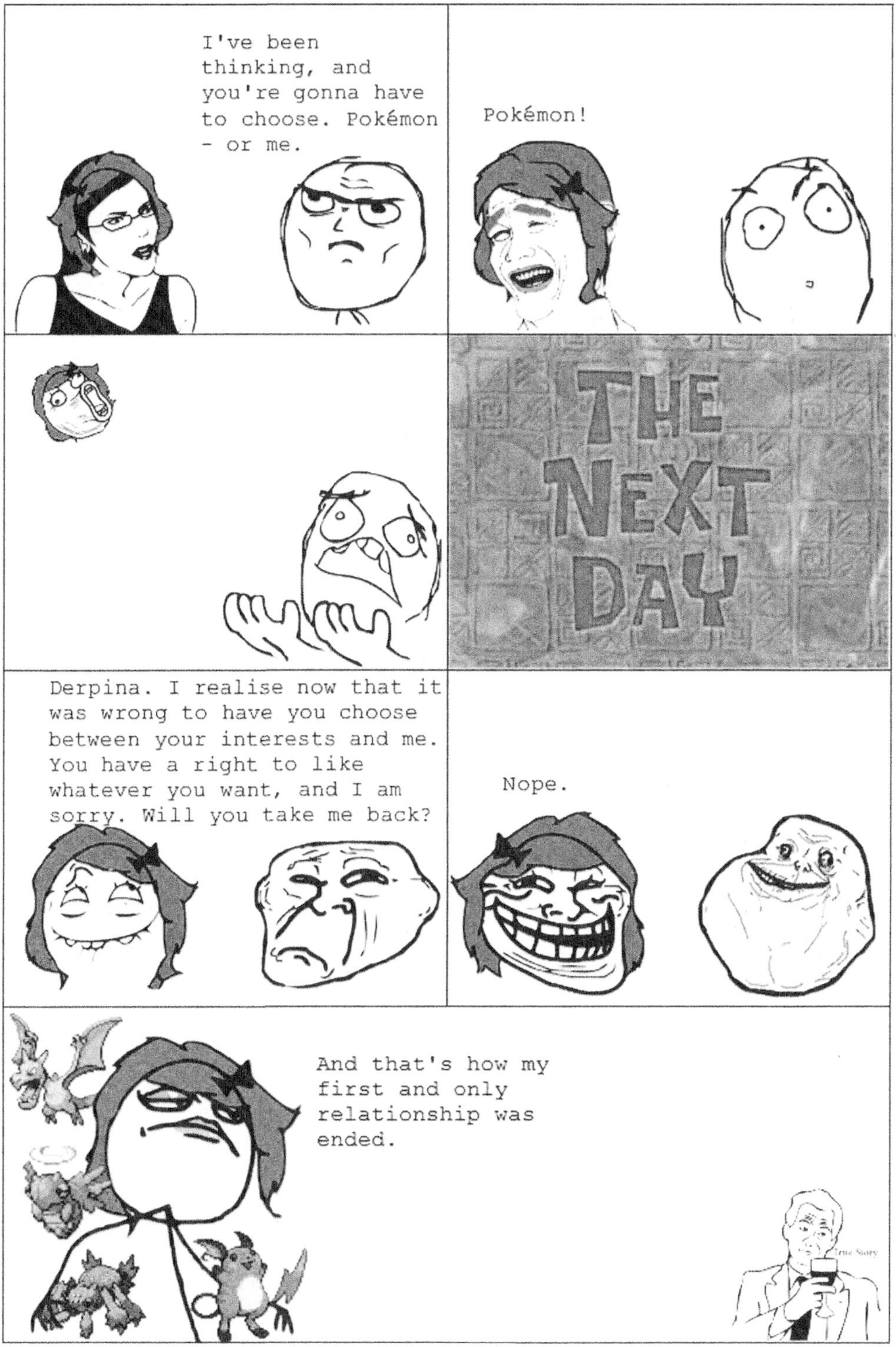
I've been thinking, and you're gonna have to choose. Pokémon - or me.
Pokémon!
THE NEXT DAY
Derpina. I realise now that it was wrong to have you choose between your interests and me. You have a right to like whatever you want, and I am sorry. Will you take me back?
Nope.
And that's how my first and only relationship was ended.

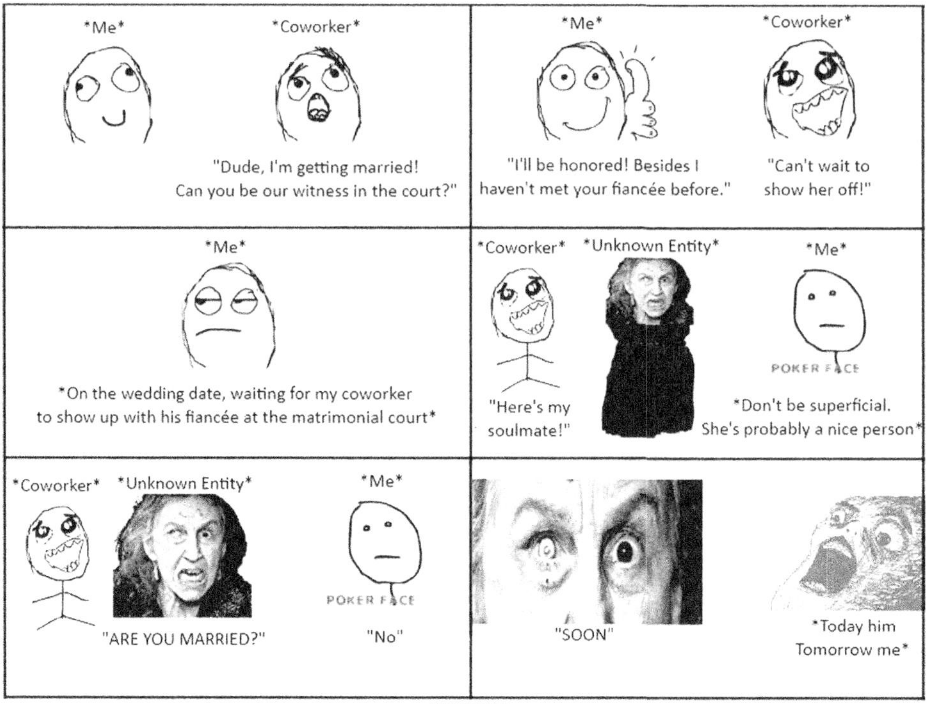
Me
Coworker
"Dude, I'm getting married!
Can you be our witness in the court?"
Me
Coworker
"I'll be honored! Besides I
haven't met your fiancée before."
"Can't wait to
show her off!"
Me
*On the wedding date, waiting for my coworker
to show up with his fiancée at the matrimonial court*
Coworker
Unknown Entity
Me
POKER FACE
"Here's my
soulmate!"
*Don't be superficial.
She's probably a nice person*
Coworker
Unknown Entity
Me
POKER FACE
"ARE YOU MARRIED?"
"No"
"SOON"
*Today him
Tomorrow me*

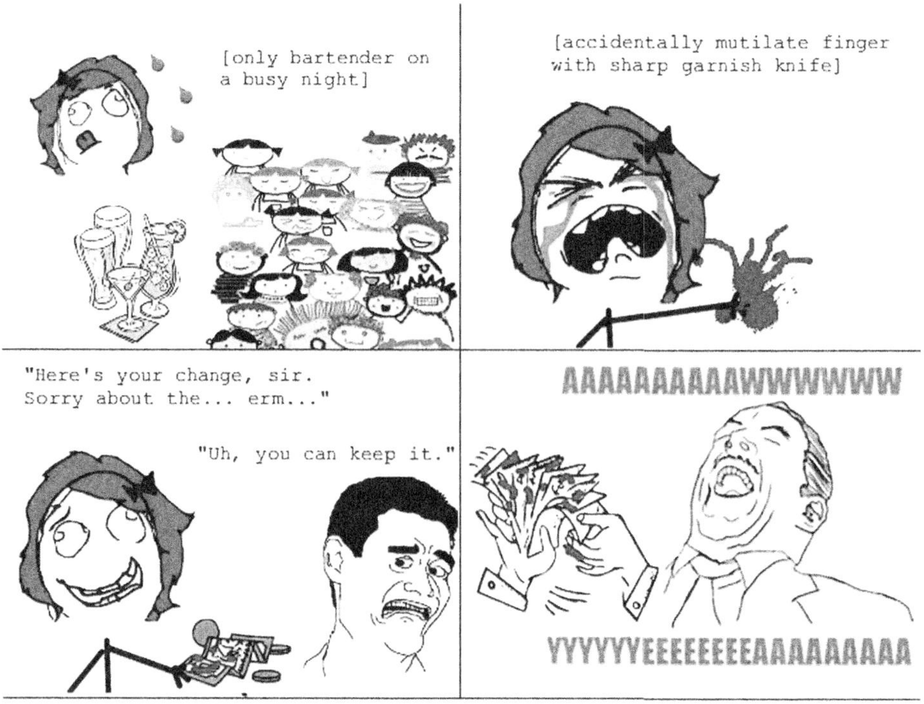
[only bartender on
a busy night]
[accidentally mutilate finger
with sharp garnish knife]
"Here's your change, sir.
Sorry about the... erm..."
"Uh, you can keep it."
AAAAAAAAAAWWWWWW
YYYYYYEEEEEEEEAAAAAAAAA

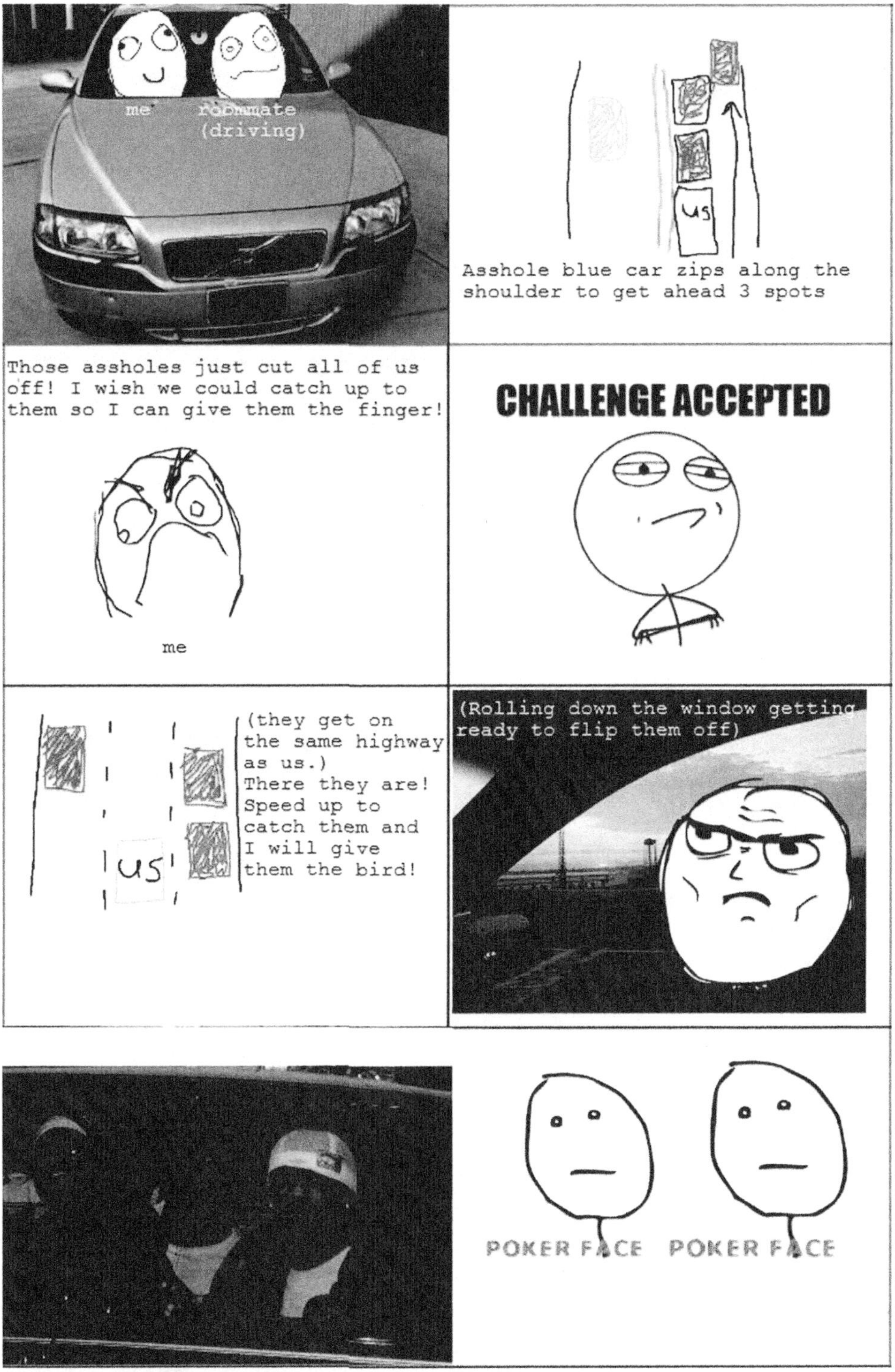
me
roommate
(driving)
Asshole blue car zips along the shoulder to get ahead 3 spots
us
Those assholes just cut all of us off! I wish we could catch up to them so I can give them the finger!
me
CHALLENGE ACCEPTED
(they get on the same highway as us.)
There they are! Speed up to catch them and I will give them the bird!
us
(Rolling down the window getting ready to flip them off)
POKER FACE
POKER FACE

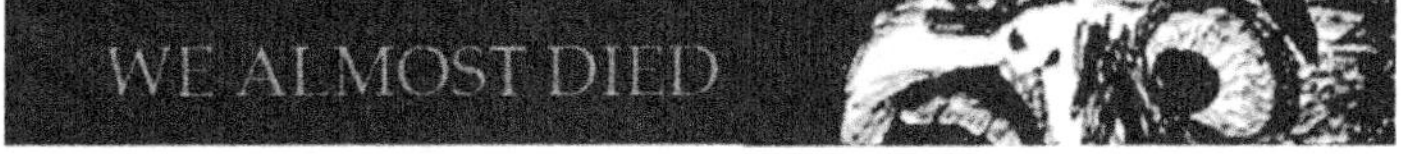
WE ALMOST DIED

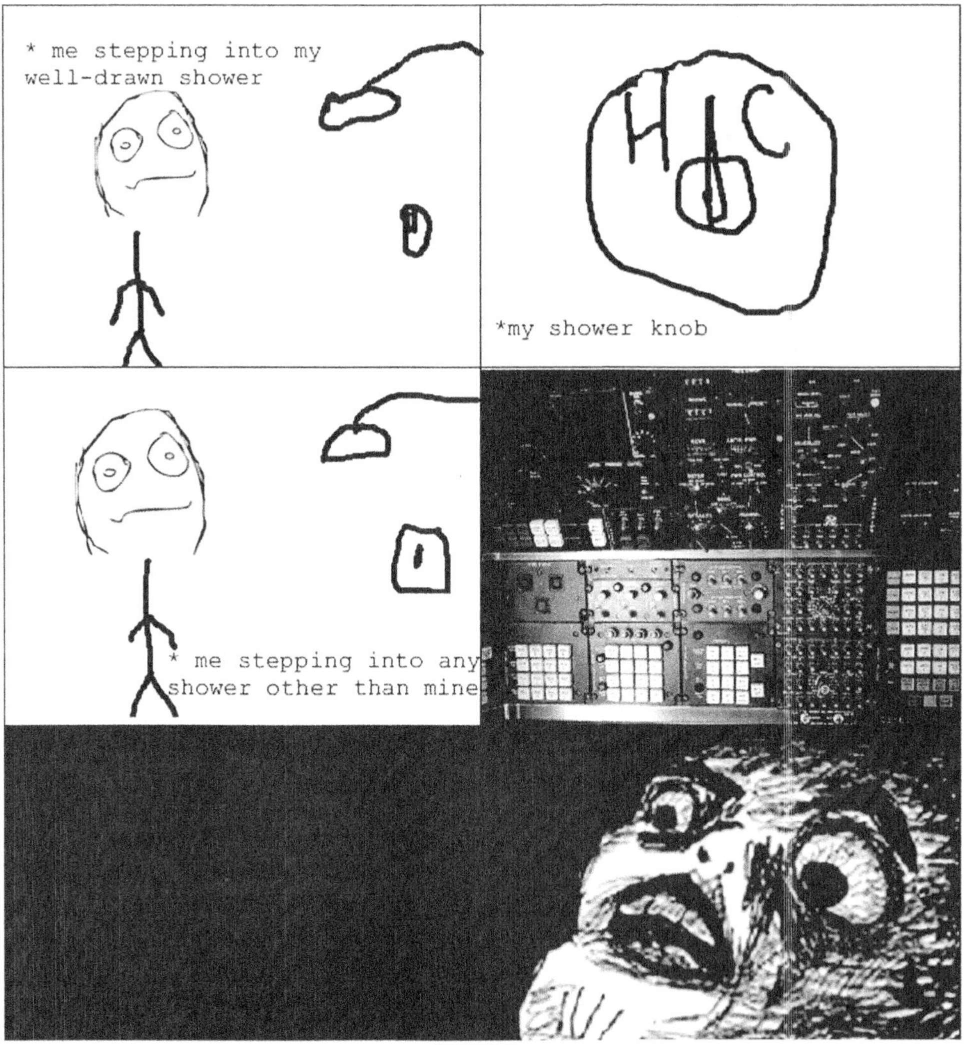
* me stepping into my well-drawn shower
*my shower knob
H
C
* me stepping into any shower other than mine

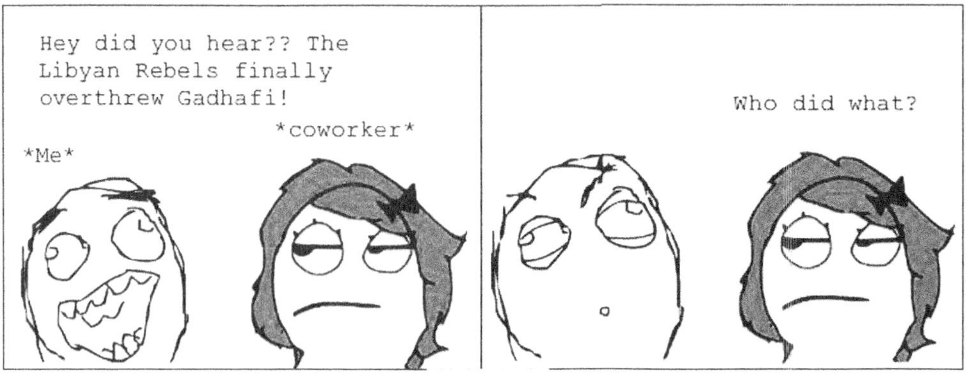
Hey did you hear?? The Libyan Rebels finally overthrew Gadhafi!
coworker
Me
Who did what?

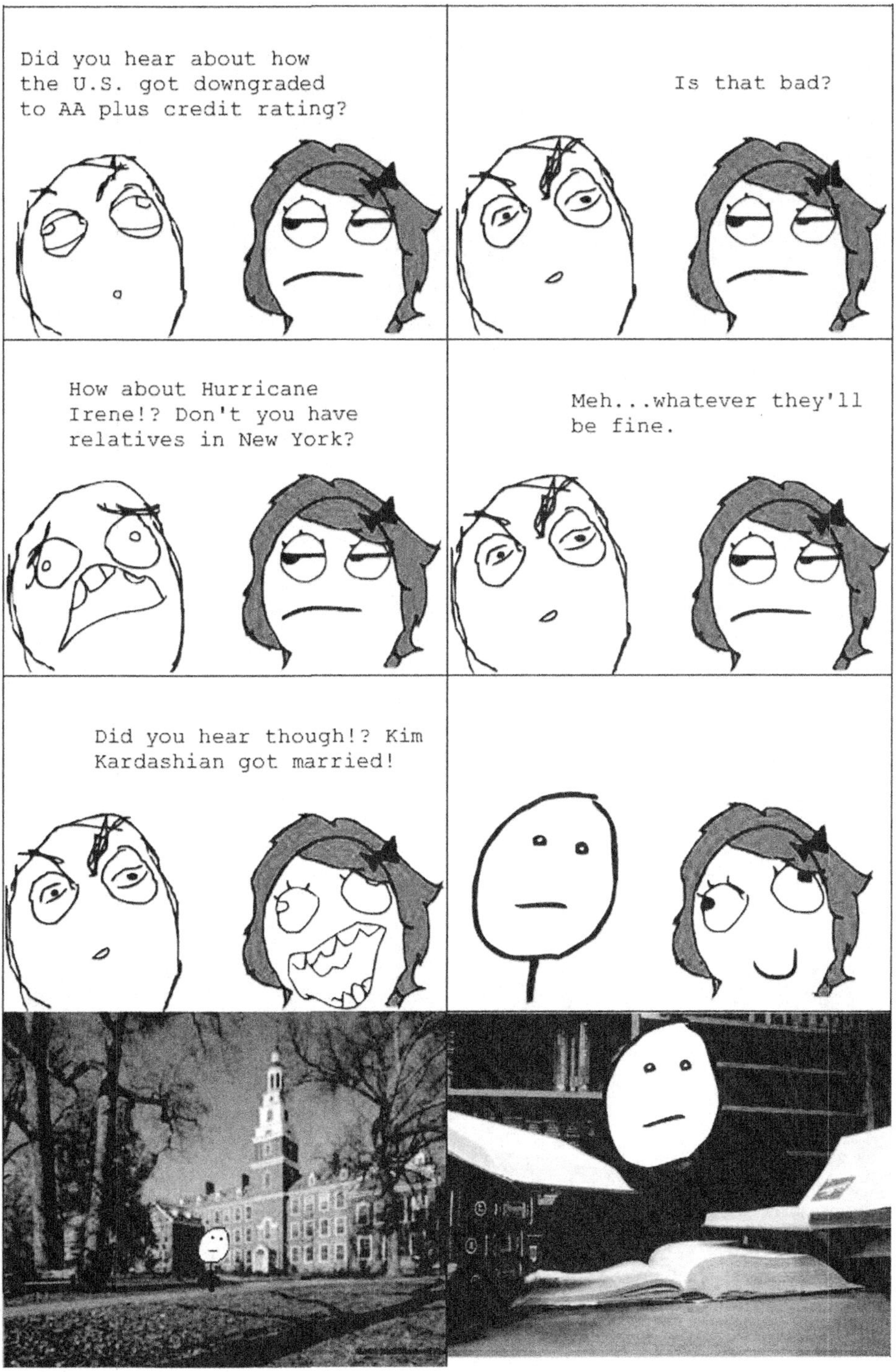
Did you hear about how the U.S. got downgraded to AA plus credit rating?
Is that bad?
How about Hurricane Irene!? Don't you have relatives in New York?
Meh...whatever they'll be fine.
Did you hear though!? Kim Kardashian got married!

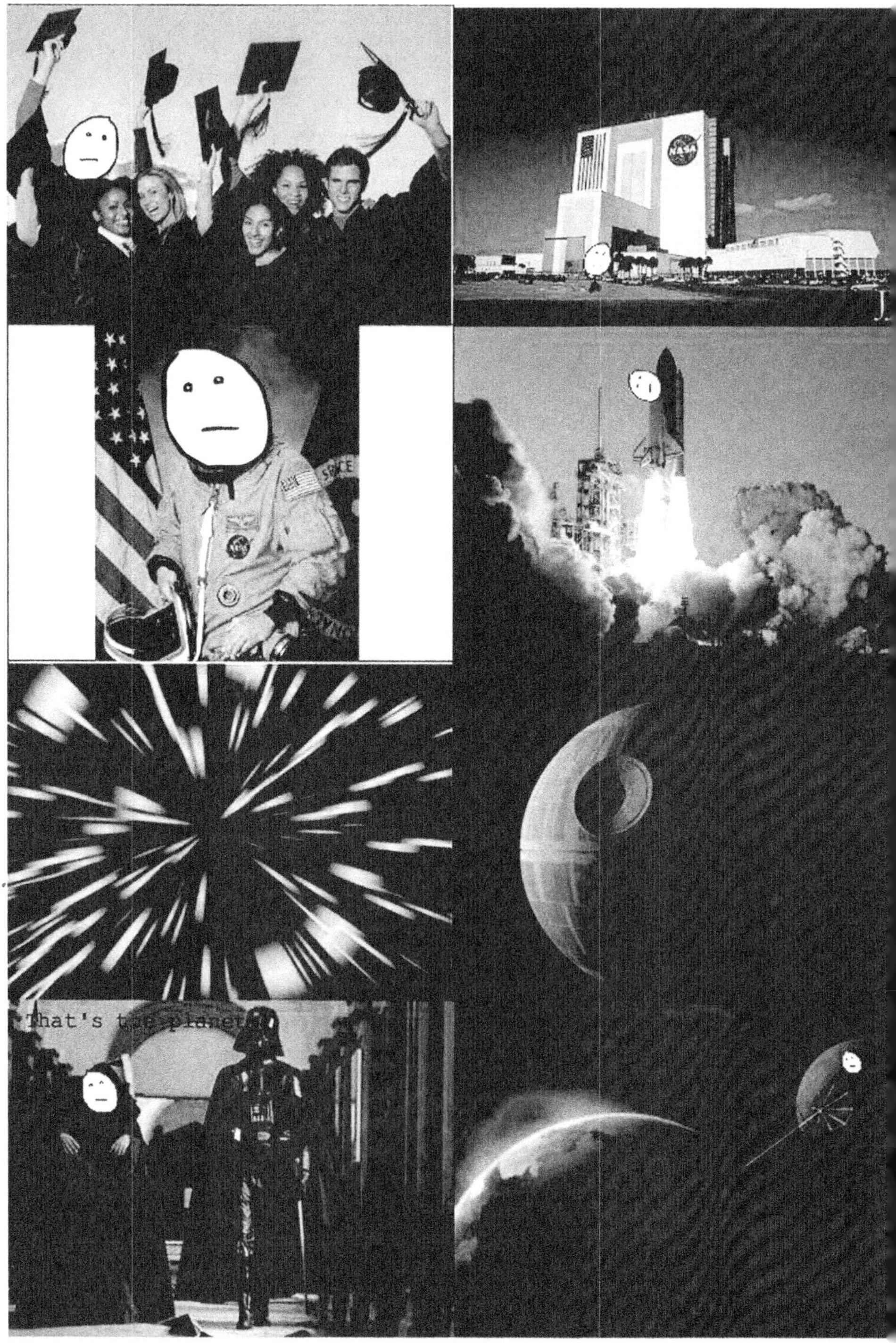

That's the planet

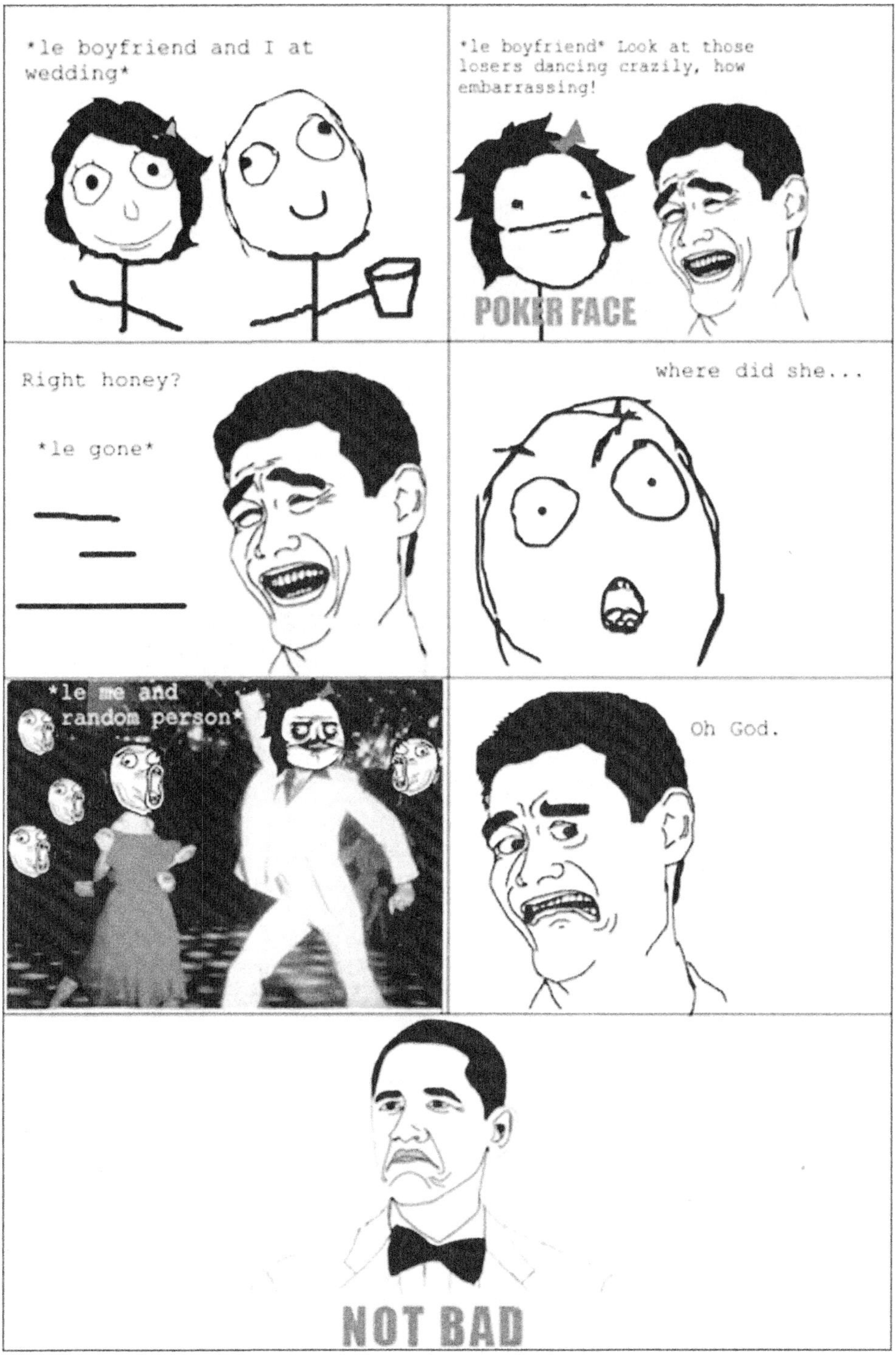
le boyfriend and I at wedding
le boyfriend Look at those losers dancing crazily, how embarrassing!
POKER FACE
Right honey?
le gone
where did she...
le me and random person
Oh God.
NOT BAD

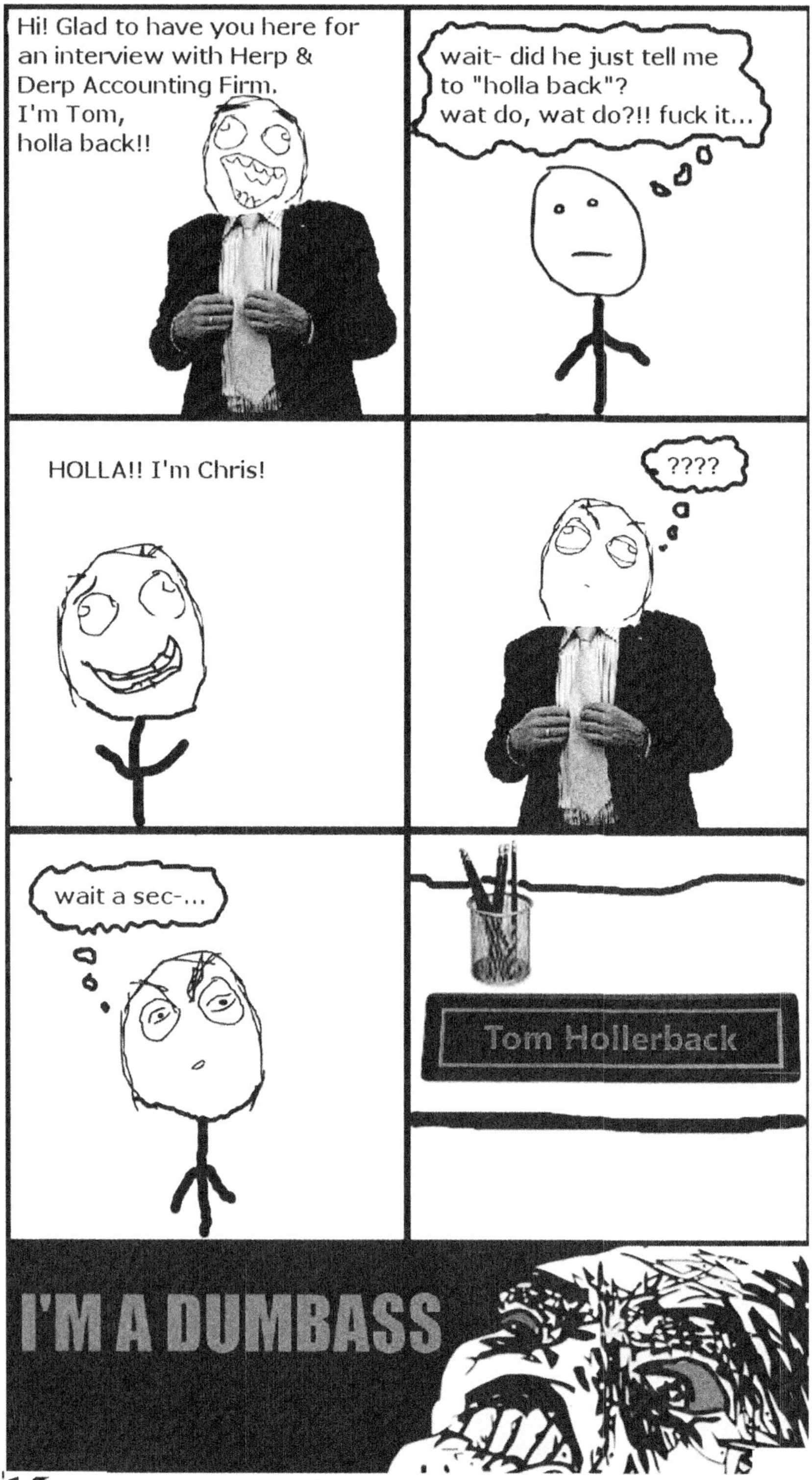
Hi! Glad to have you here for an interview with Herp & Derp Accounting Firm.
I'm Tom, holla back!!
wait- did he just tell me to "holla back"?
wat do, wat do?!! fuck it...
HOLLA!! I'm Chris!
????
wait a sec-...
Tom Hollerback
I'M A DUMBASS

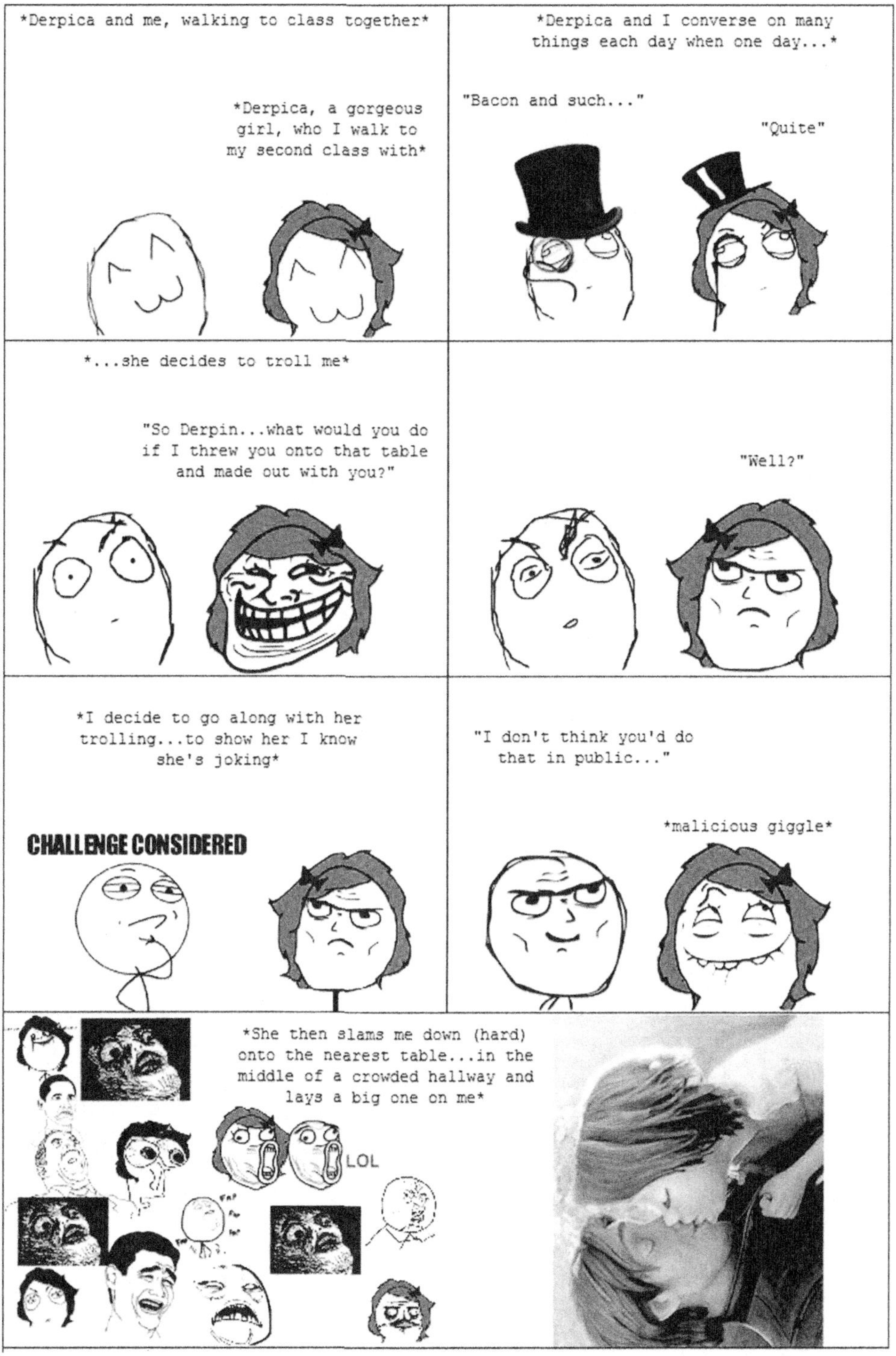
Derpica and me, walking to class together
Derpica, a gorgeous girl, who I walk to my second class with
Derpica and I converse on many things each day when one day...
"Bacon and such..."
"Quite"
...she decides to troll me
"So Derpin...what would you do if I threw you onto that table and made out with you?"
"Well?"
I decide to go along with her trolling...to show her I know she's joking
CHALLENGE CONSIDERED
"I don't think you'd do that in public..."
malicious giggle
She then slams me down (hard) onto the nearest table...in the middle of a crowded hallway and lays a big one on me
LOL

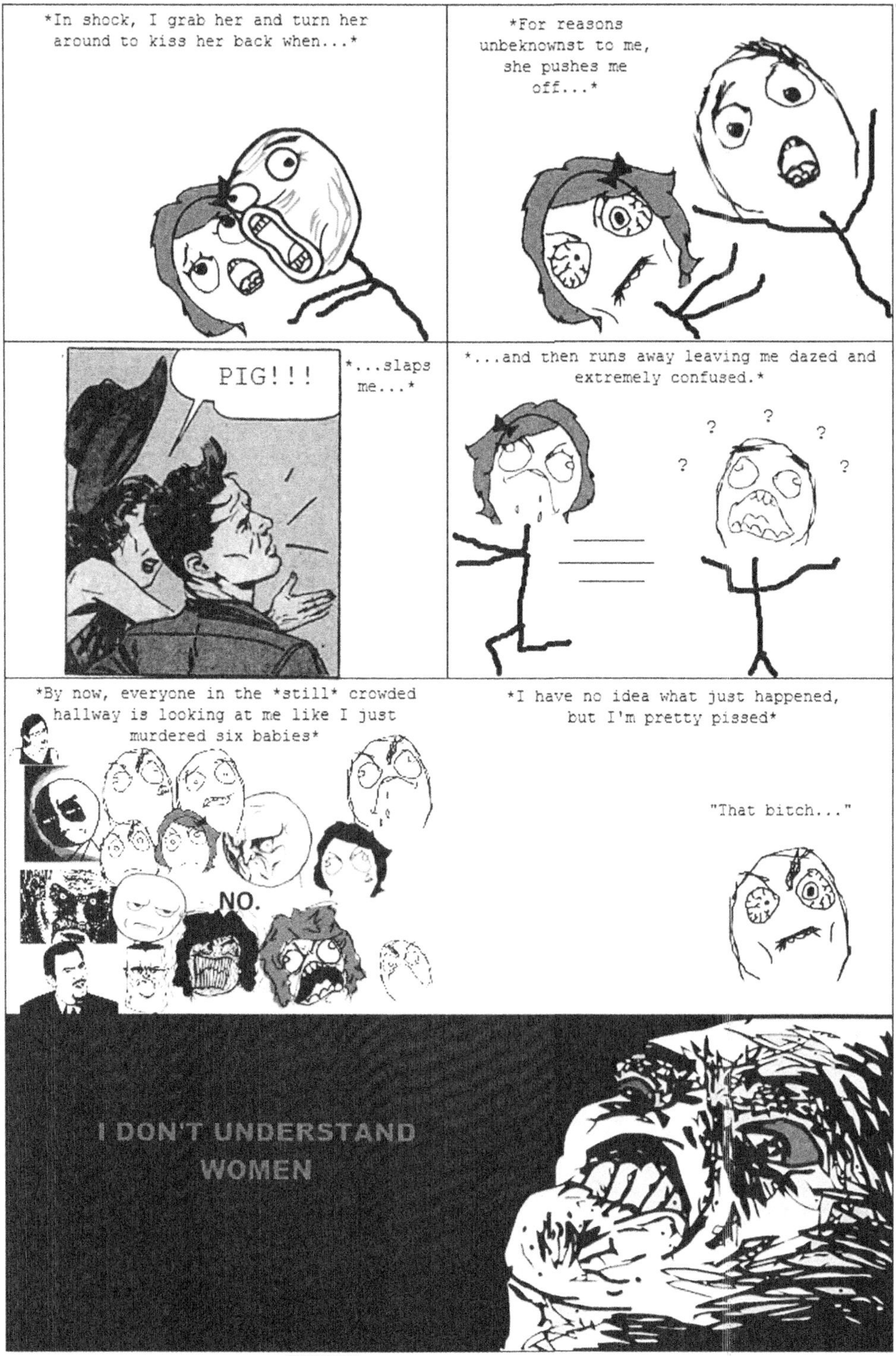
In shock, I grab her and turn her around to kiss her back when...
For reasons unbeknownst to me, she pushes me off...
PIG!!!
...slaps me...
...and then runs away leaving me dazed and extremely confused.
? ? ? ? ?
*By now, everyone in the *still* crowded hallway is looking at me like I just murdered six babies*
NO.
I have no idea what just happened, but I'm pretty pissed
"That bitch..."
I DON'T UNDERSTAND WOMEN

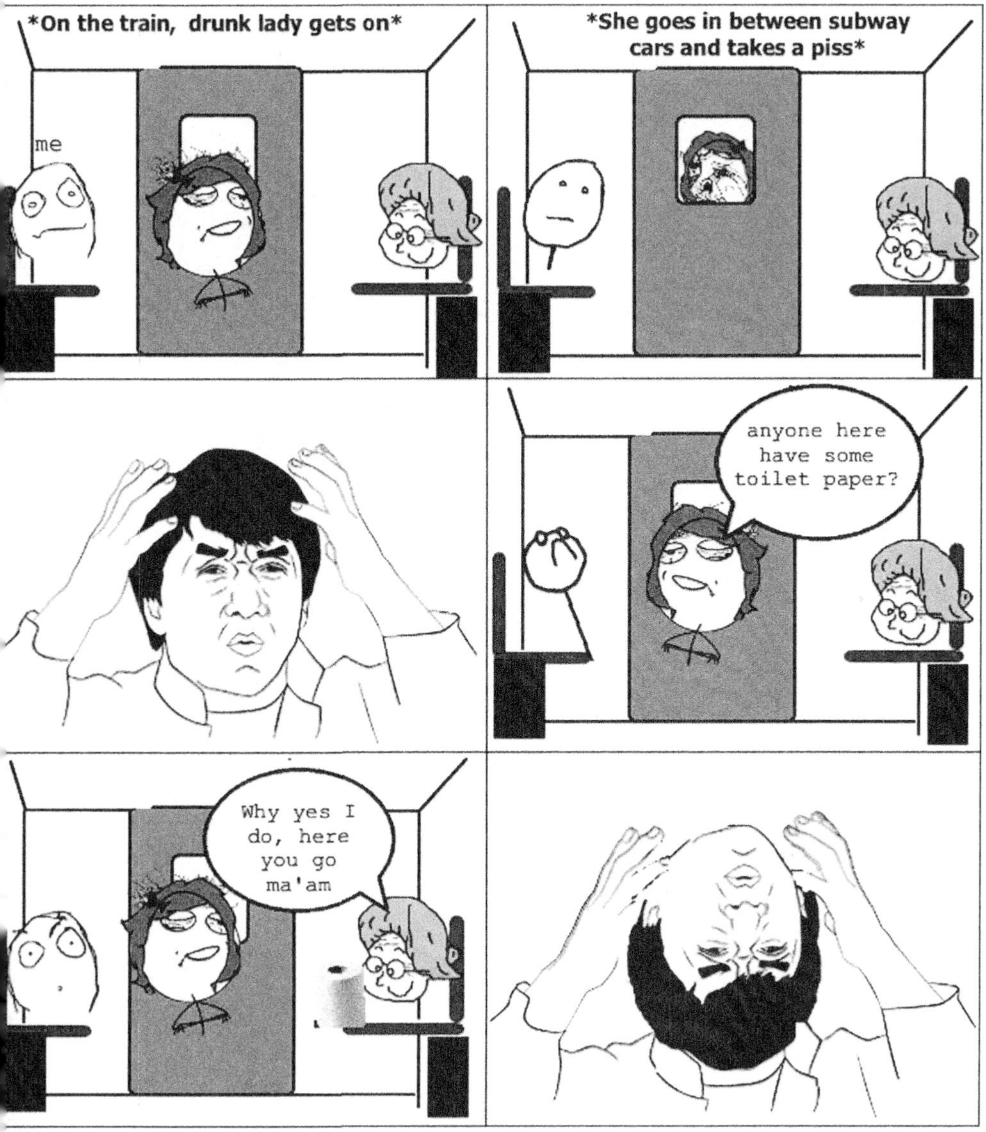
On the train, drunk lady gets on
me
She goes in between subway cars and takes a piss
anyone here have some toilet paper?
Why yes I do, here you go ma'am

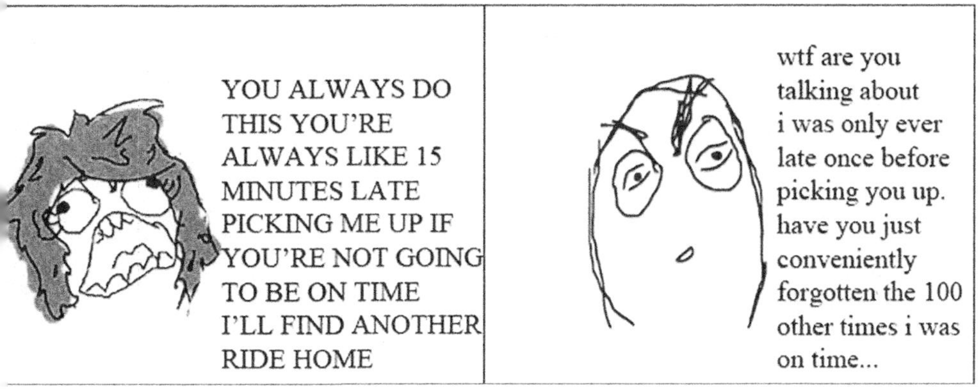
YOU ALWAYS DO THIS YOU'RE ALWAYS LIKE 15 MINUTES LATE PICKING ME UP IF YOU'RE NOT GOING TO BE ON TIME I'LL FIND ANOTHER RIDE HOME
wtf are you talking about i was only ever late once before picking you up. have you just conveniently forgotten the 100 other times i was on time...

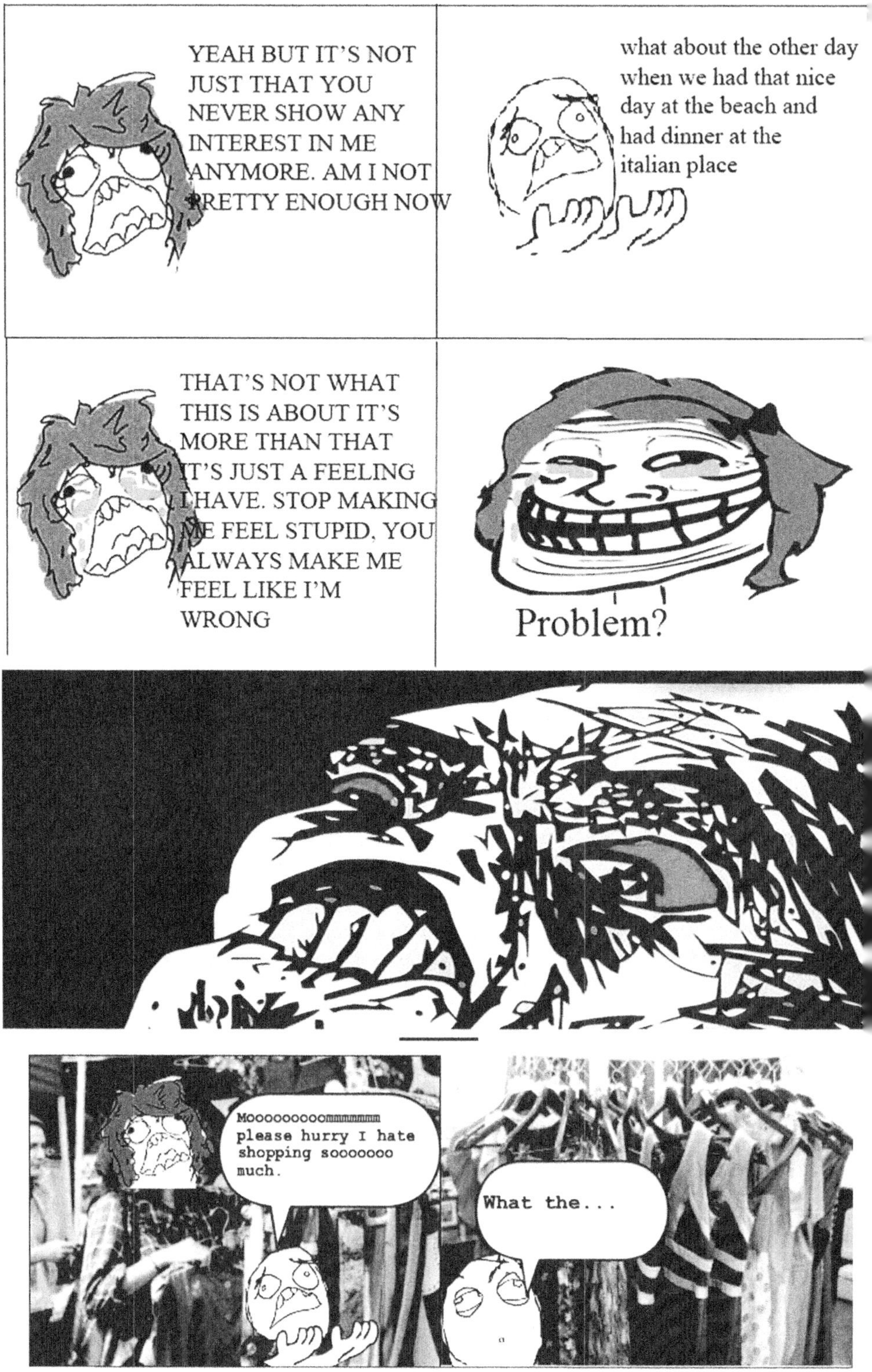

YEAH BUT IT'S NOT JUST THAT YOU NEVER SHOW ANY INTEREST IN ME ANYMORE. AM I NOT PRETTY ENOUGH NOW
what about the other day when we had that nice day at the beach and had dinner at the italian place
THAT'S NOT WHAT THIS IS ABOUT IT'S MORE THAN THAT IT'S JUST A FEELING I HAVE. STOP MAKING ME FEEL STUPID, YOU ALWAYS MAKE ME FEEL LIKE I'M WRONG
Problem?
Moooooooommmmmm please hurry I hate shopping sooooooo much.
What the...

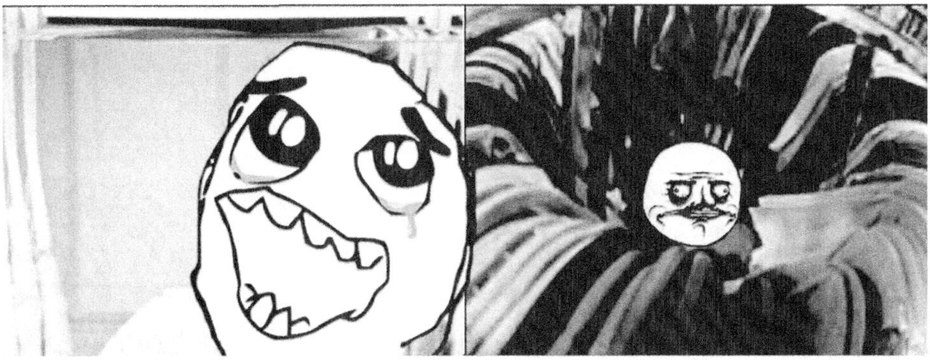

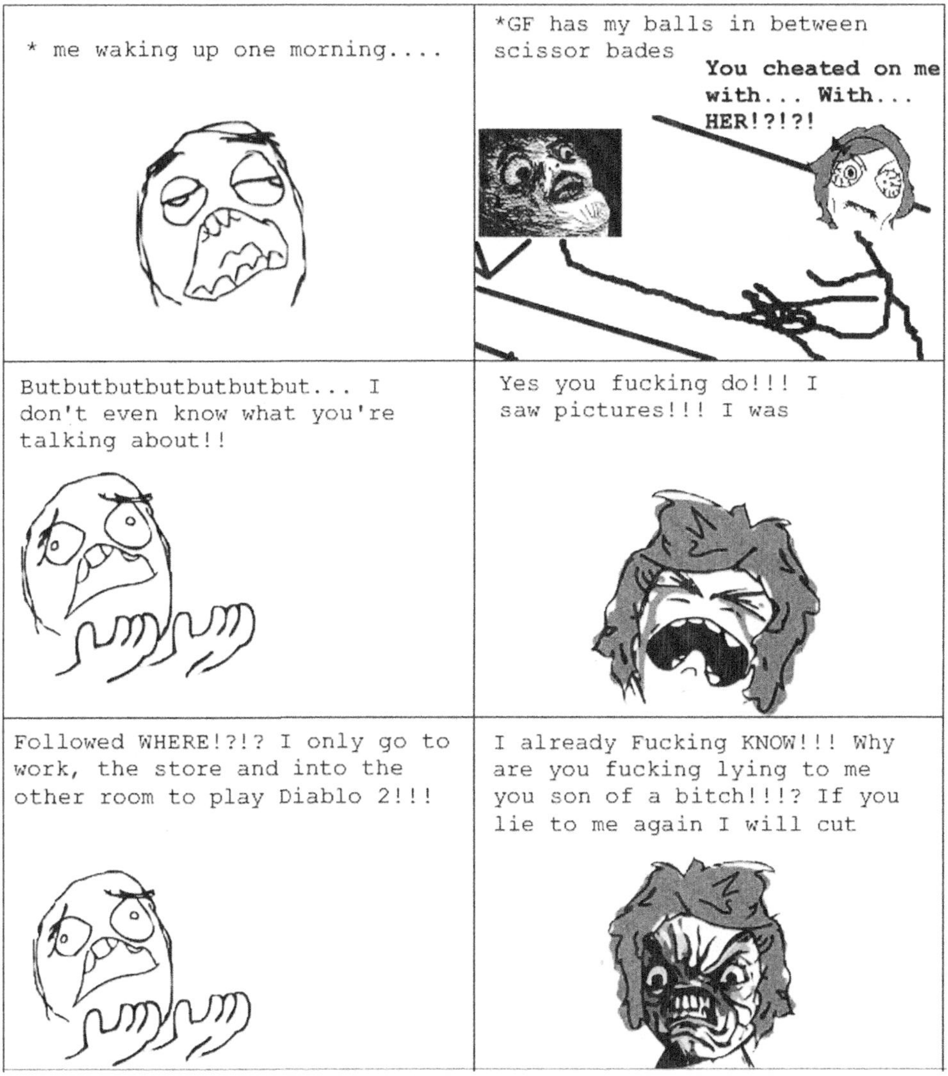
* me waking up one morning....
*GF has my balls in between scissor bades
You cheated on me with... With... HER!?!?!
Butbutbutbutbutbutbut... I don't even know what you're talking about!!
Yes you fucking do!!! I saw pictures!!! I was
Followed WHERE!?!? I only go to work, the store and into the other room to play Diablo 2!!!
I already Fucking KNOW!!! Why are you fucking lying to me you son of a bitch!!!? If you lie to me again I will cut

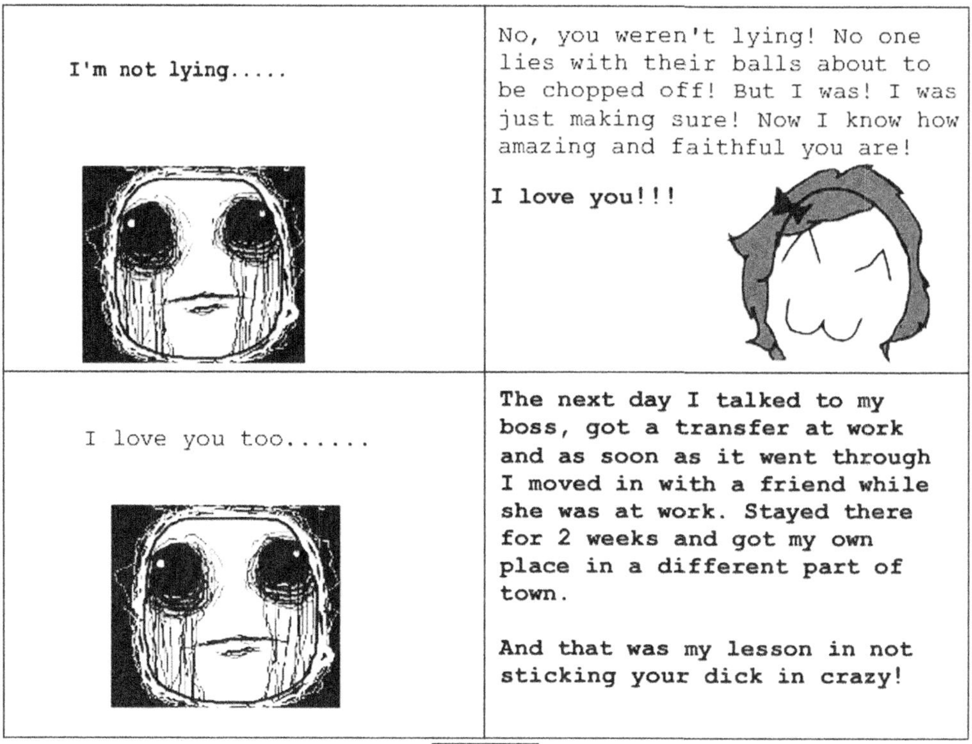
I'm not lying.....
No, you weren't lying! No one lies with their balls about to be chopped off! But I was! I was just making sure! Now I know how amazing and faithful you are!
I love you!!!
I love you too......
The next day I talked to my boss, got a transfer at work and as soon as it went through I moved in with a friend while she was at work. Stayed there for 2 weeks and got my own place in a different part of town.
And that was my lesson in not sticking your dick in crazy!

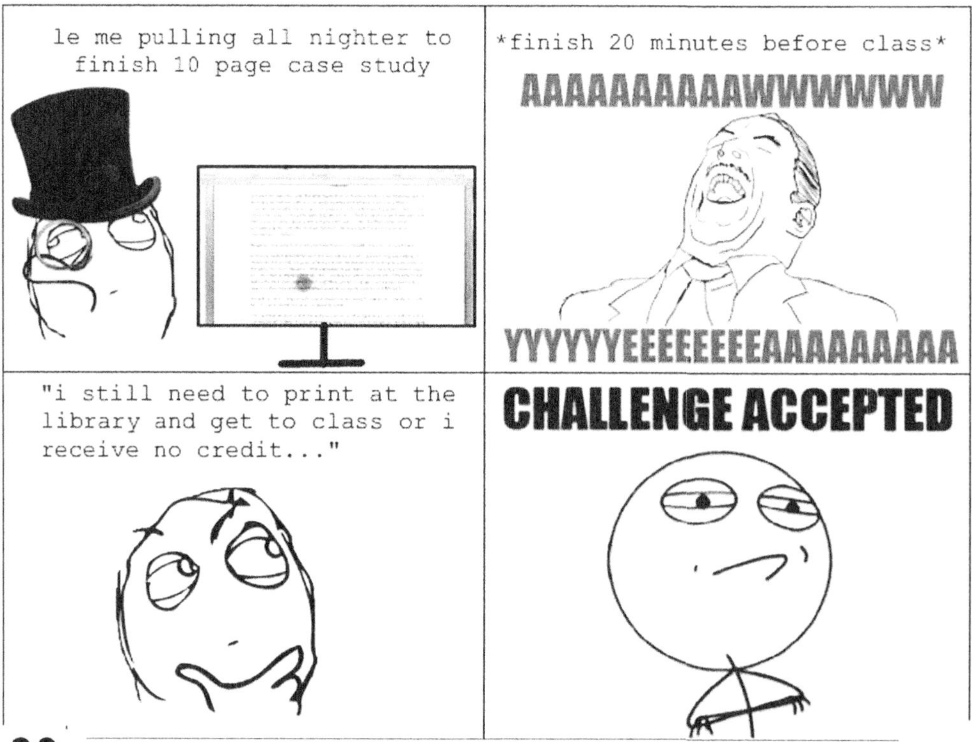
le me pulling all nighter to finish 10 page case study
finish 20 minutes before class
AAAAAAAAAAWWWWWW
YYYYYYEEEEEEEEAAAAAAAAA
"i still need to print at the library and get to class or i receive no credit..."
CHALLENGE ACCEPTED

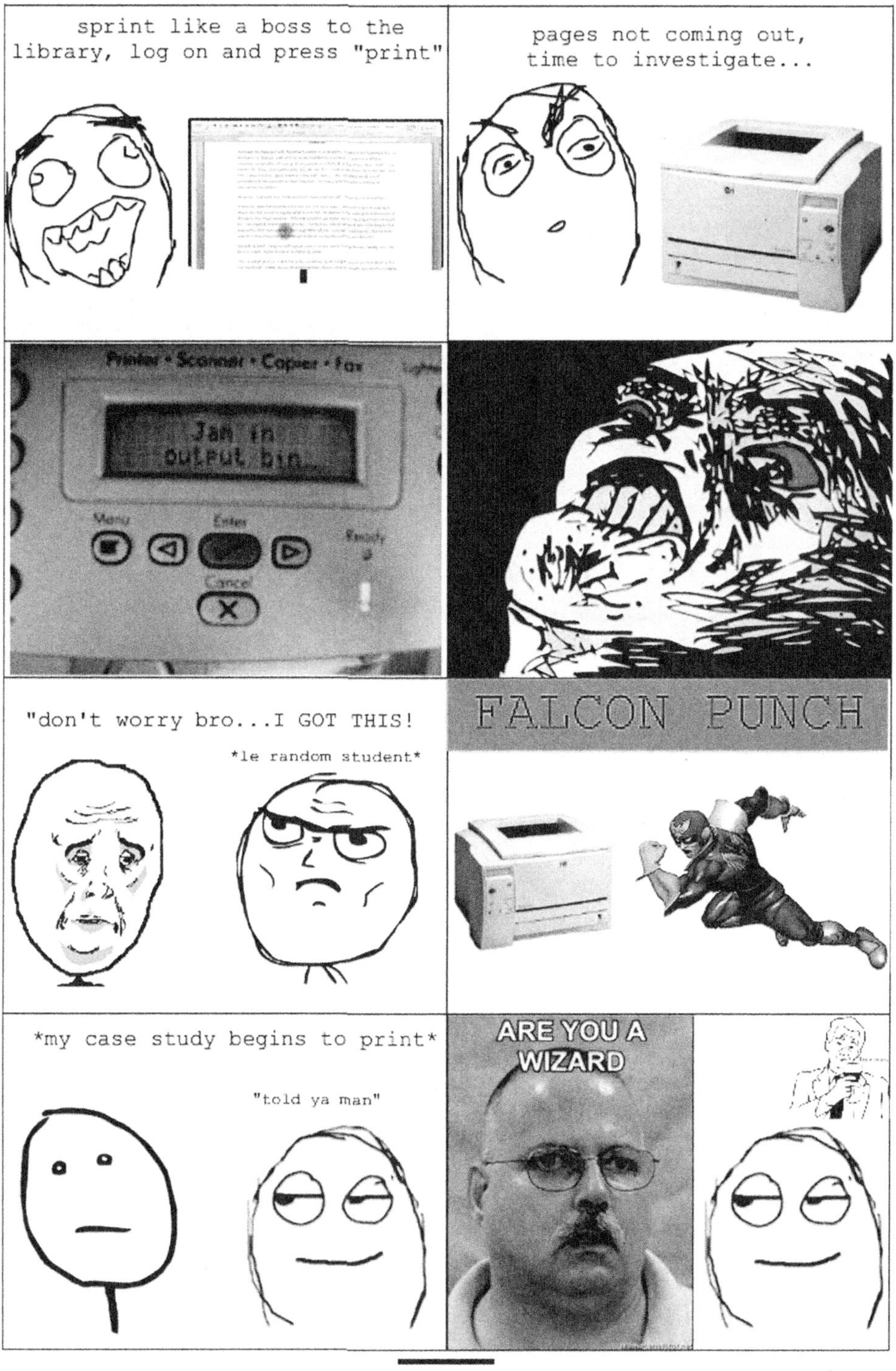
sprint like a boss to the library, log on and press "print"
pages not coming out, time to investigate...
Printer • Scanner • Copier • Fax
Jam in output bin
Menu
Enter
Ready
Cancel
"don't worry bro...I GOT THIS!
le random student
FALCON PUNCH
my case study begins to print
"told ya man"
ARE YOU A WIZARD

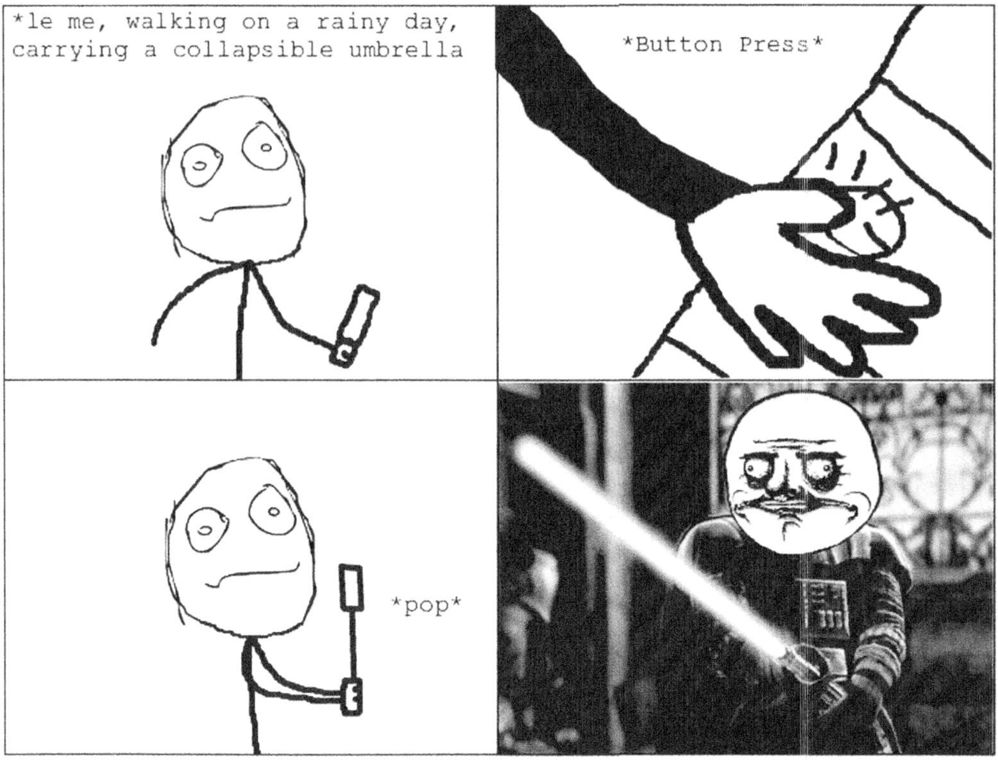
*le me, walking on a rainy day, carrying a collapsible umbrella
Button Press
pop

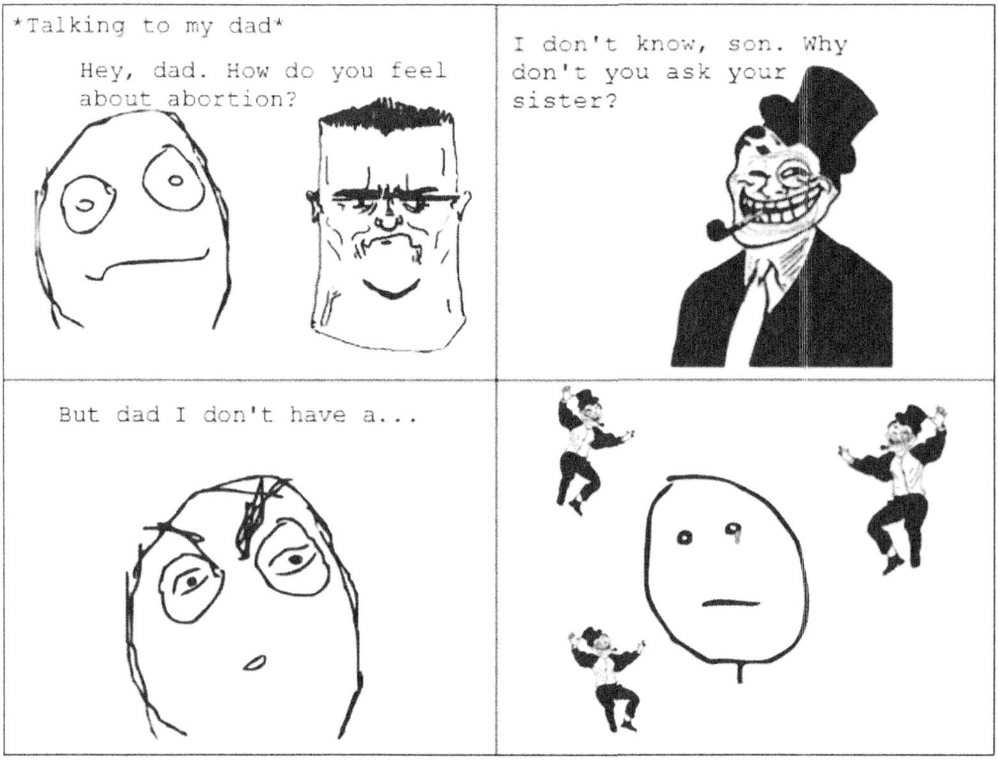
Talking to my dad
Hey, dad. How do you feel about abortion?
I don't know, son. Why don't you ask your sister?
But dad I don't have a...

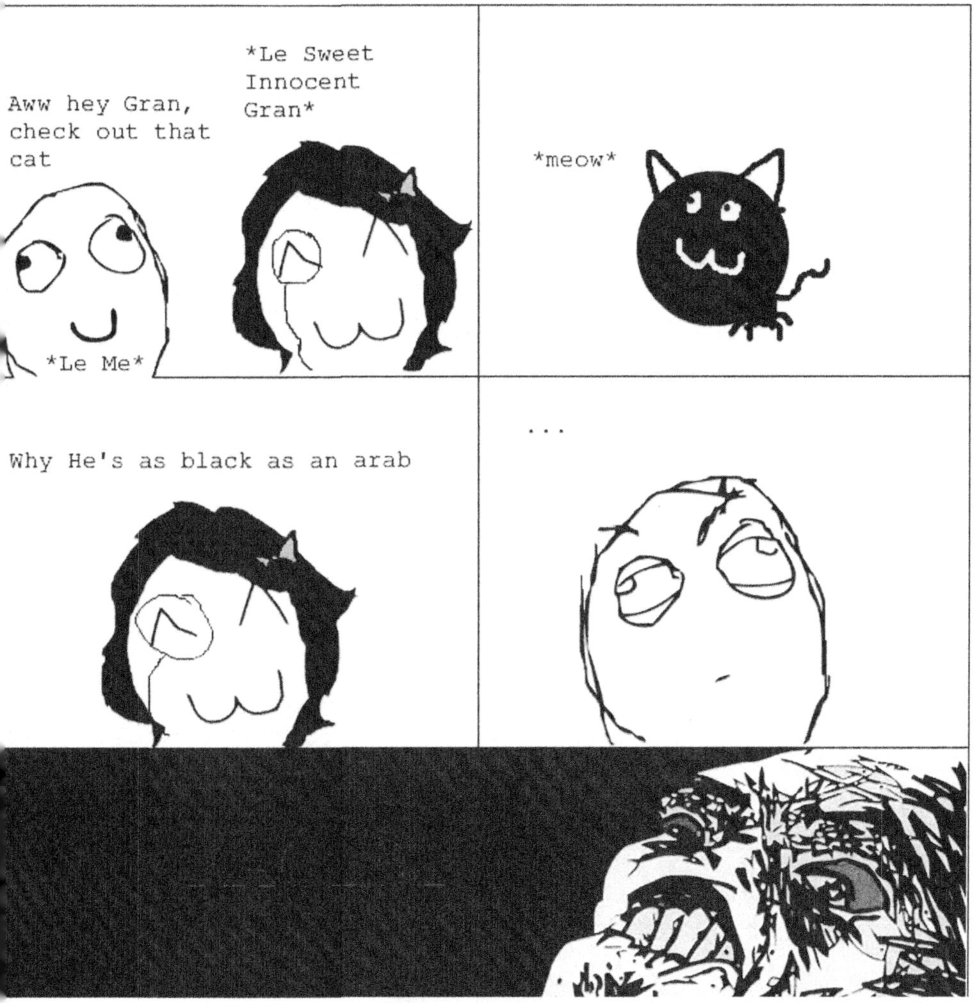

Aww hey Gran, check out that cat
Le Sweet Innocent Gran
Le Me
meow
Why He's as black as an arab
...

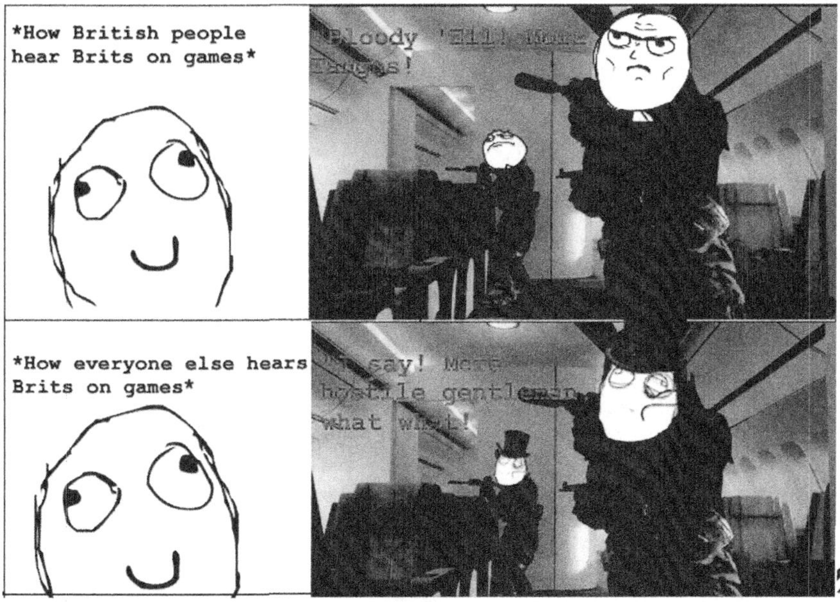

How British people hear Brits on games
Bloody 'Ell! More
How everyone else hears Brits on games
say! More
what

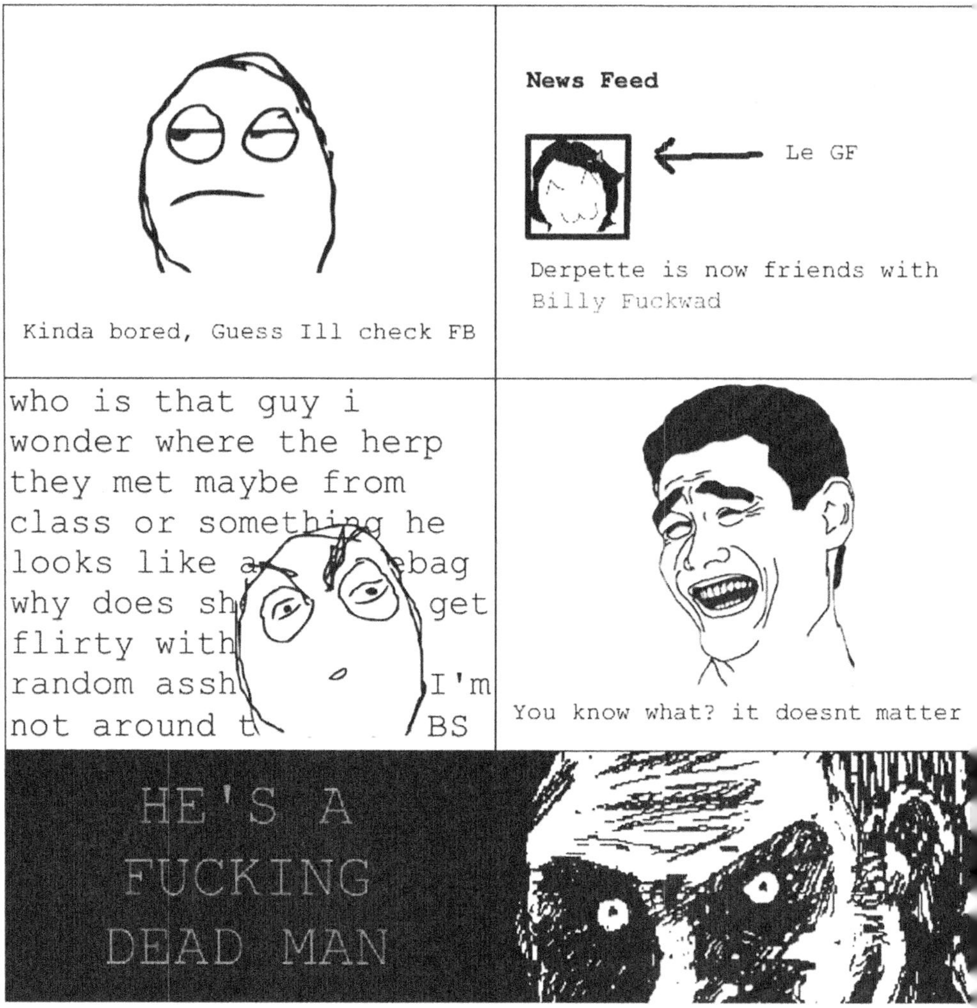
Kinda bored, Guess Ill check FB
News Feed
Le GF
Derpette is now friends with Billy Fuckwad
who is that guy i
wonder where the herp
they met maybe from
class or someth he
looks like a ebag
why does sh get
flirty with
random assh I'm
not around t BS
You know what? it doesnt matter
HE'S A FUCKING DEAD MAN

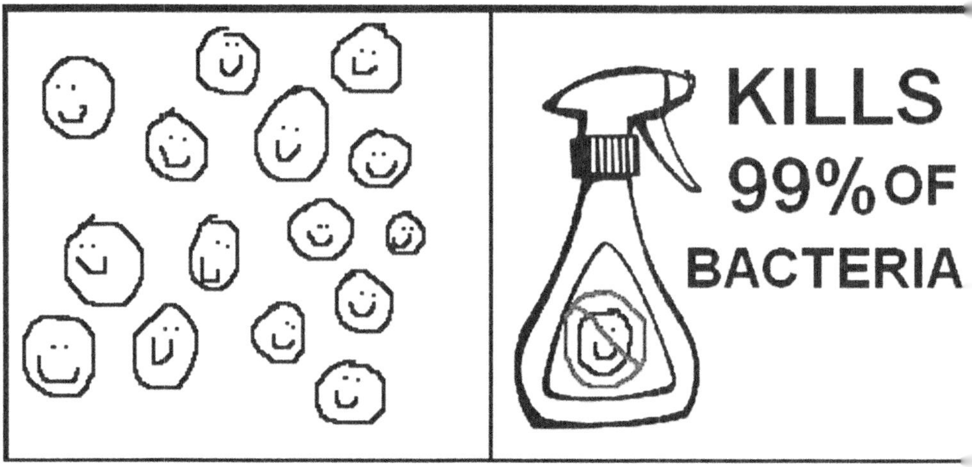
KILLS 99% OF BACTERIA

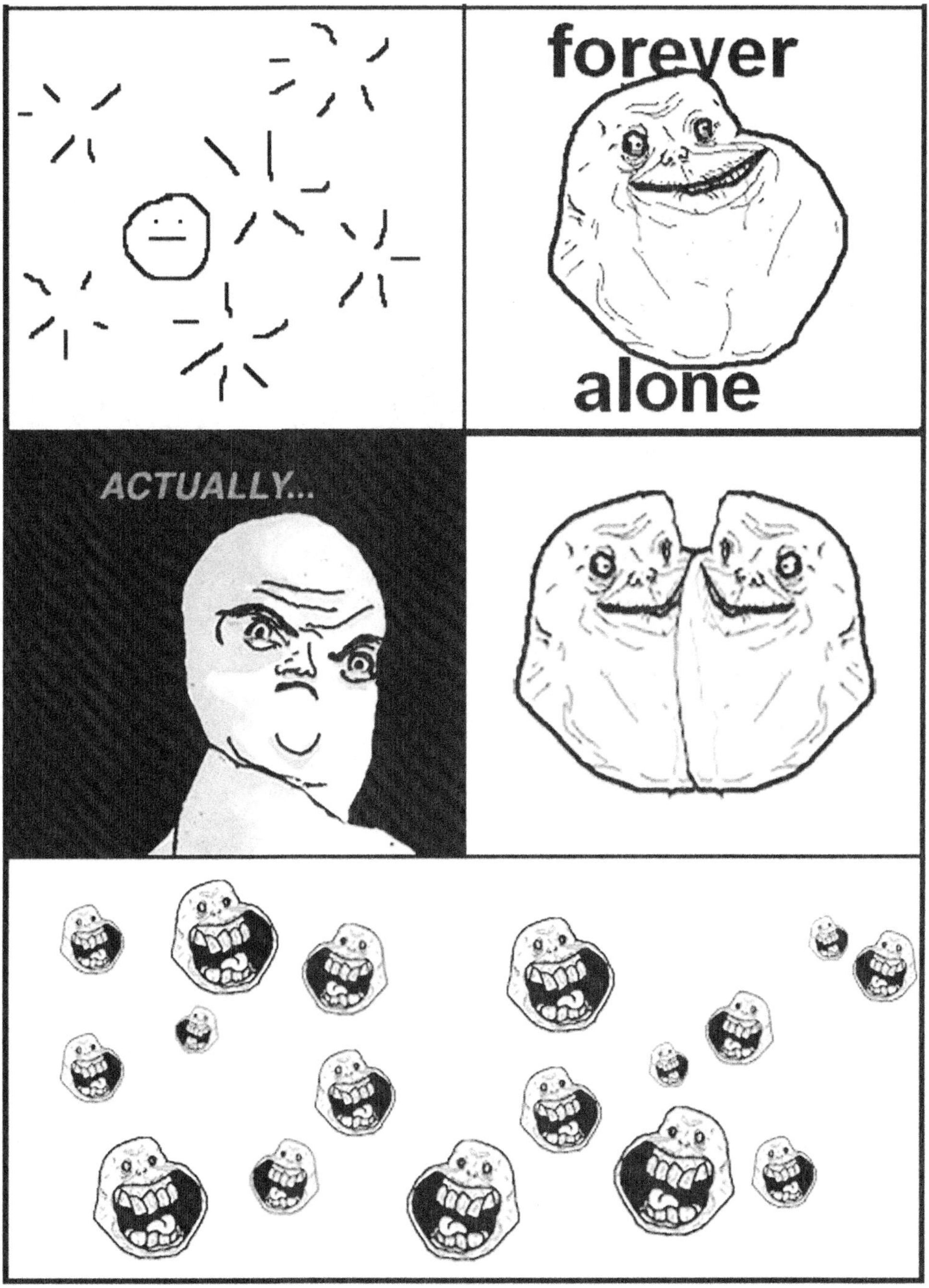
forever
alone
ACTUALLY...

*me, after working outside all day

I'm so hungry but way too tired to move...

Time to get delivery!

Hello...can i have a scallion pancake, pork and cabbage dumplings, hot and sour soup, hunan beef, and a large order of rice?

LATER...

Yay, food's here! Time to eat!

*unpacking food...

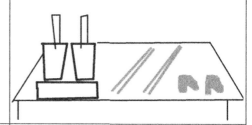

Hmmm...two sets of chopsticks... two fortune cookies...

28.

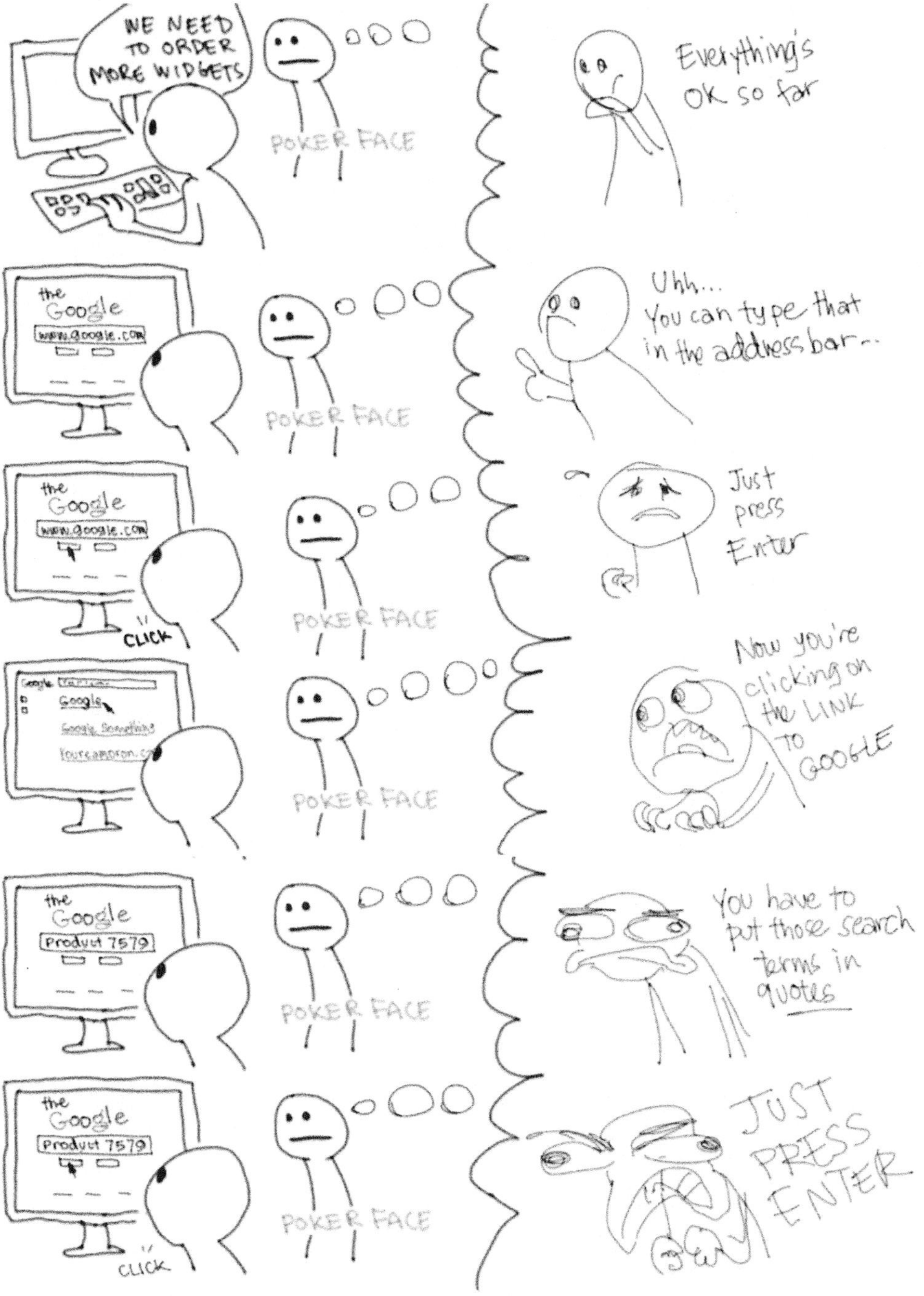

WE NEED TO ORDER MORE WIDGETS
POKER FACE
Everything's ok so far
the Google
www.google.com
POKER FACE
Uhh... You can type that in the address bar...
the Google
www.google.com
CLICK
POKER FACE
Just press Enter
Google
POKER FACE
Now you're clicking on the LINK TO GOOGLE
the Google
Product 7579
POKER FACE
You have to put those search terms in quotes
the Google
Product 7579
CLICK
POKER FACE
JUST PRESS ENTER

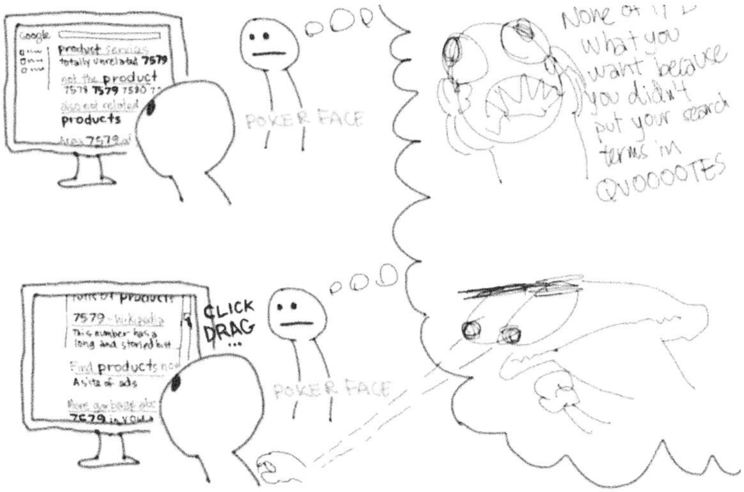
Google
product
totally unrelated 7579
not the product
7578 7579 7580
products
POKER FACE
what you want because you didn't put your search terms in QUOOOOTES
7579 - Wikipedia
This number has a long and storied hist
Find products now
A site of ads
7579 in YOUR
CLICK DRAG ...
POKER FACE

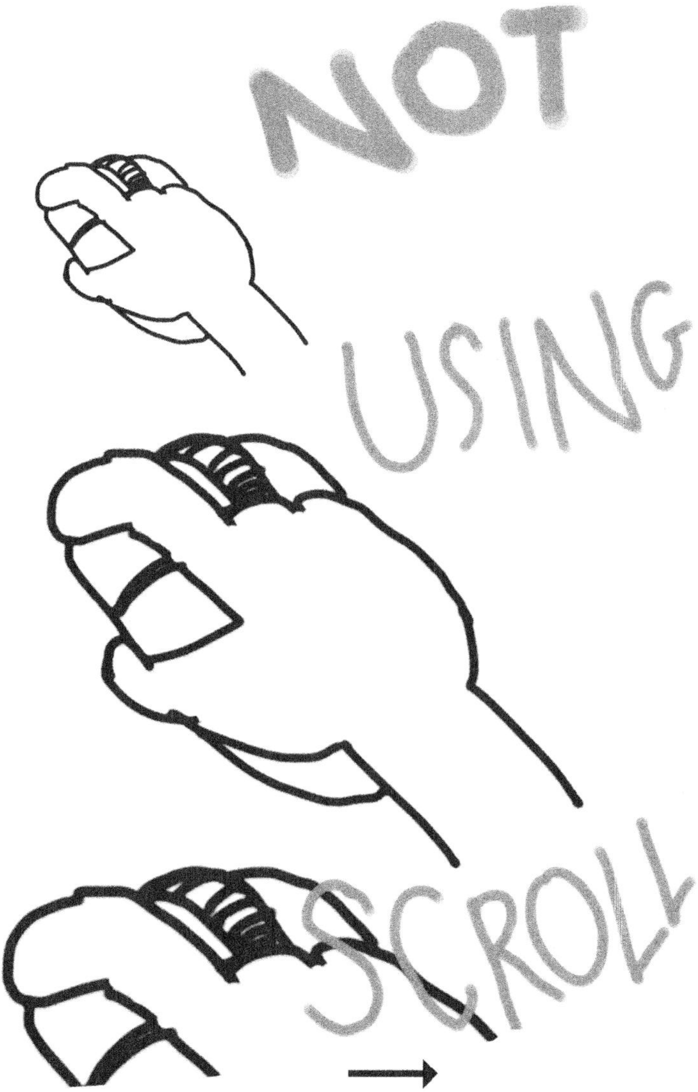
NOT
USING
SCROLL

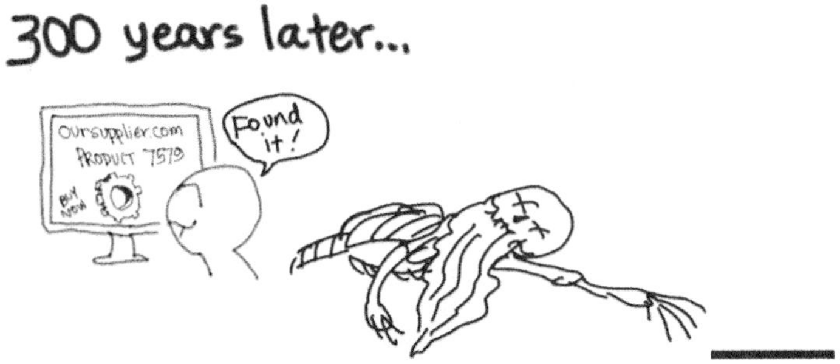
300 years later...
Oursupplier.com
PRODUCT 7579
BUY NOW
Found it!

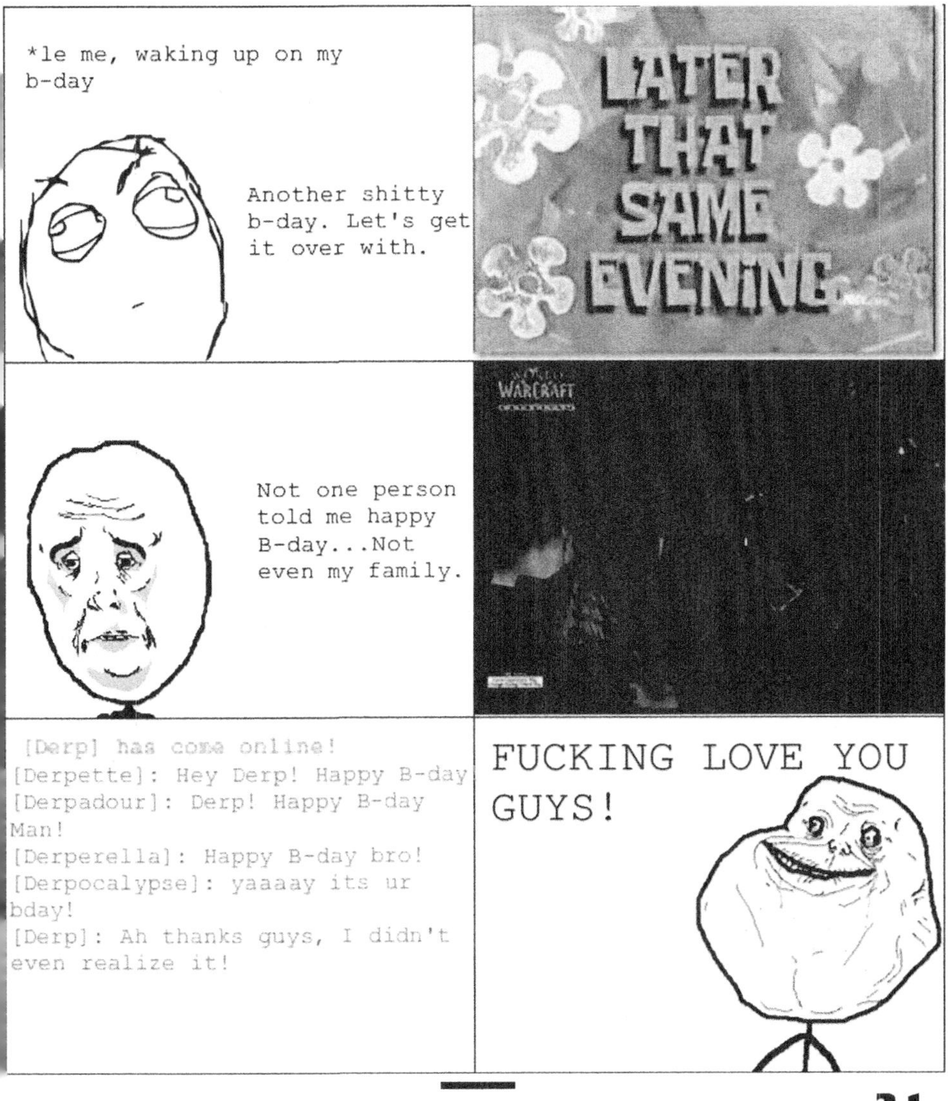
*le me, waking up on my b-day
Another shitty b-day. Let's get it over with.
LATER THAT SAME EVENING
Not one person told me happy B-day...Not even my family.
WARCRAFT
[Derp] has come online!
[Derpette]: Hey Derp! Happy B-day
[Derpadour]: Derp! Happy B-day Man!
[Derperella]: Happy B-day bro!
[Derpocalypse]: yaaaay its ur bday!
[Derp]: Ah thanks guys, I didn't even realize it!
FUCKING LOVE YOU GUYS!

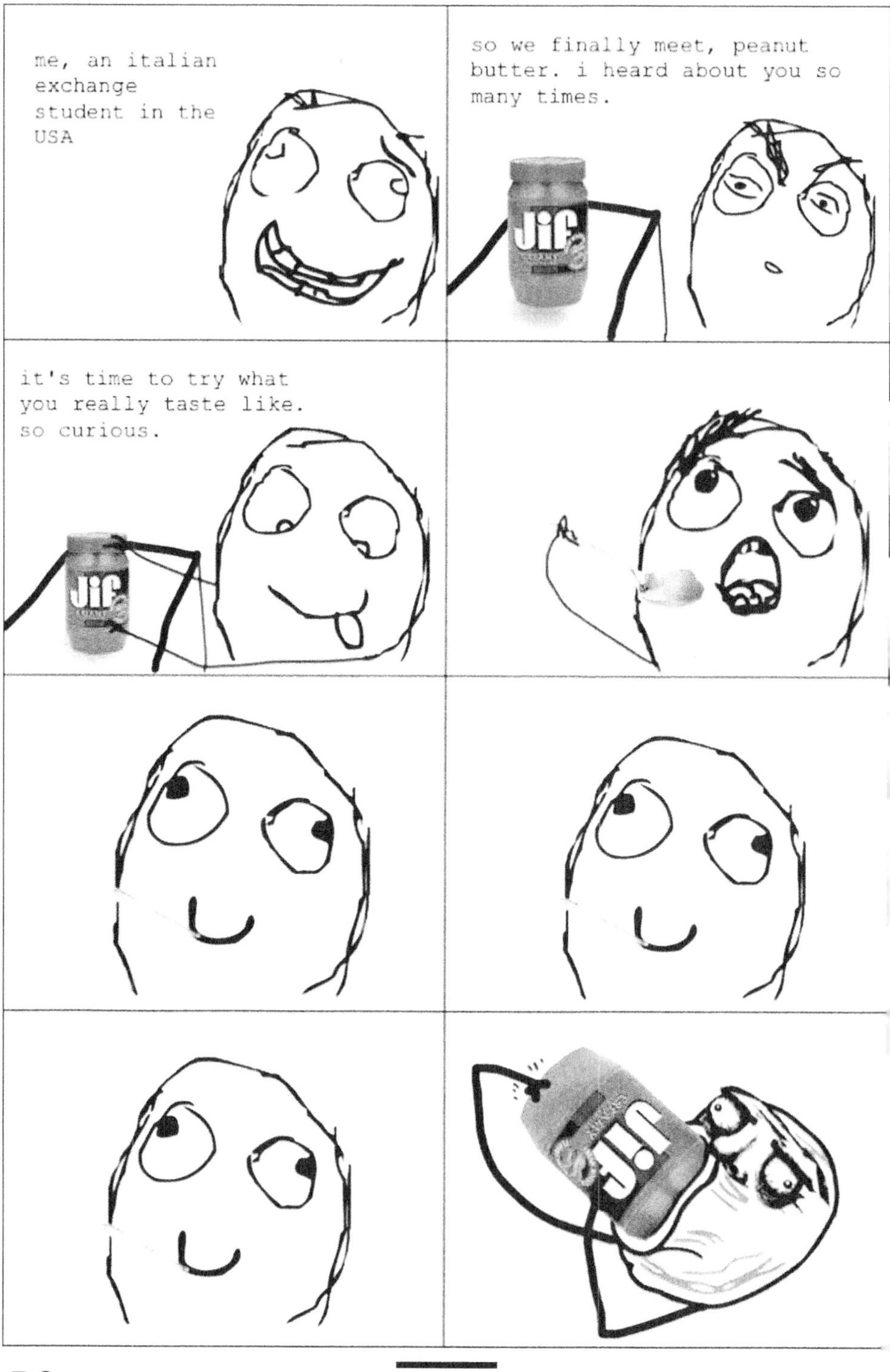
me, an italian exchange student in the USA
so we finally meet, peanut butter. i heard about you so many times.
Jif
it's time to try what you really taste like. so curious.
Jif
Jif

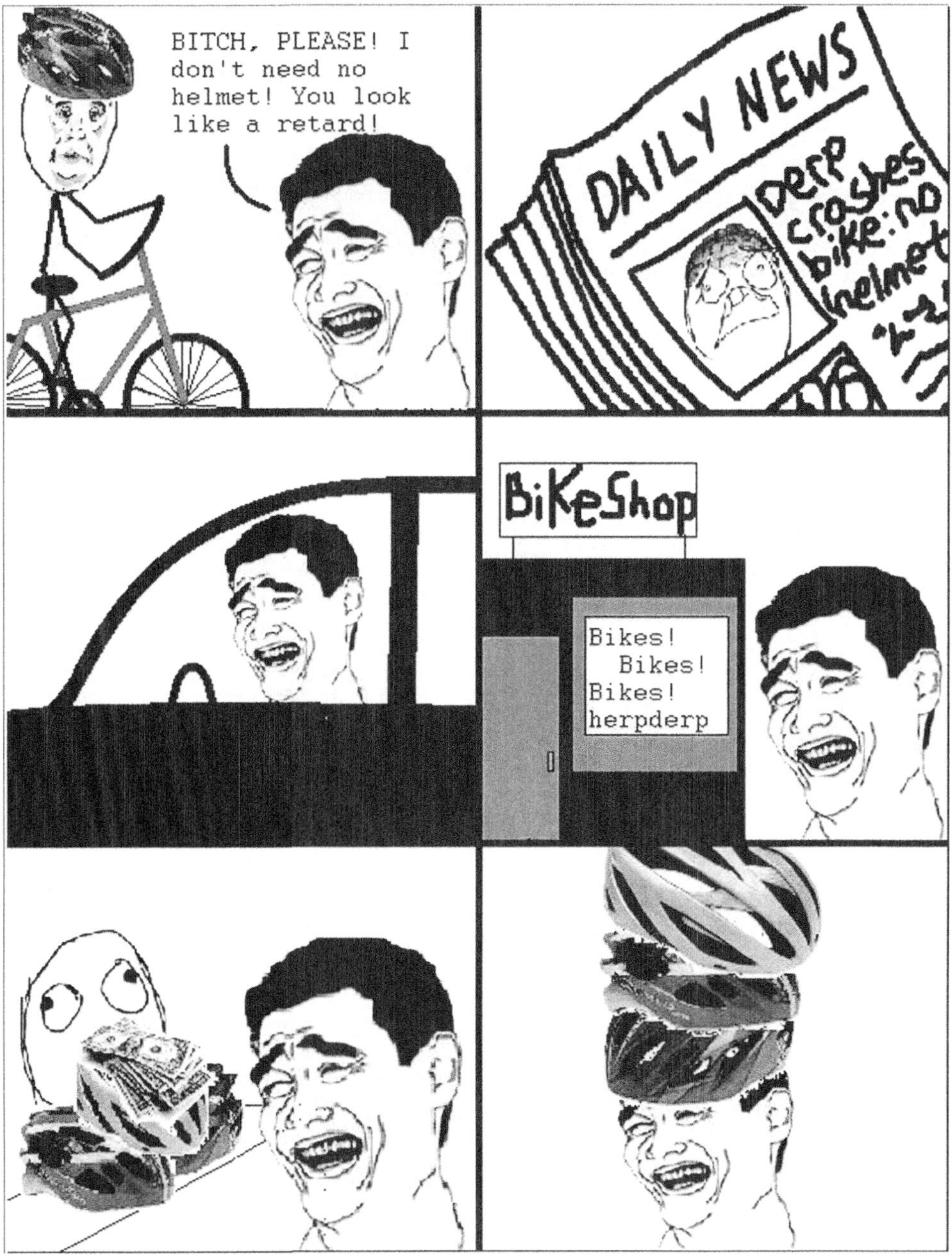
BITCH, PLEASE! I don't need no helmet! You look like a retard!
DAILY NEWS
derp crashes bike: no helmet
BikeShop
Bikes!
Bikes!
Bikes!
herpderp

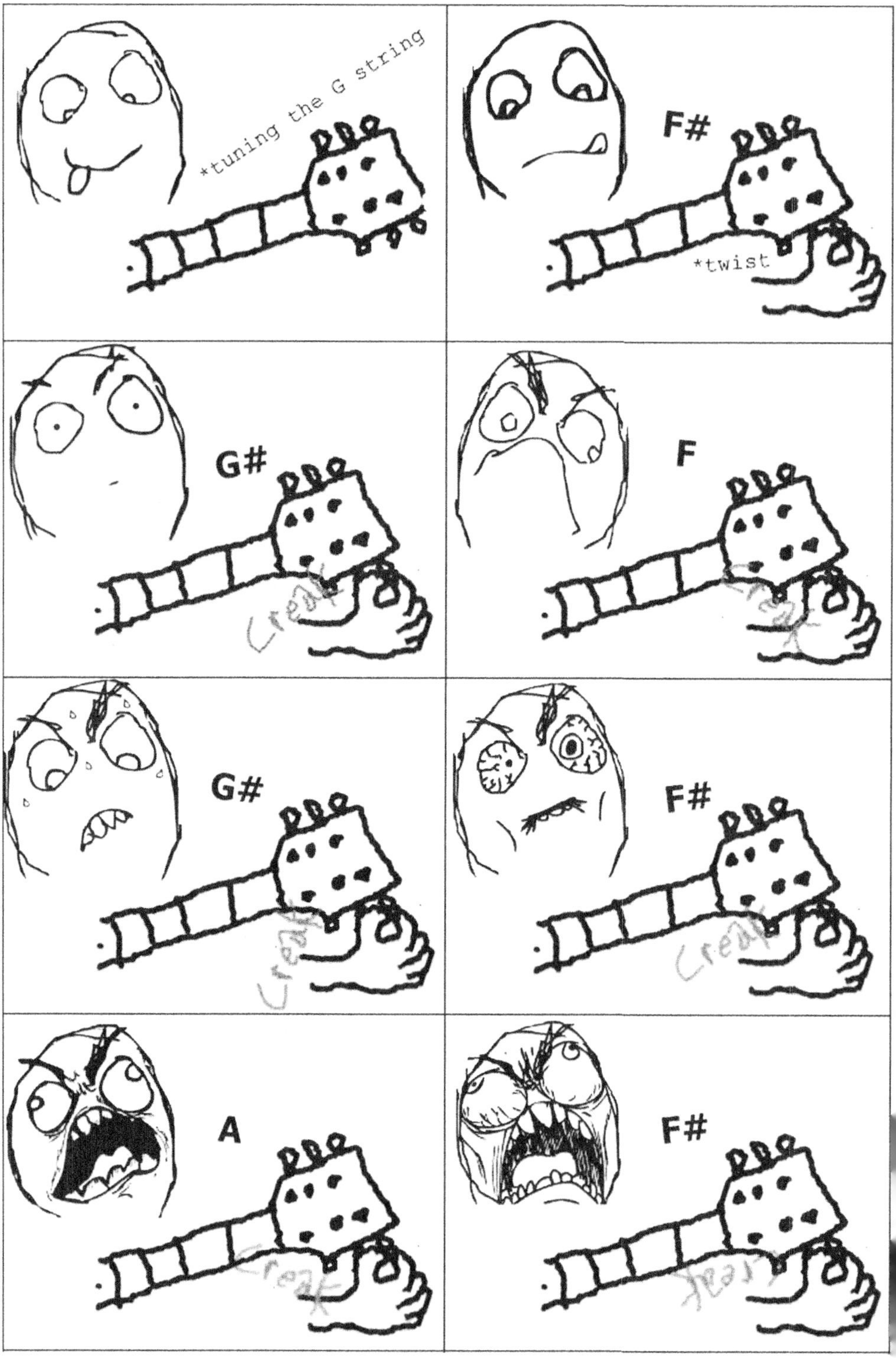
*tuning the G string
F#
*twist
G#
F
creak
G#
F#
creak
A
F#
creak

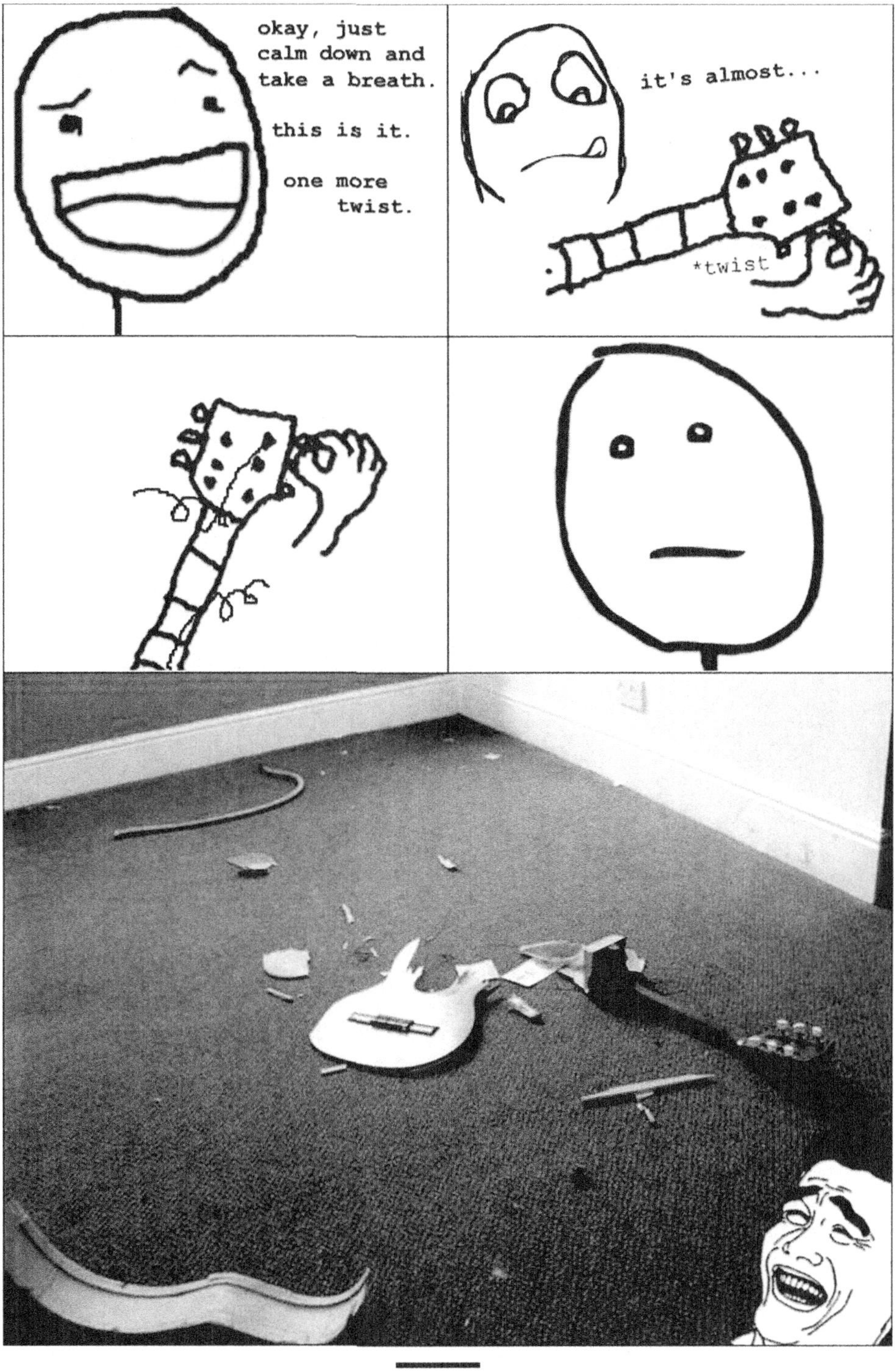
okay, just calm down and take a breath.
this is it.
one more twist.
it's almost...
*twist

YOU'VE REALLY FORGOTTEN WHAT DAY IT IS?!?

JESUS FUCK!

NO PRESENT, NOT EVEN A CARD

N..no.
I didn't forget.

Let me get your present...

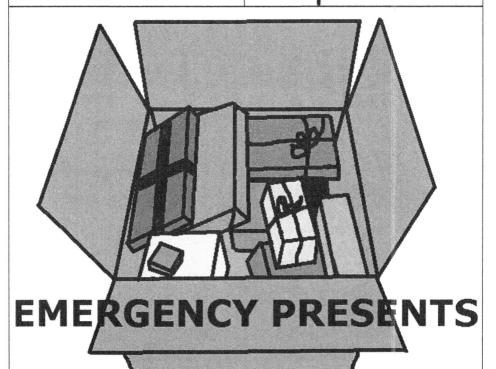

EMERGENCY PRESENTS

OMG
You remembered!
I love you.

I'm so sorry I doubted you!

NO IDEA WHAT THE OCCASION IS.

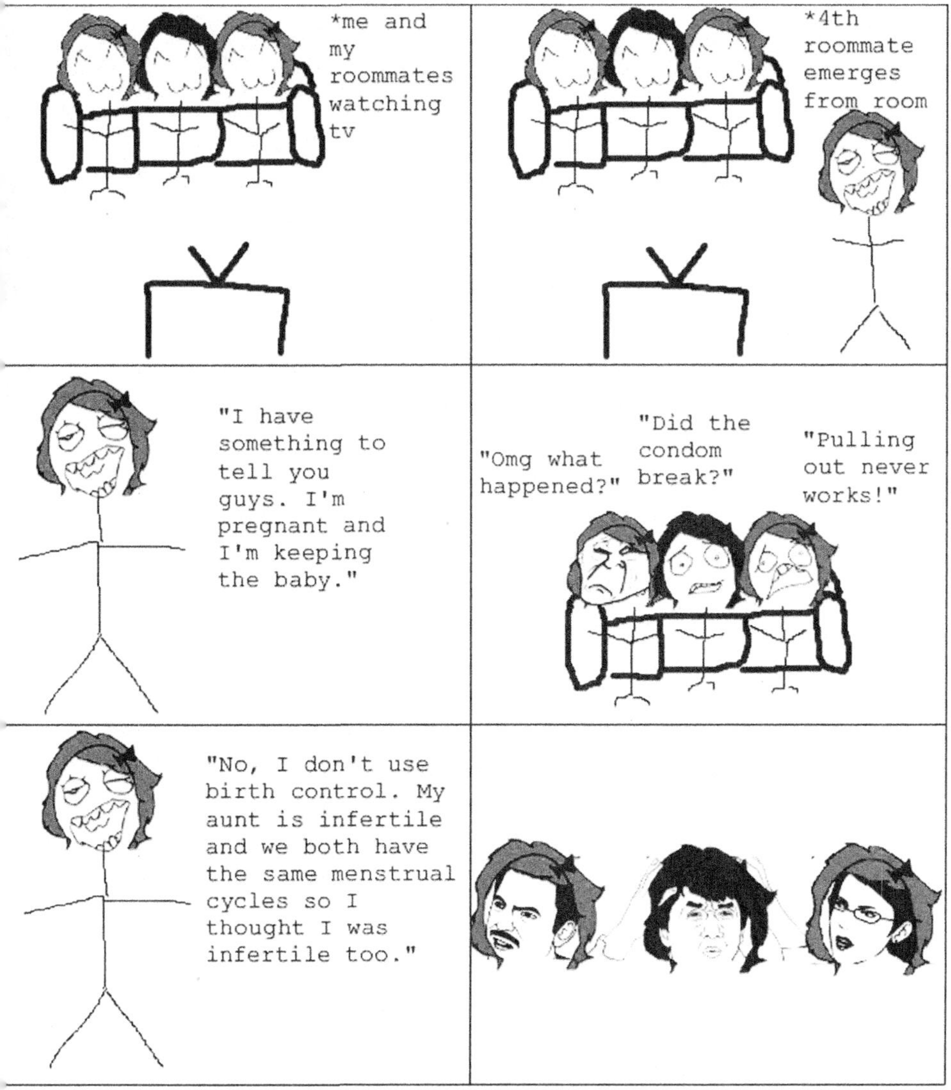
*me and my roommates watching tv
*4th roommate emerges from room
"I have something to tell you guys. I'm pregnant and I'm keeping the baby."
"Omg what happened?"
"Did the condom break?"
"Pulling out never works!"
"No, I don't use birth control. My aunt is infertile and we both have the same menstrual cycles so I thought I was infertile too."

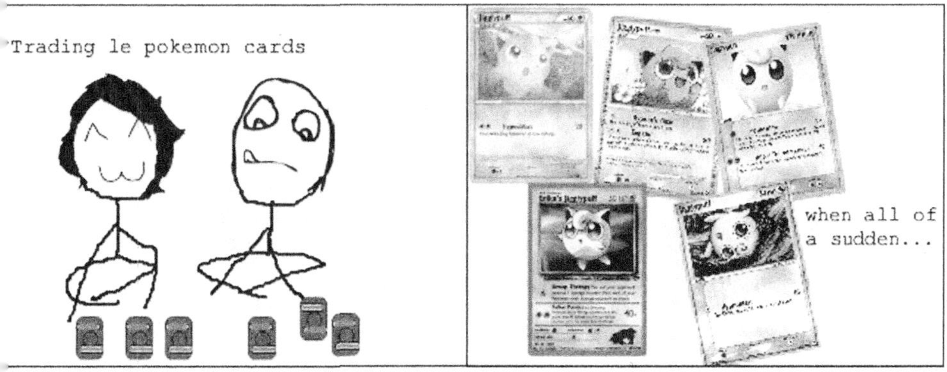
Trading le pokemon cards
when all of a sudden...

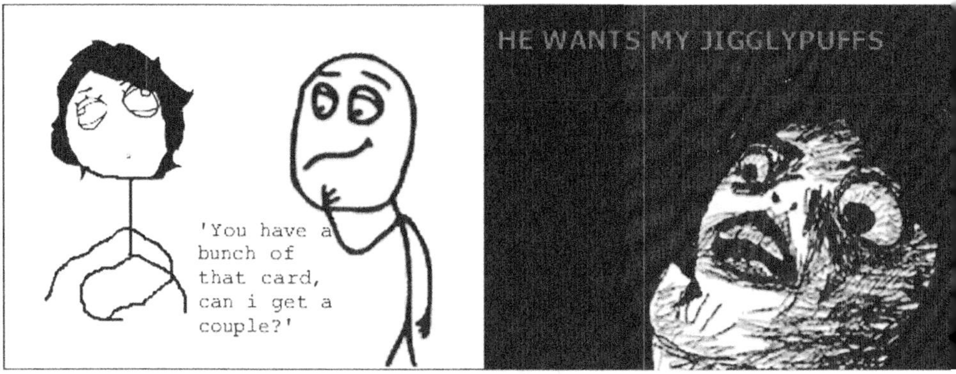
'You have a bunch of that card, can i get a couple?'
HE WANTS MY JIGGLYPUFFS

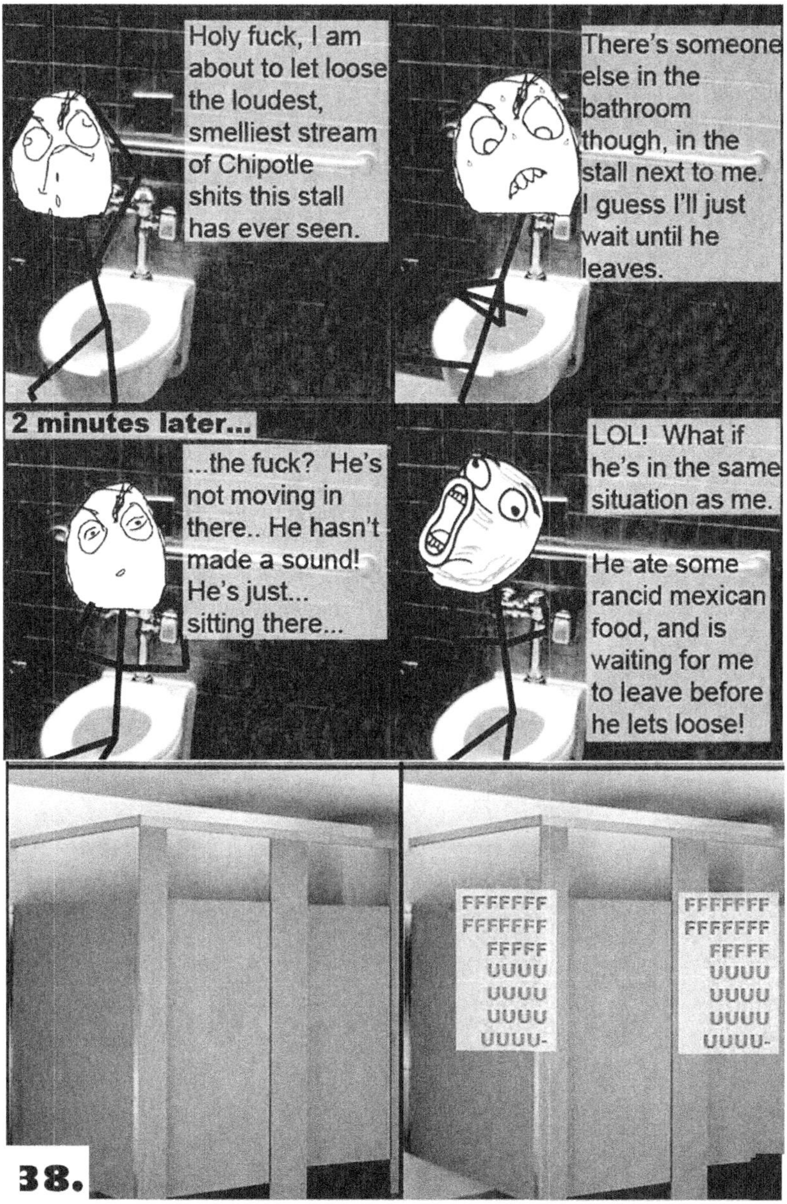
Holy fuck, I am about to let loose the loudest, smelliest stream of Chipotle shits this stall has ever seen.
There's someone else in the bathroom though, in the stall next to me. I guess I'll just wait until he leaves.
2 minutes later...
...the fuck? He's not moving in there.. He hasn't made a sound! He's just... sitting there...
LOL! What if he's in the same situation as me.
He ate some rancid mexican food, and is waiting for me to leave before he lets loose!
FFFFFFF FFFFFFF FFFFF UUUU UUUU UUUU UUUU-
FFFFFFF FFFFFFF FFFFF UUUU UUUU UUUU UUUU-

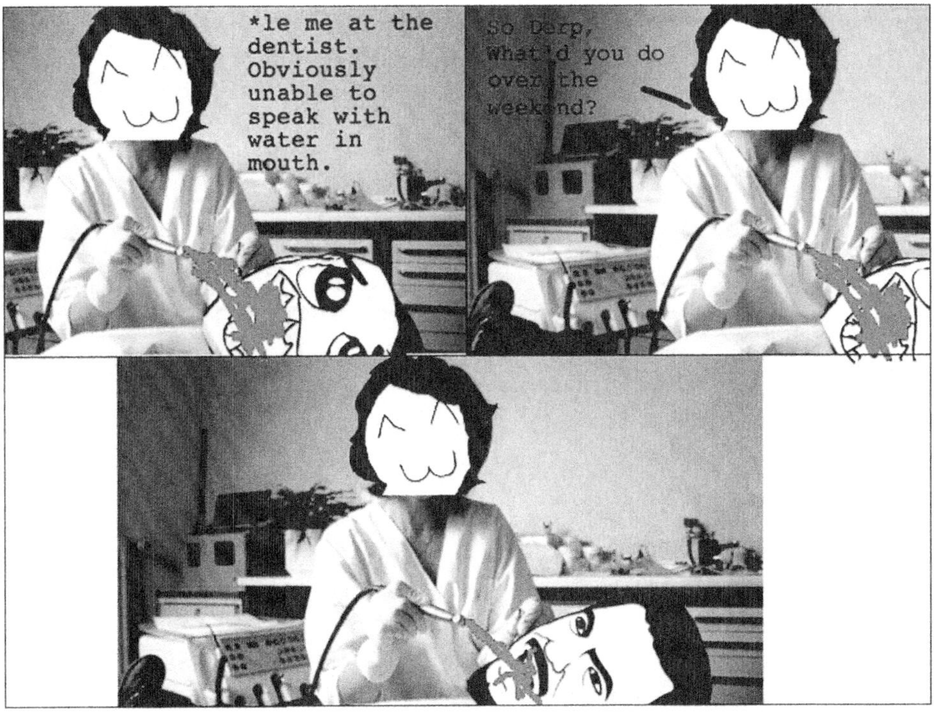
*le me at the dentist. Obviously unable to speak with water in mouth.
So Derp, What'd you do over the weekend?

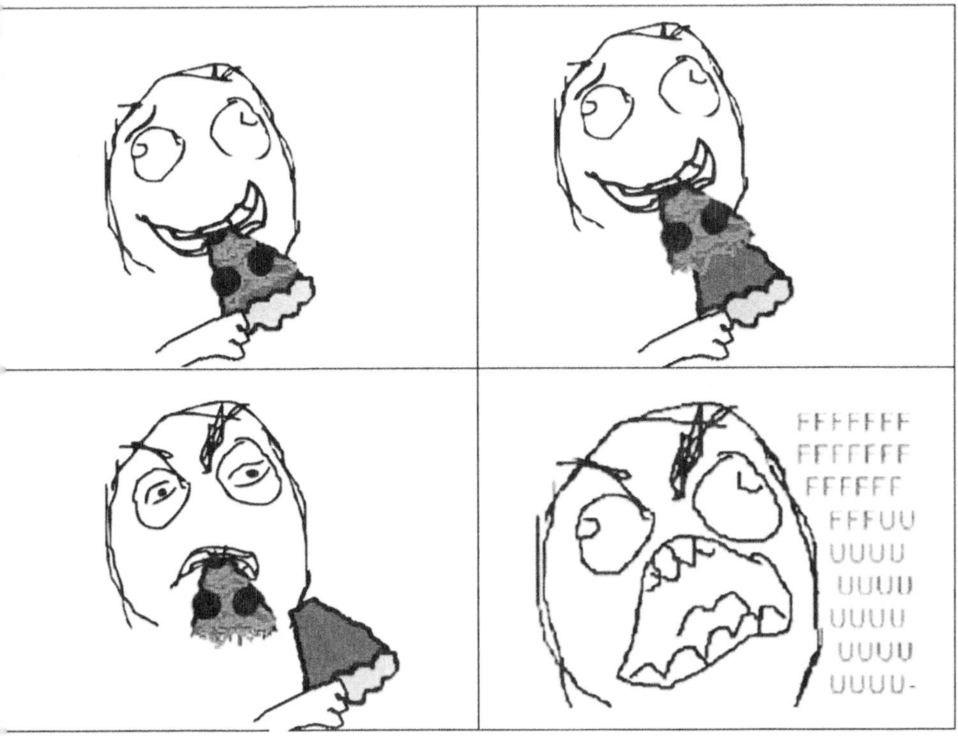
FFFFFFF
FFFFFFF
FFFFFF
FFFUU
UUUU
UUUU
UUUU
UUUU
UUUU-

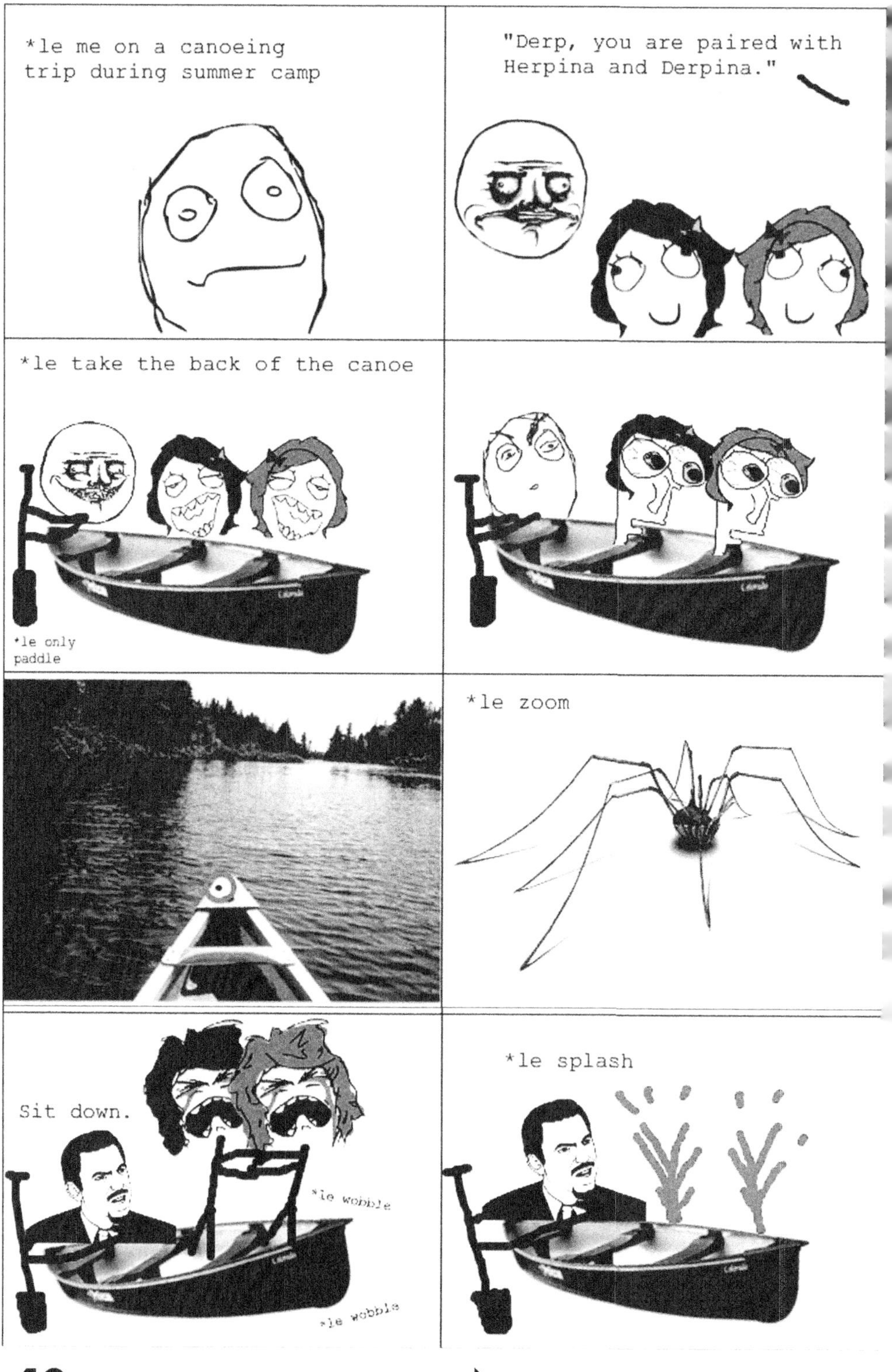
*le me on a canoeing trip during summer camp
"Derp, you are paired with Herpina and Derpina."
*le take the back of the canoe
*le only paddle
*le zoom
Sit down.
*le wobble
*le wobble
*le splash

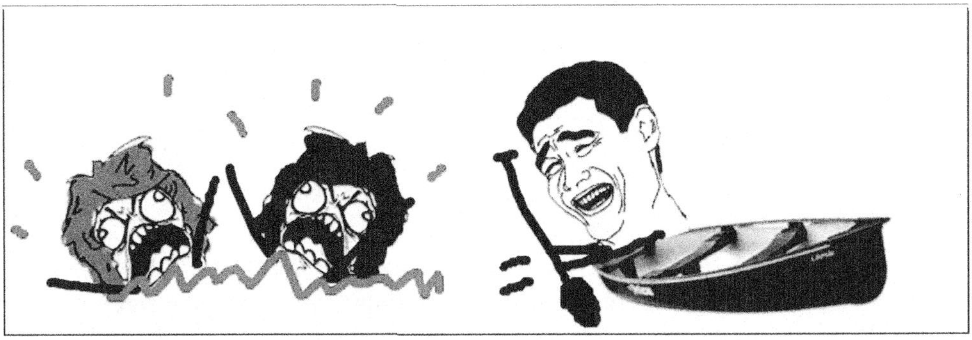

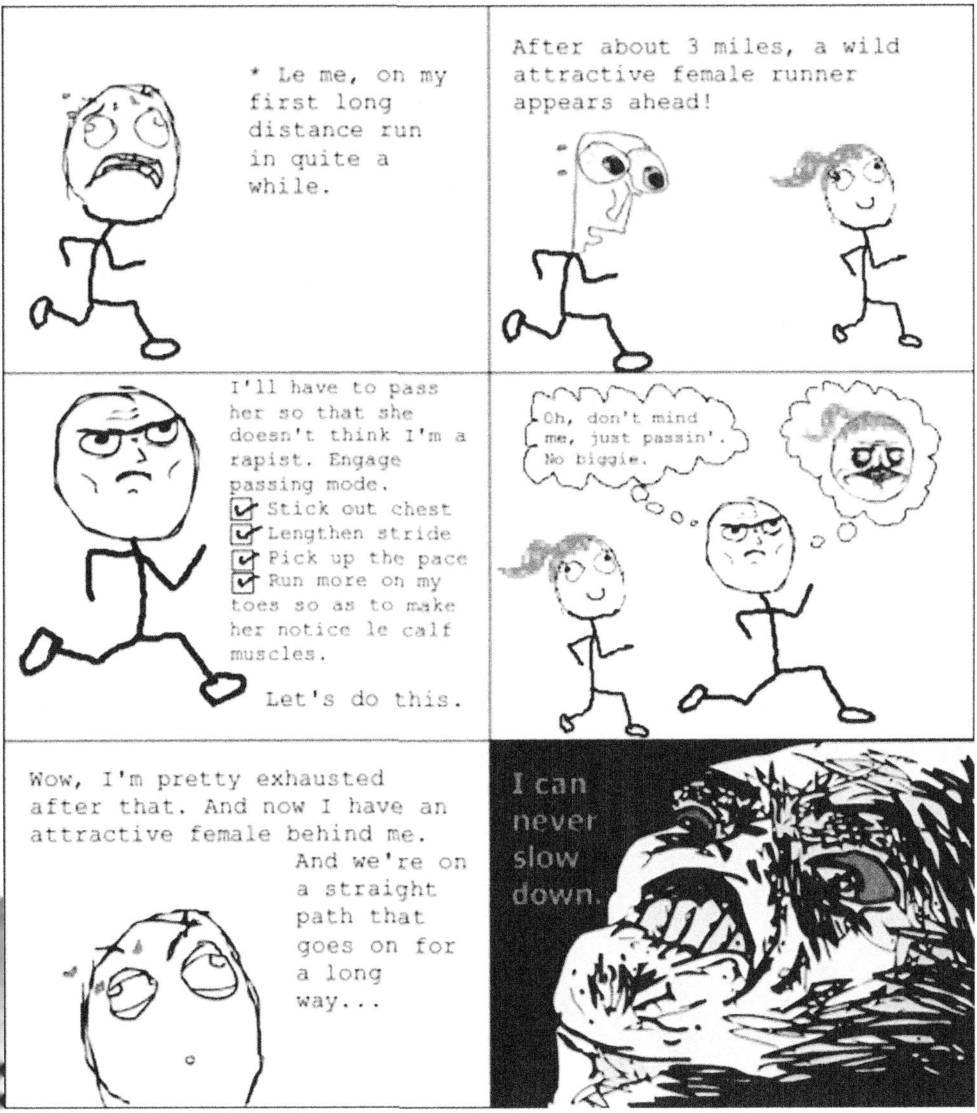
* Le me, on my first long distance run in quite a while.
After about 3 miles, a wild attractive female runner appears ahead!
I'll have to pass her so that she doesn't think I'm a rapist. Engage passing mode.
Stick out chest
Lengthen stride
Pick up the pace
Run more on my toes so as to make her notice le calf muscles.
Let's do this.
Oh, don't mind me, just passin'. No biggie.
Wow, I'm pretty exhausted after that. And now I have an attractive female behind me.
And we're on a straight path that goes on for a long way...
I can never slow down.

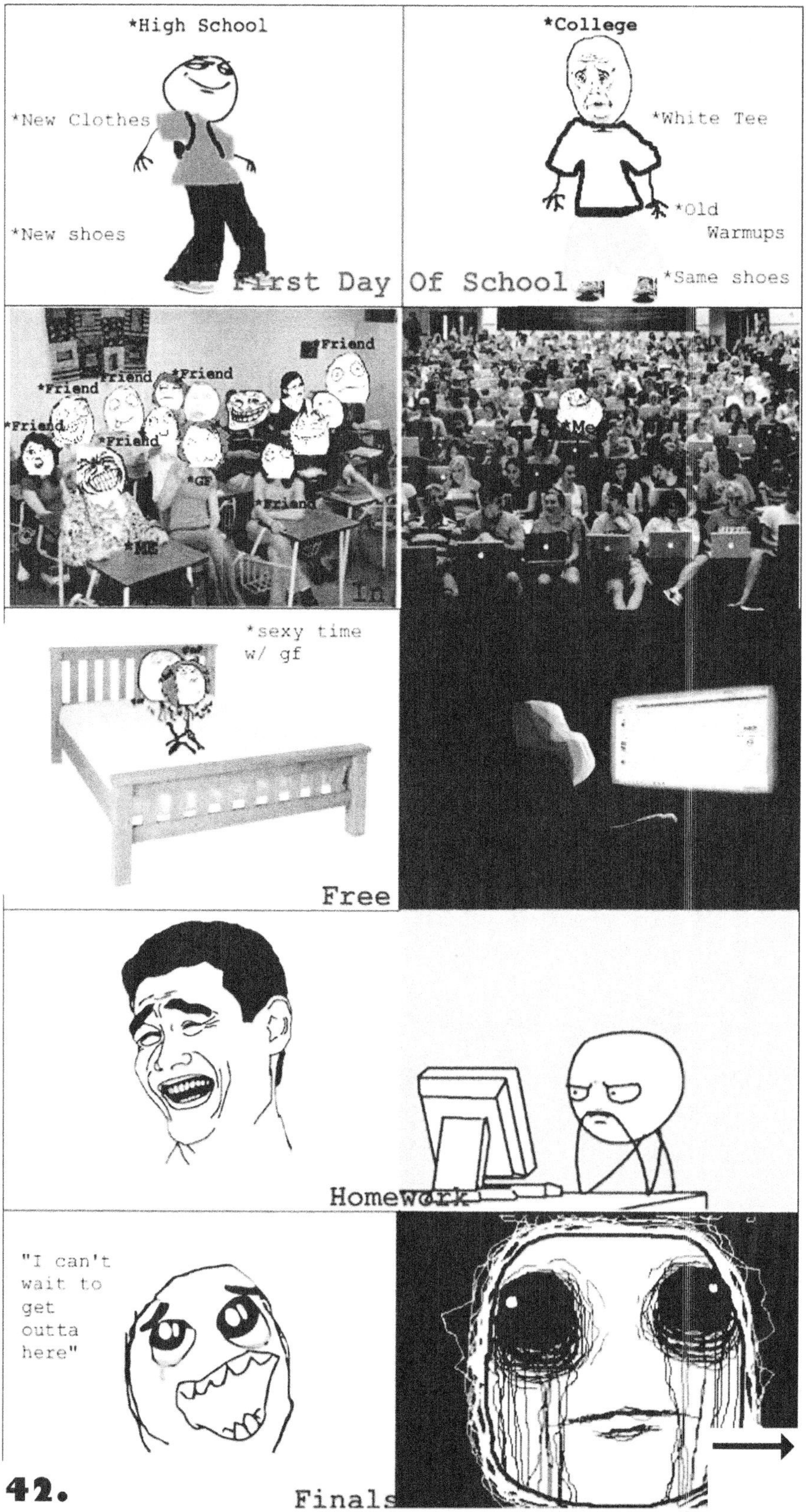
*High School
*New Clothes
*New shoes
*College
*White Tee
*Old Warmups
*Same shoes
First Day Of School
*Friend
*Friend
*Friend
*Friend
*Friend
*Friend
*GF
*Friend
*ME
*Me
In
*sexy time w/ gf
Free
Homework
"I can't wait to get outta here"
Finals

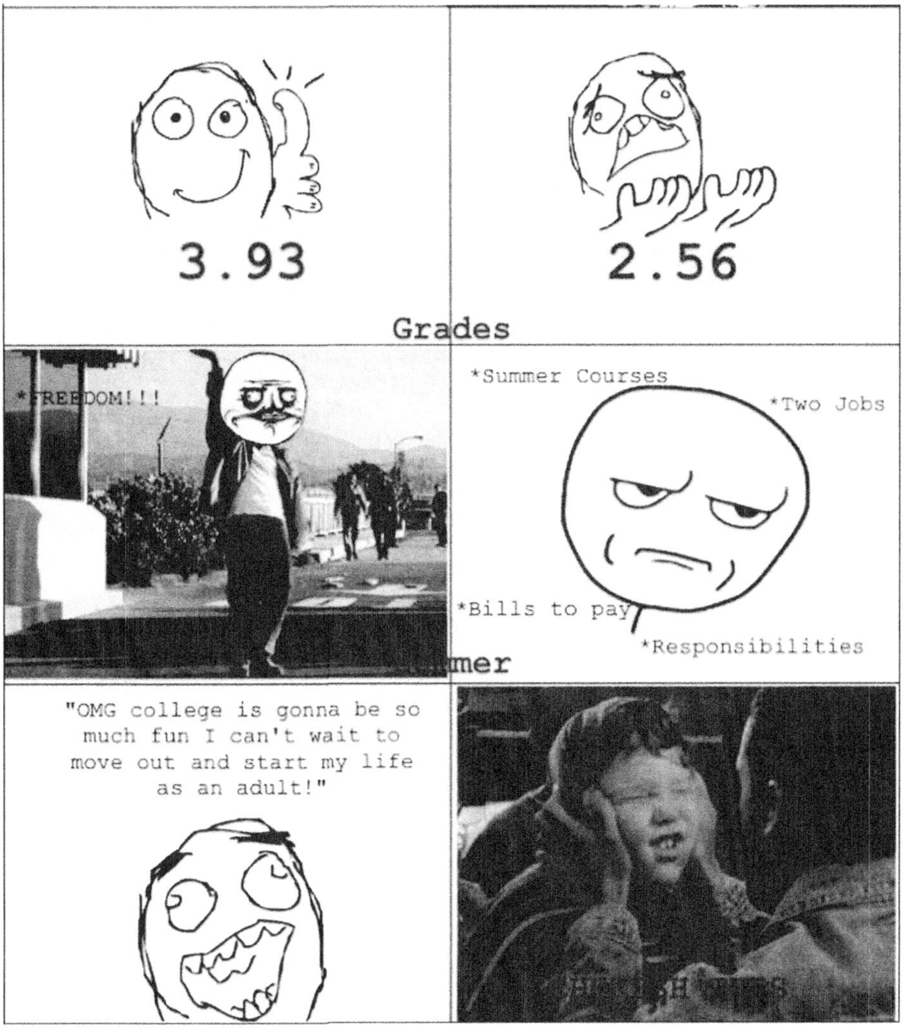
3.93
2.56
Grades
*FREEDOM!!!
*Summer Courses
*Two Jobs
*Bills to pay
*Responsibilities
mer
"OMG college is gonna be so much fun I can't wait to move out and start my life as an adult!"

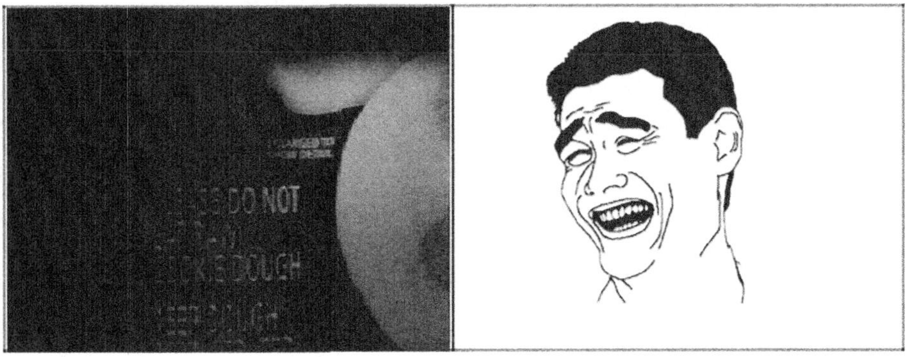
DO NOT

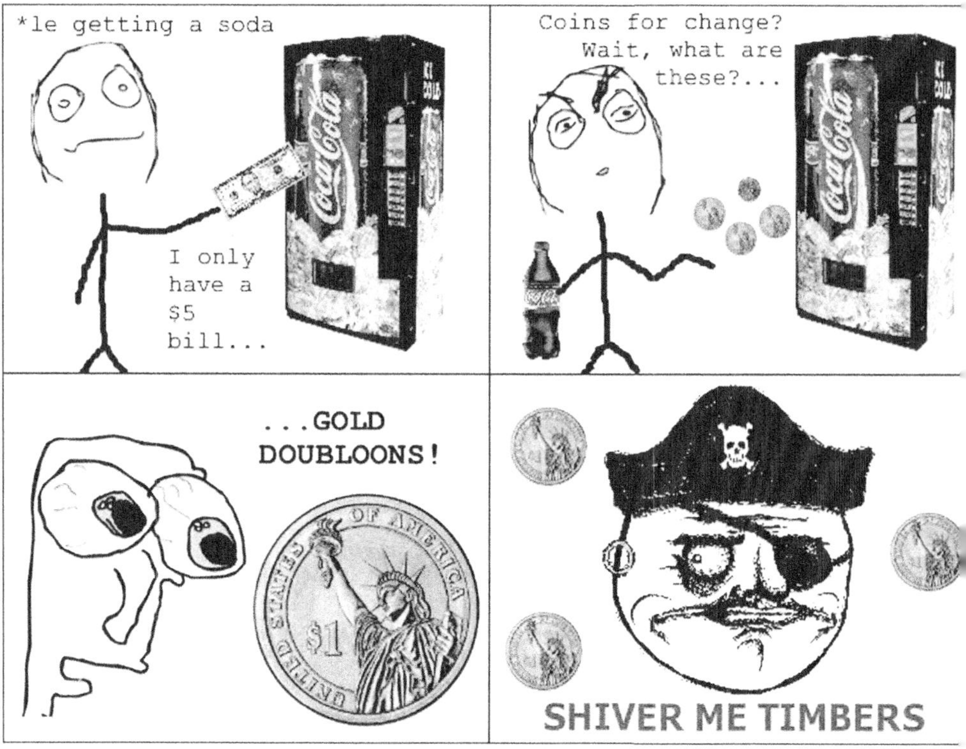
*le getting a soda
I only have a $5 bill...
Coins for change? Wait, what are these?...
...GOLD DOUBLOONS!
SHIVER ME TIMBERS

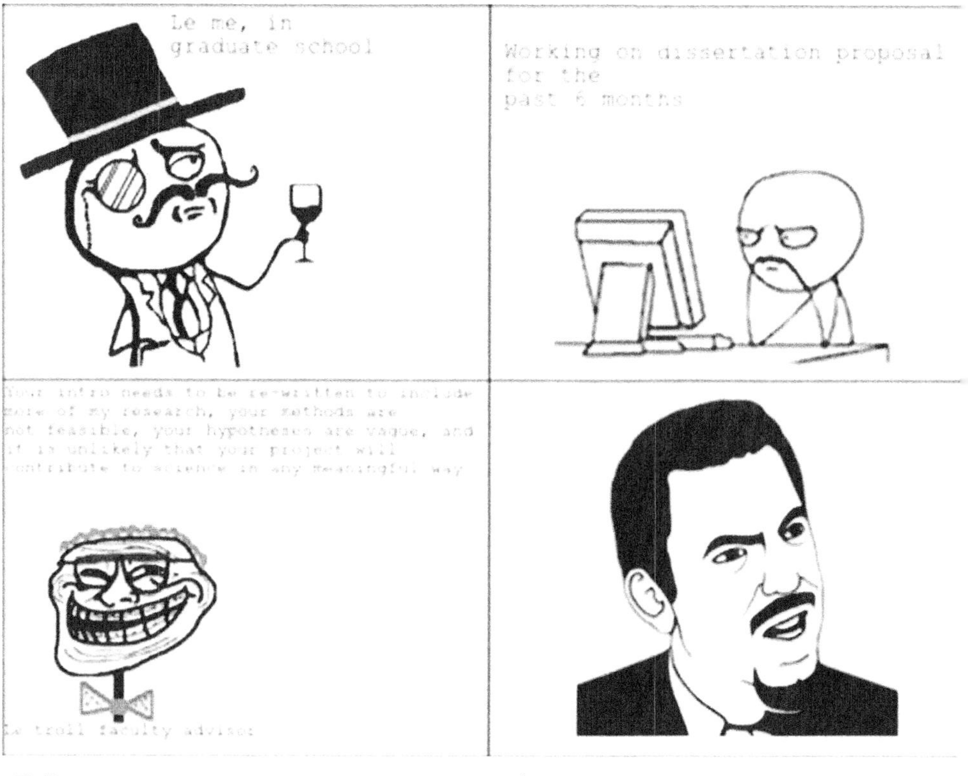
Le me, in graduate school
Working on dissertation proposal for the past 6 months
Your intro needs to be re-written to include more of my research, your methods are not feasible, your hypotheses are vague, and it is unlikely that your project will contribute to science in any meaningful way
Le troll faculty advisor

44.

→

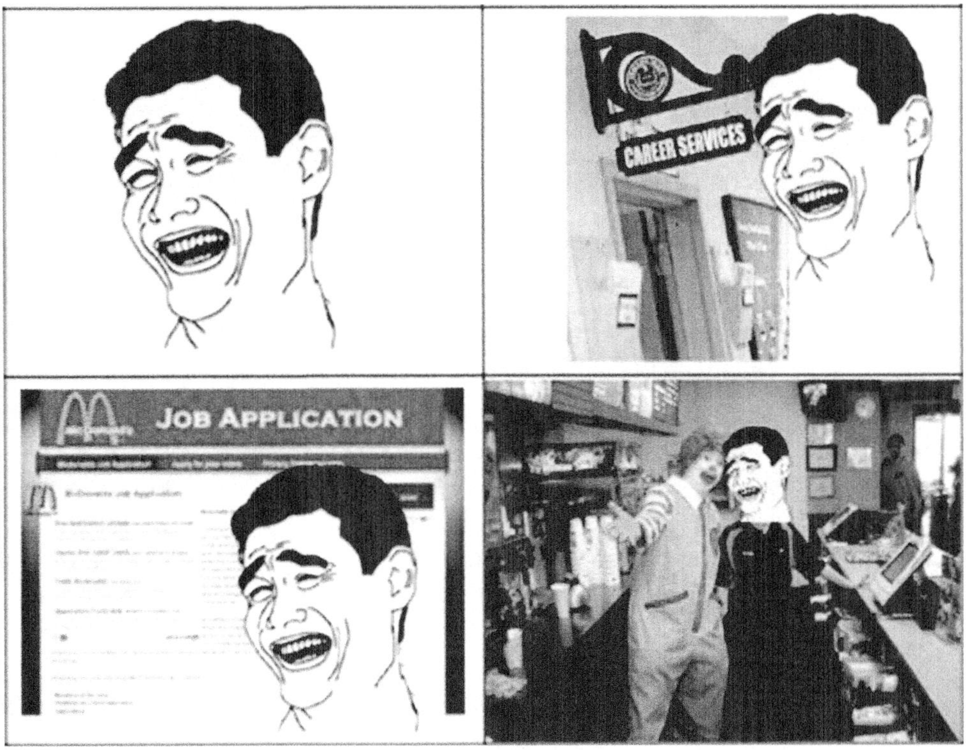
CAREER SERVICES
JOB APPLICATION

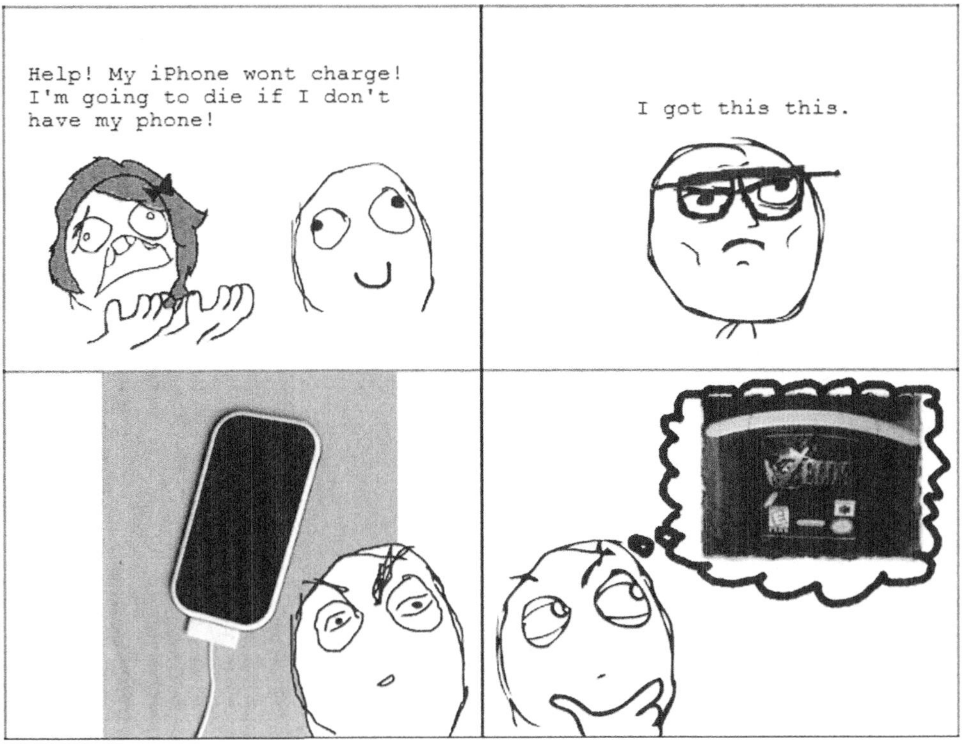
Help! My iPhone wont charge! I'm going to die if I don't have my phone!
I got this this.

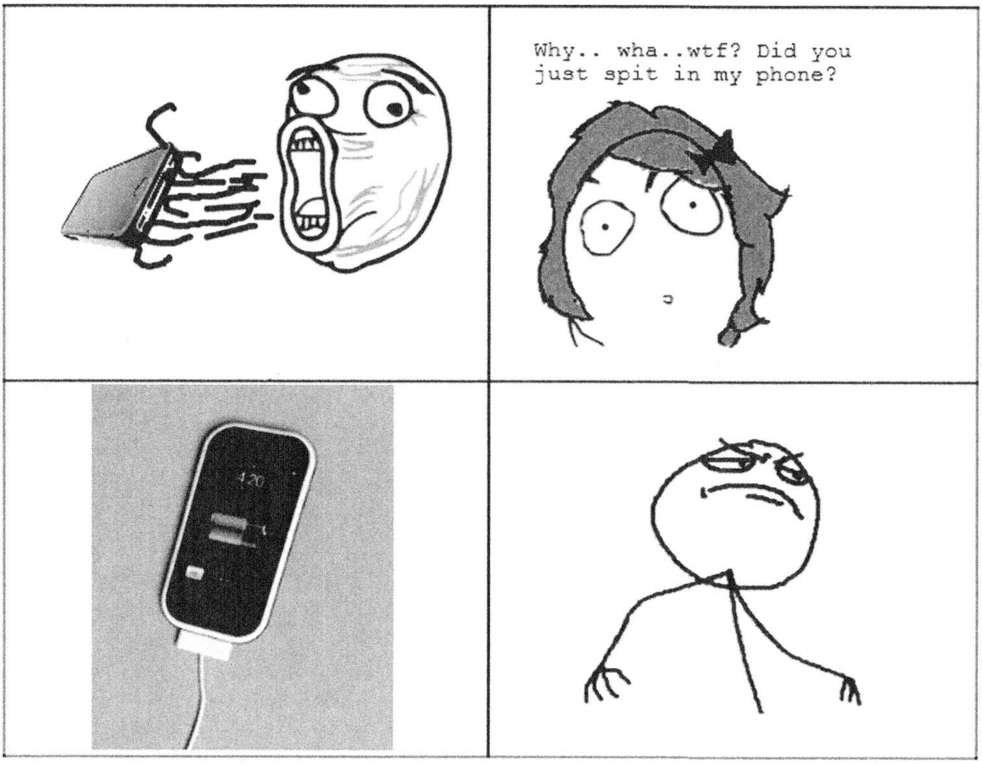
Why.. wha..wtf? Did you just spit in my phone?
4:20

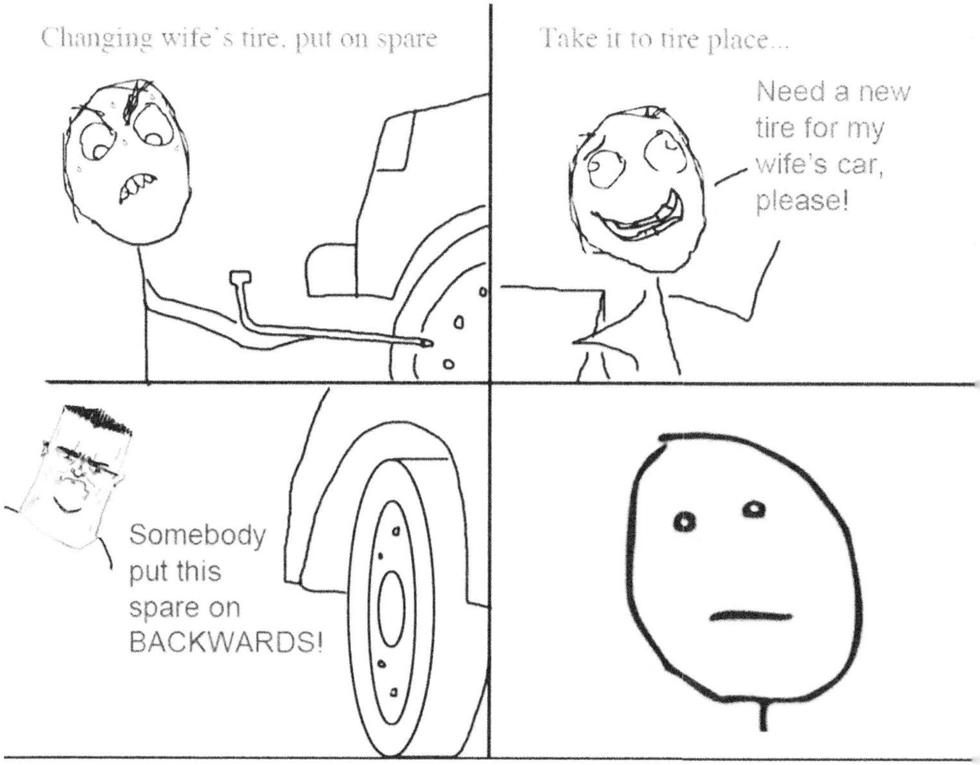
Changing wife's tire, put on spare
Take it to tire place...
Need a new tire for my wife's car, please!
Somebody put this spare on BACKWARDS!

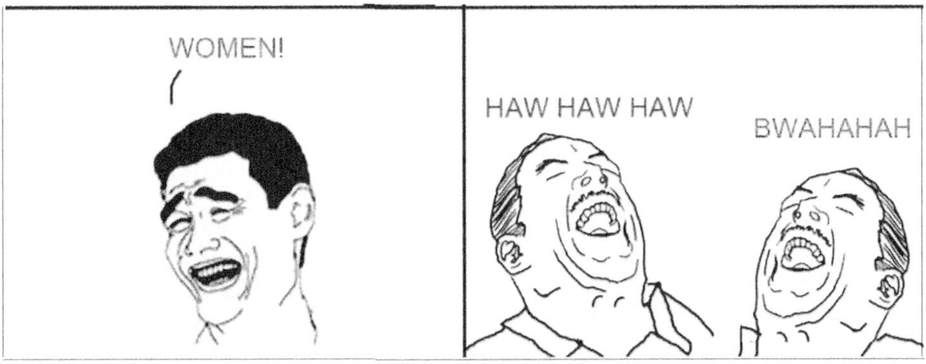
WOMEN!
HAW HAW HAW
BWAHAHAH

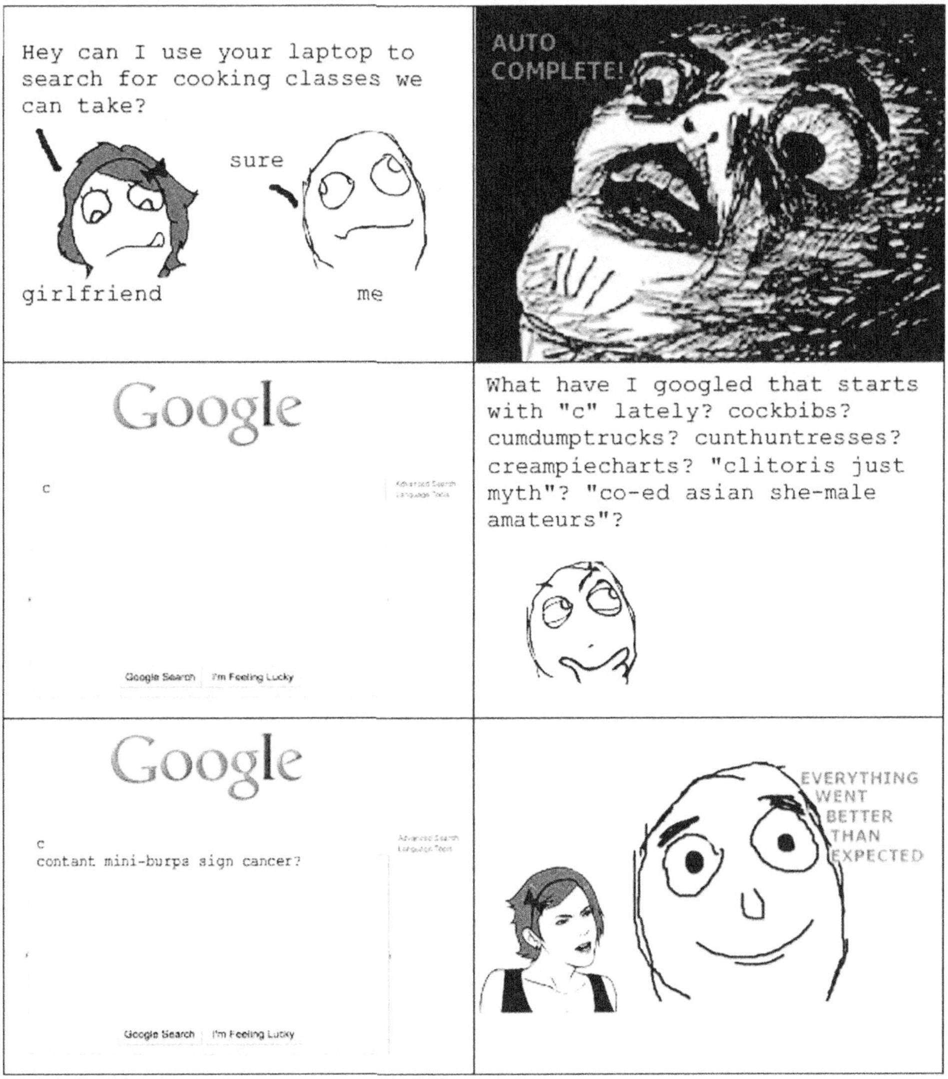
Hey can I use your laptop to search for cooking classes we can take?
sure
girlfriend
me
AUTO COMPLETE!
Google
c
Google Search
I'm Feeling Lucky
What have I googled that starts with "c" lately? cockbibs? cumdumptrucks? cunthuntresses? creampiecharts? "clitoris just myth"? "co-ed asian she-male amateurs"?
Google
c
contant mini-burps sign cancer?
Google Search
I'm Feeling Lucky
EVERYTHING WENT BETTER THAN EXPECTED

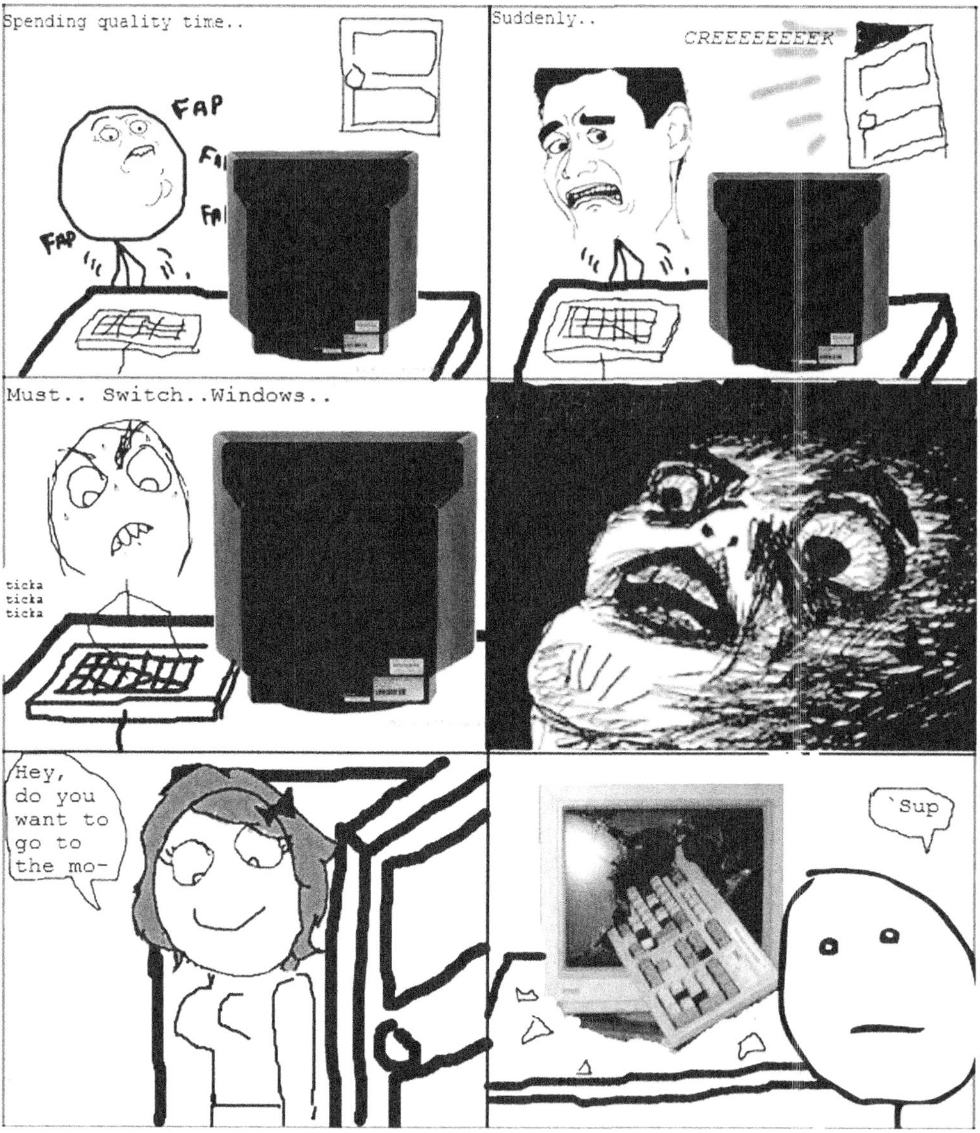
Spending quality time..
FAP
FA
FA
FAP
Suddenly..
CREEEEEEEEK
Must.. Switch..Windows..
ticka
ticka
ticka
Hey,
do you
want to
go to
the mo-
`Sup

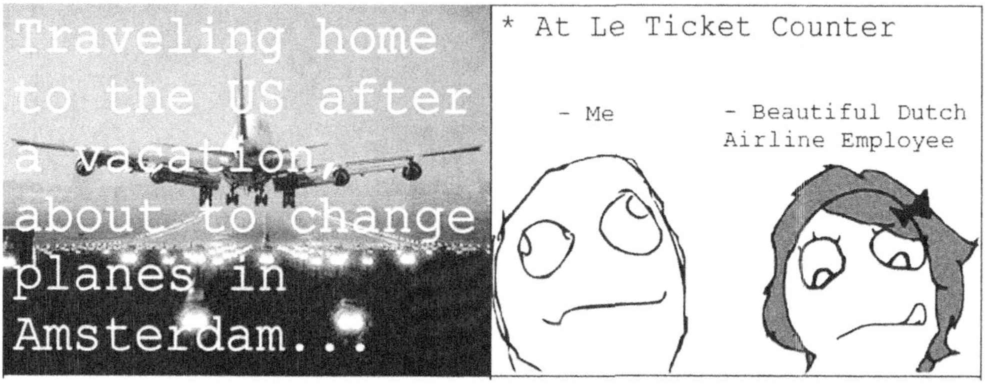
Traveling home to the US after a vacation, about to change planes in Amsterdam...
* At Le Ticket Counter
- Me
- Beautiful Dutch Airline Employee

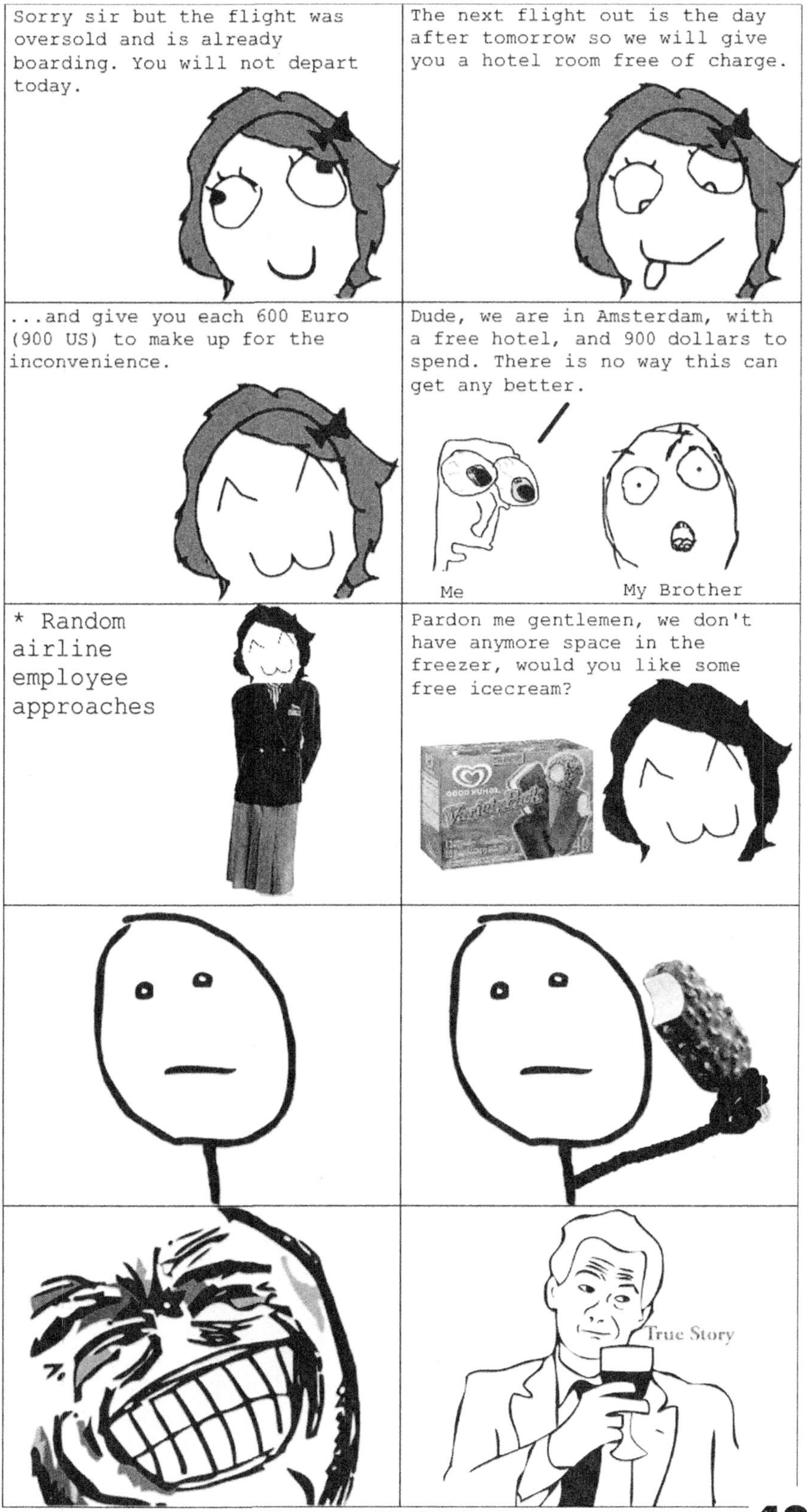
Sorry sir but the flight was oversold and is already boarding. You will not depart today.
The next flight out is the day after tomorrow so we will give you a hotel room free of charge.
...and give you each 600 Euro (900 US) to make up for the inconvenience.
Dude, we are in Amsterdam, with a free hotel, and 900 dollars to spend. There is no way this can get any better.
Me
My Brother
* Random airline employee approaches
Pardon me gentlemen, we don't have anymore space in the freezer, would you like some free icecream?
True Story

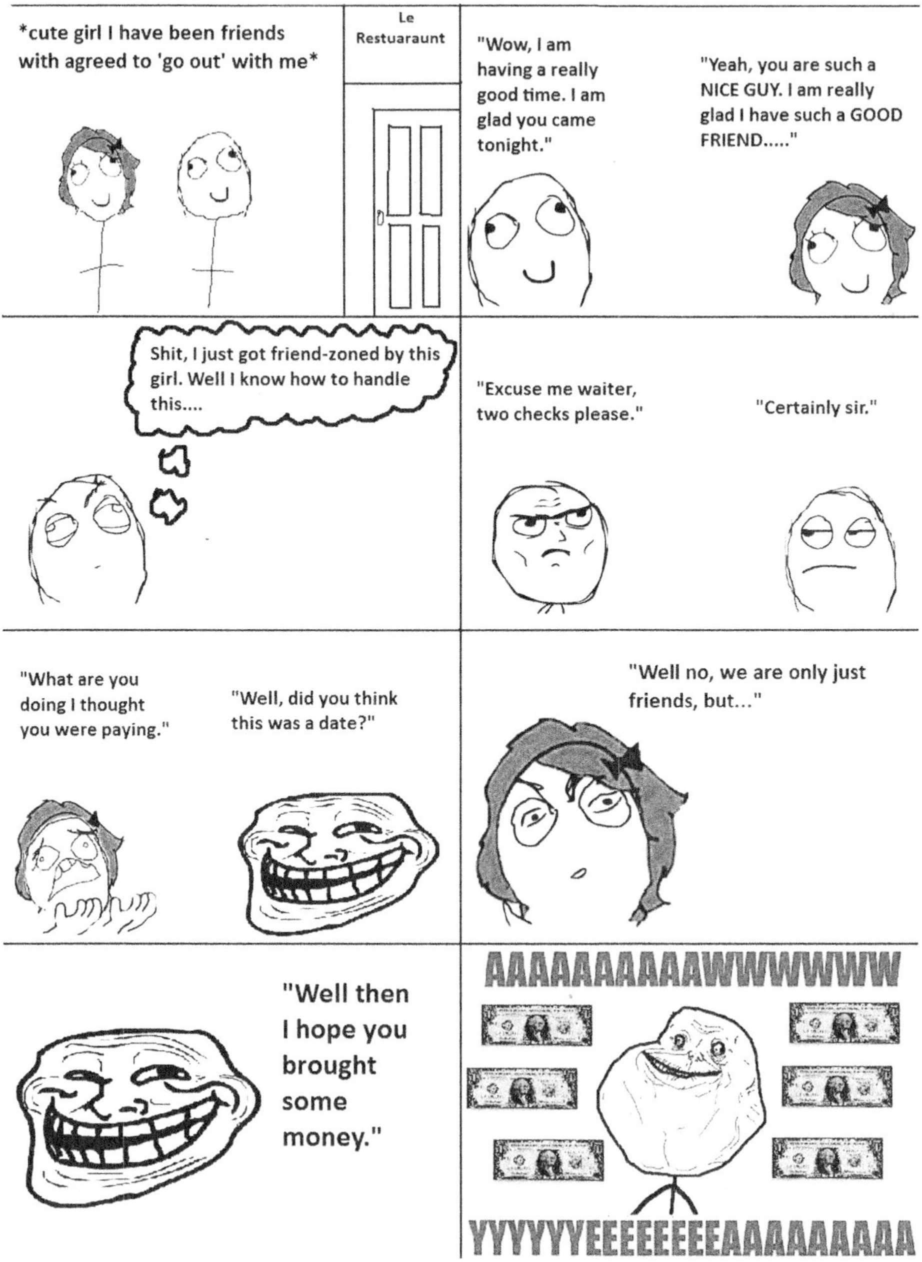
cute girl I have been friends with agreed to 'go out' with me
Le Restuaraunt
"Wow, I am having a really good time. I am glad you came tonight."
"Yeah, you are such a NICE GUY. I am really glad I have such a GOOD FRIEND....."
Shit, I just got friend-zoned by this girl. Well I know how to handle this....
"Excuse me waiter, two checks please."
"Certainly sir."
"What are you doing I thought you were paying."
"Well, did you think this was a date?"
"Well no, we are only just friends, but..."
"Well then I hope you brought some money."
AAAAAAAAAAWWWWWW
YYYYYYEEEEEEEEAAAAAAAAA

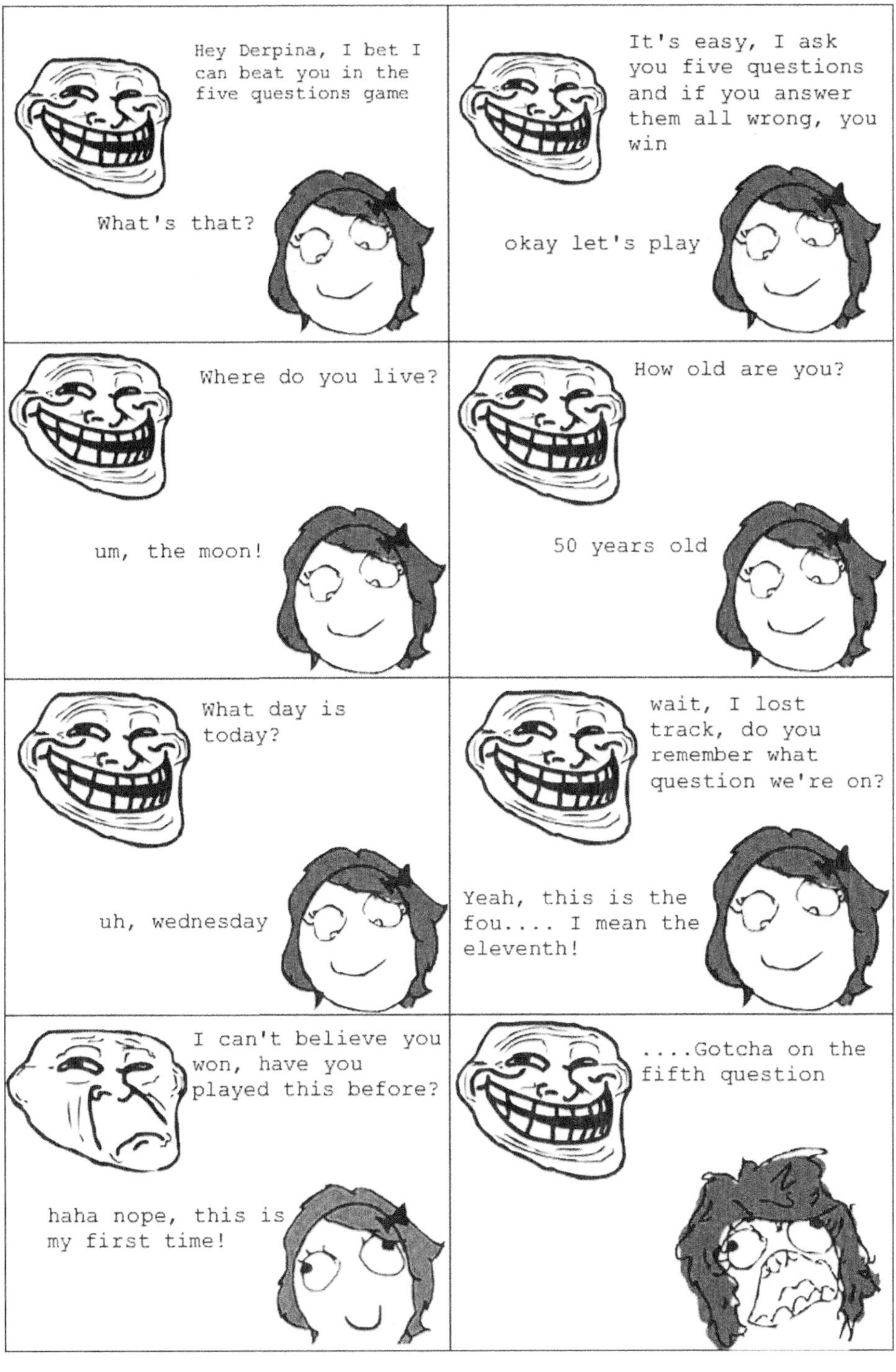
Hey Derpina, I bet I can beat you in the five questions game
What's that?
It's easy, I ask you five questions and if you answer them all wrong, you win
okay let's play
Where do you live?
um, the moon!
How old are you?
50 years old
What day is today?
uh, wednesday
wait, I lost track, do you remember what question we're on?
Yeah, this is the fou.... I mean the eleventh!
I can't believe you won, have you played this before?
haha nope, this is my first time!
....Gotcha on the fifth question

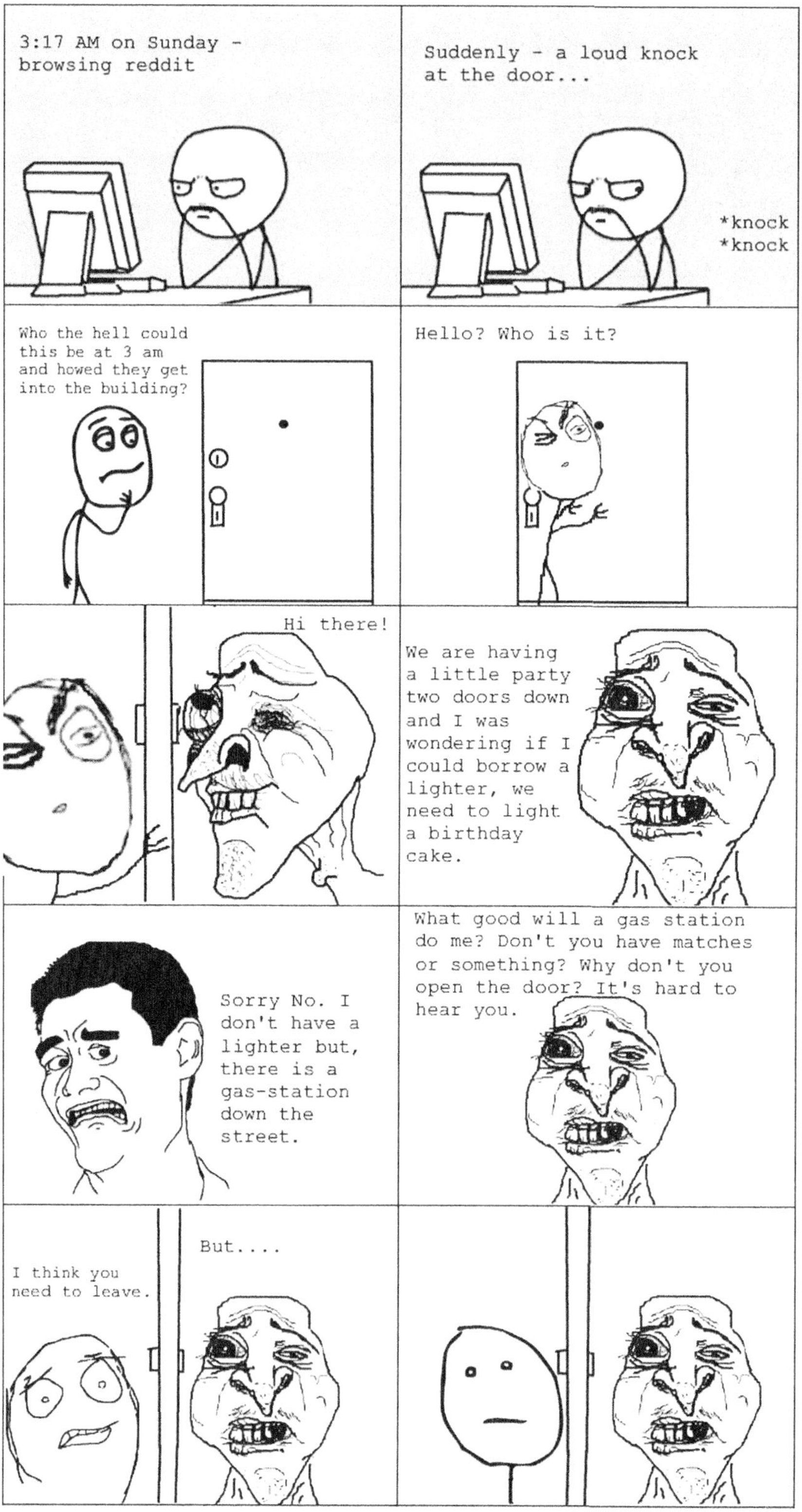
3:17 AM on Sunday - browsing reddit
Suddenly - a loud knock at the door...
*knock
*knock
Who the hell could this be at 3 am and howed they get into the building?
Hello? Who is it?
Hi there!
We are having a little party two doors down and I was wondering if I could borrow a lighter, we need to light a birthday cake.
Sorry No. I don't have a lighter but, there is a gas-station down the street.
What good will a gas station do me? Don't you have matches or something? Why don't you open the door? It's hard to hear you.
I think you need to leave.
But....

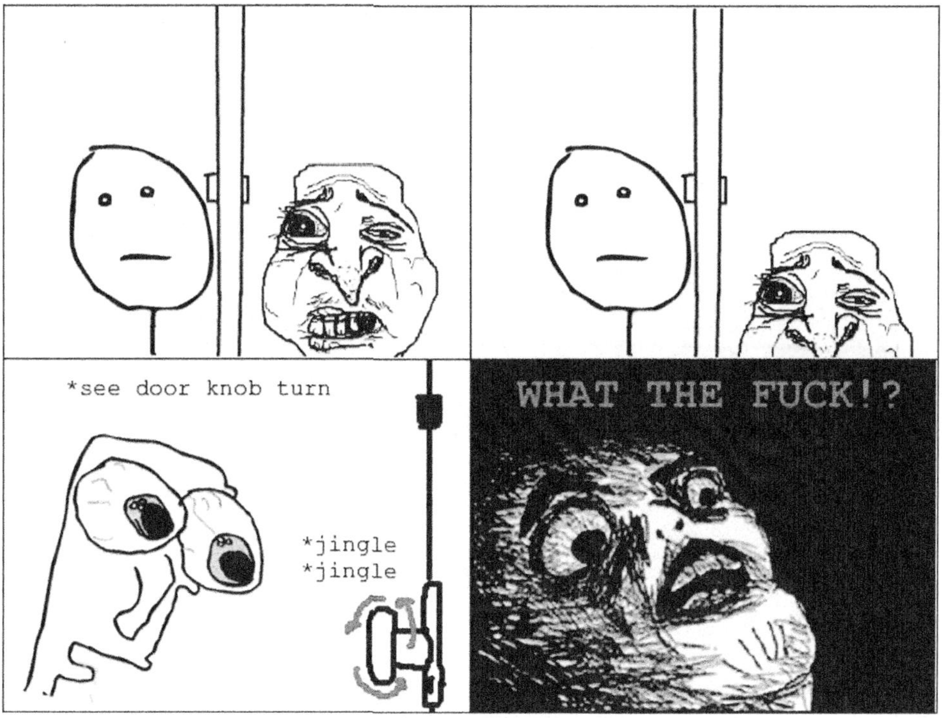
*see door knob turn
*jingle
*jingle
WHAT THE FUCK!?

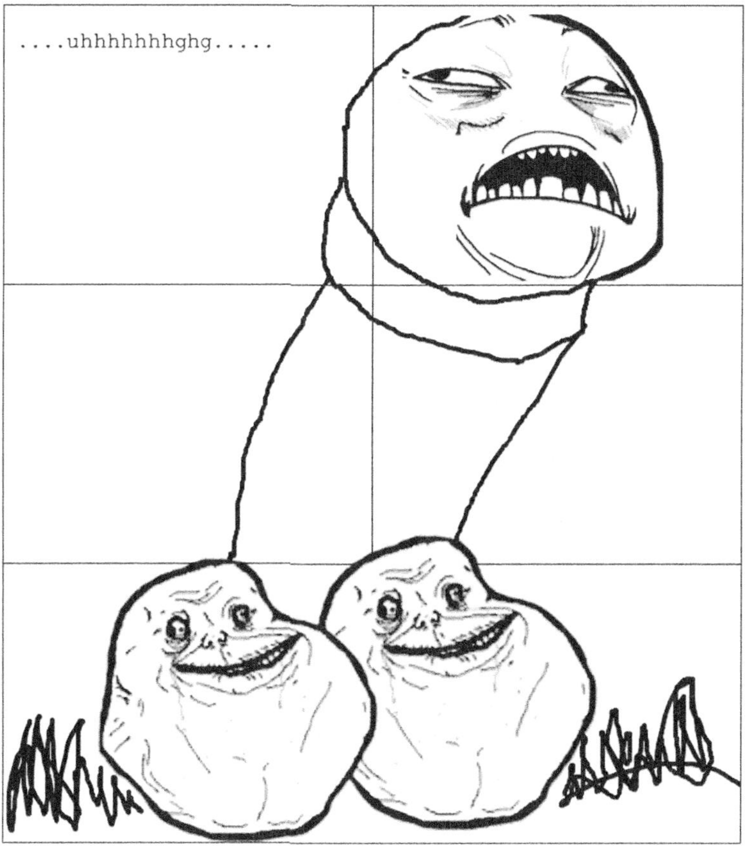
....uhhhhhhhghg.....

Me, taking my friend to an abortion clinic like a non-judgmental gentleman, when I spot something on the entrance.
"No way..."
Abortion Clinic
Office Hours: 7-?
Dr. Herp & Derp
No Children Allowed.
Enhanced
No Children Allowed.
"That's...hilarious!"
I then began laughing all the way into the near silent waiting area.
Very Angry Stares
Inner Monologue: "Why do they look so angry at me? Do they.."
"Fuck it! That's even funnier!"

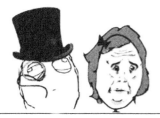

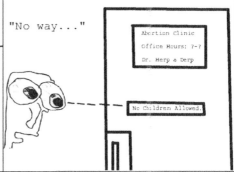

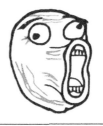

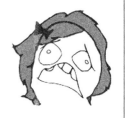

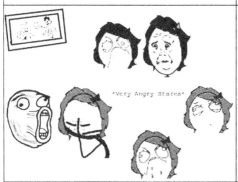

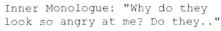

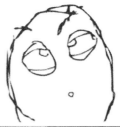

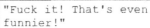

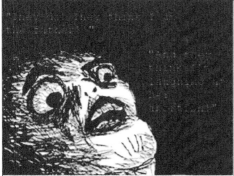

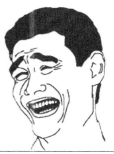

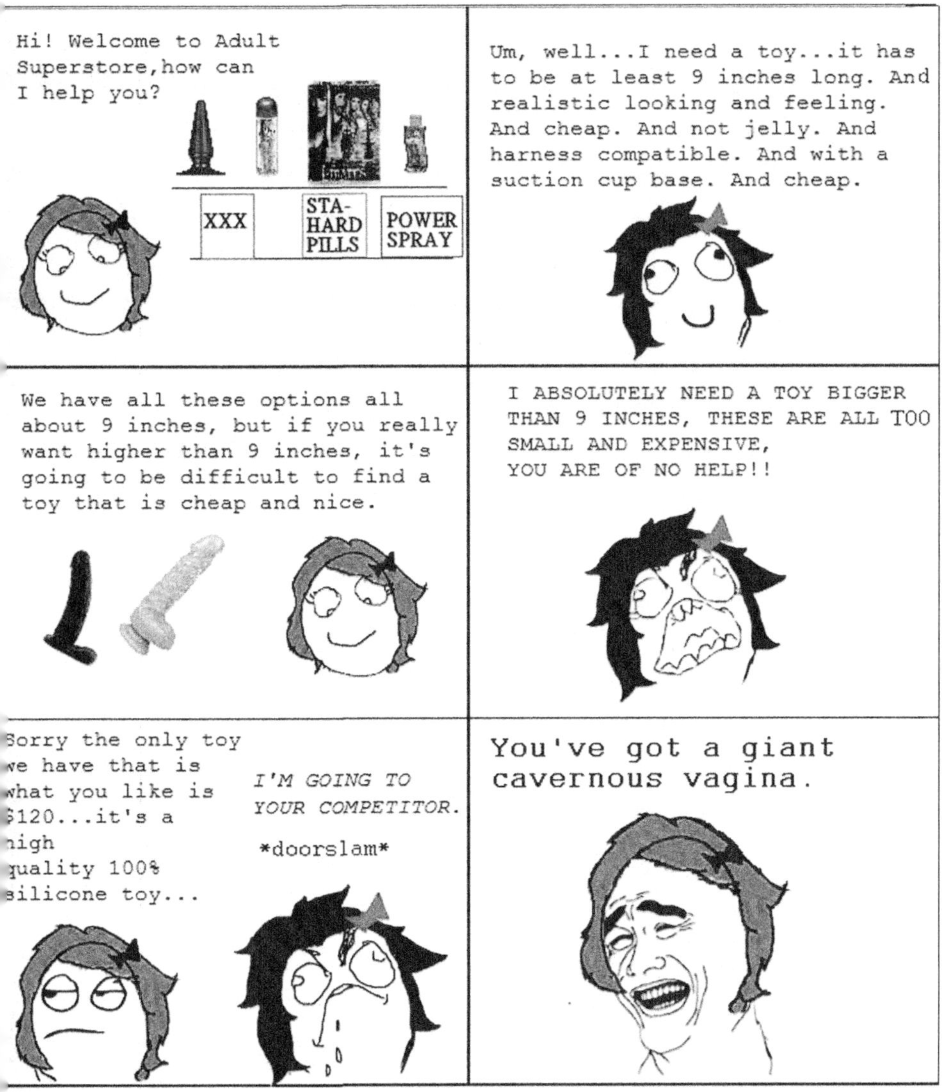
Hi! Welcome to Adult Superstore,how can I help you?
XXX
STA-HARD PILLS
POWER SPRAY
Um, well...I need a toy...it has to be at least 9 inches long. And realistic looking and feeling. And cheap. And not jelly. And harness compatible. And with a suction cup base. And cheap.
We have all these options all about 9 inches, but if you really want higher than 9 inches, it's going to be difficult to find a toy that is cheap and nice.
I ABSOLUTELY NEED A TOY BIGGER THAN 9 INCHES, THESE ARE ALL TOO SMALL AND EXPENSIVE, YOU ARE OF NO HELP!!
Sorry the only toy we have that is what you like is $120...it's a high quality 100% silicone toy...
I'M GOING TO YOUR COMPETITOR.
doorslam
You've got a giant cavernous vagina.

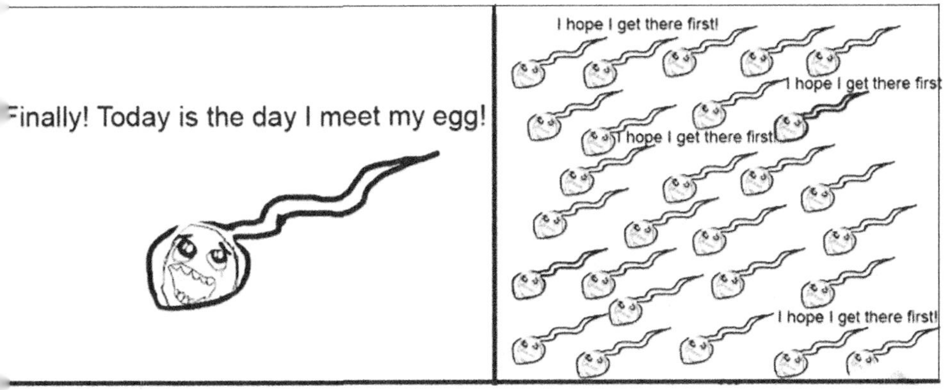
Finally! Today is the day I meet my egg!
I hope I get there first!
I hope I get there first
I hope I get there first!
I hope I get there first!

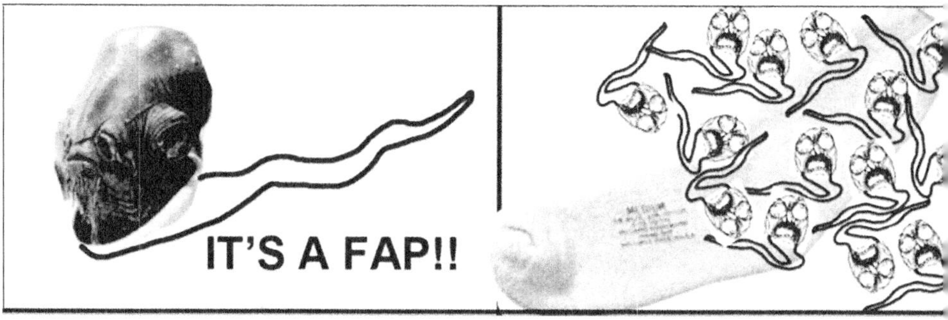
IT'S A FAP!!

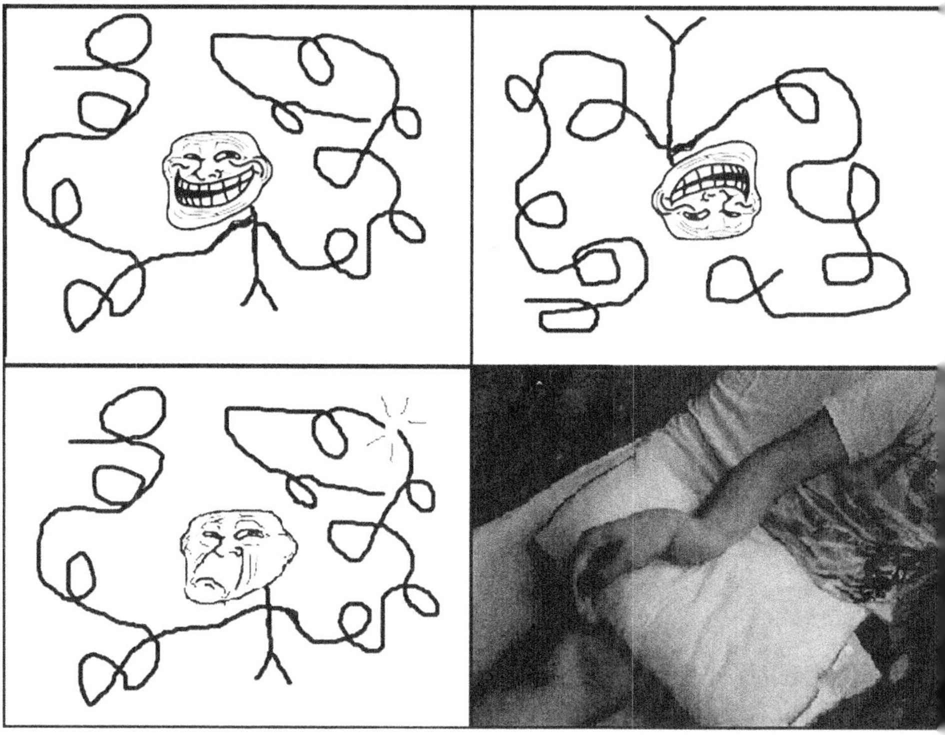

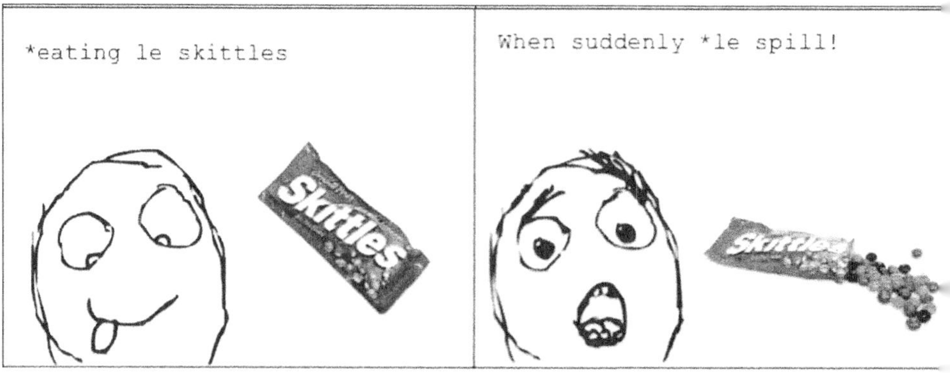
*eating le skittles
Skittles
When suddenly *le spill!
Skittles

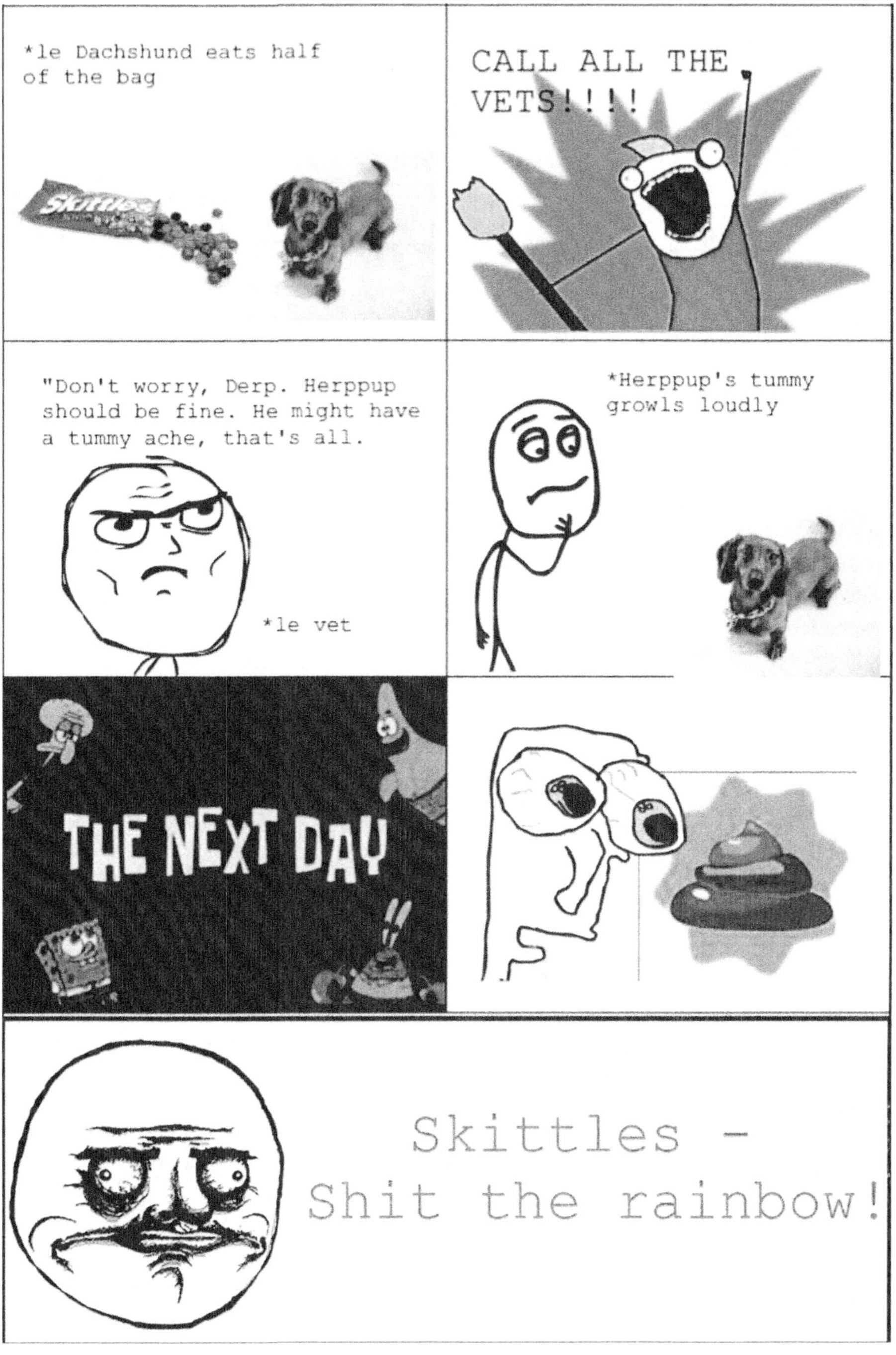
*le Dachshund eats half of the bag
Skittles
CALL ALL THE VETS!!!!
"Don't worry, Derp. Herppup should be fine. He might have a tummy ache, that's all.
*le vet
*Herppup's tummy growls loudly
THE NEXT DAY
Skittles - Shit the rainbow!

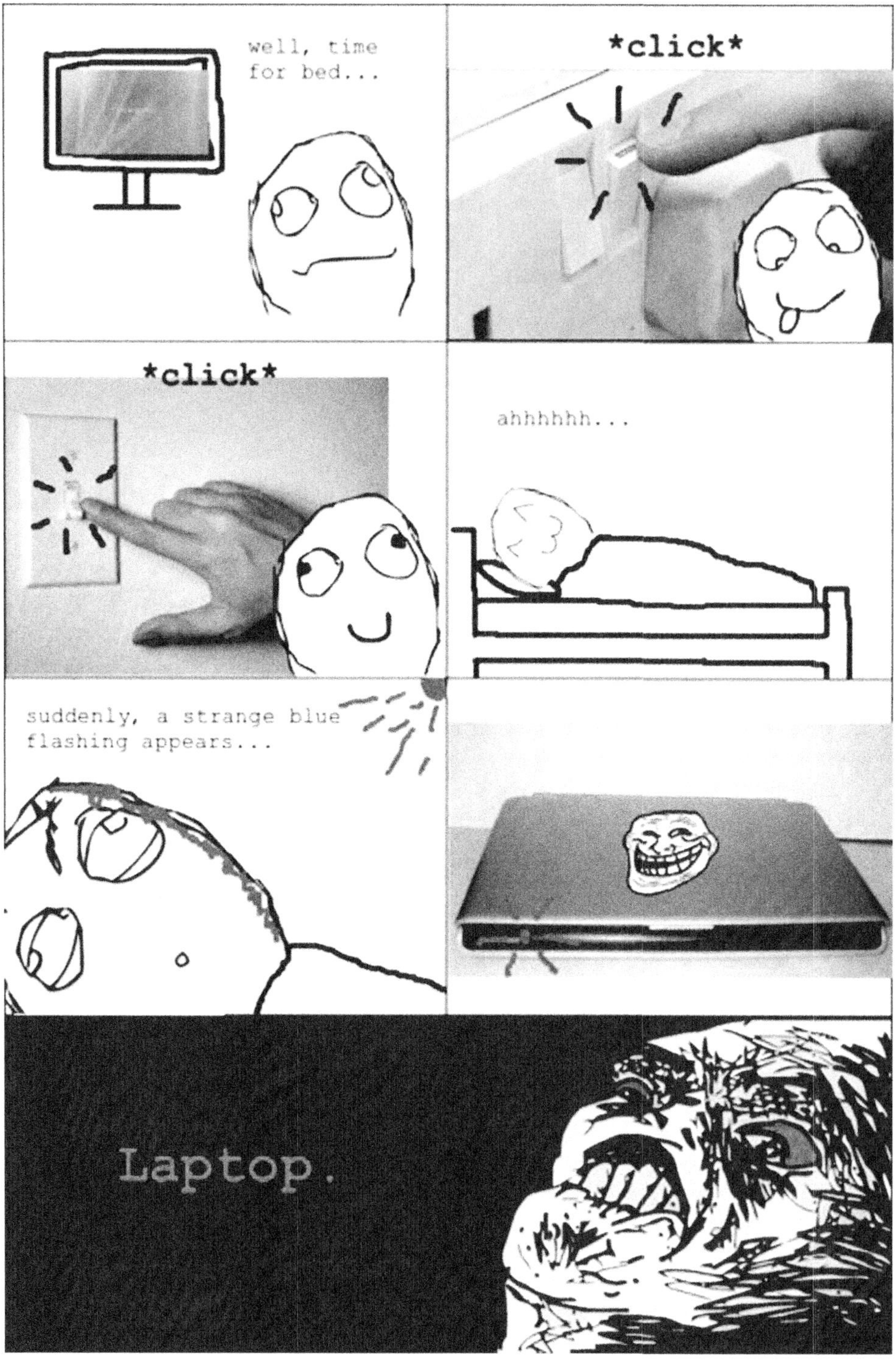
well, time for bed...
click
click
ahhhhhh...
suddenly, a strange blue flashing appears...
Laptop.

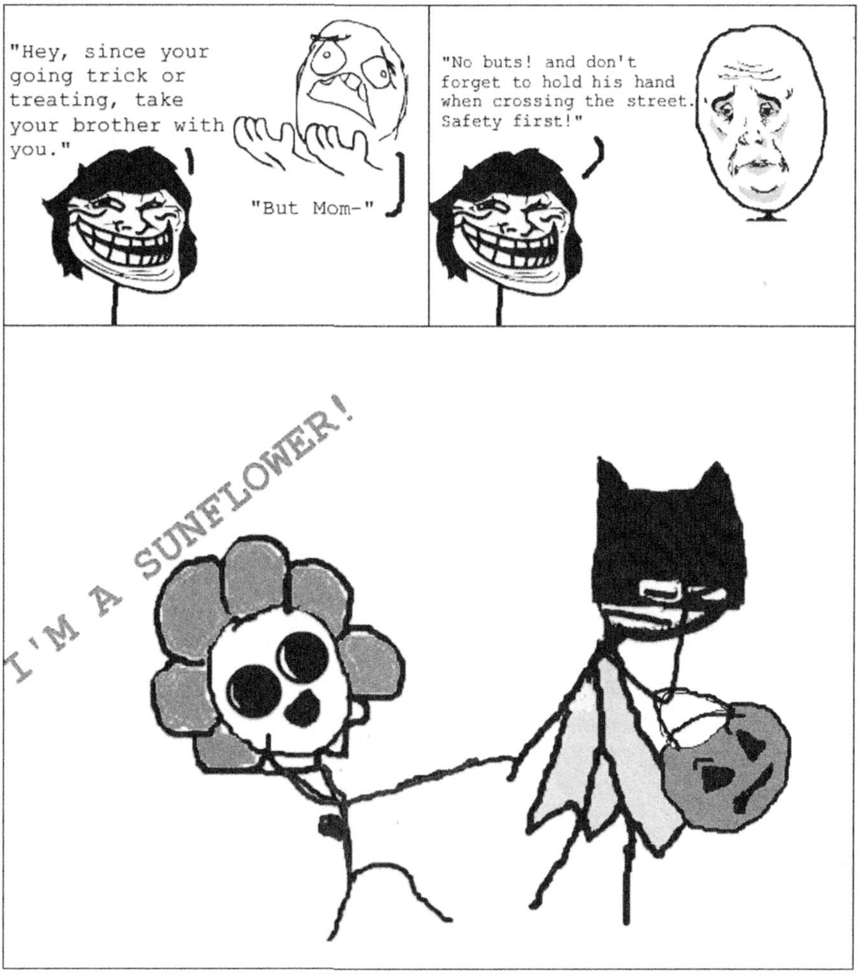
"Hey, since your going trick or treating, take your brother with you."
"But Mom-"
"No buts! and don't forget to hold his hand when crossing the street. Safety first!"
I'M A SUNFLOWER!

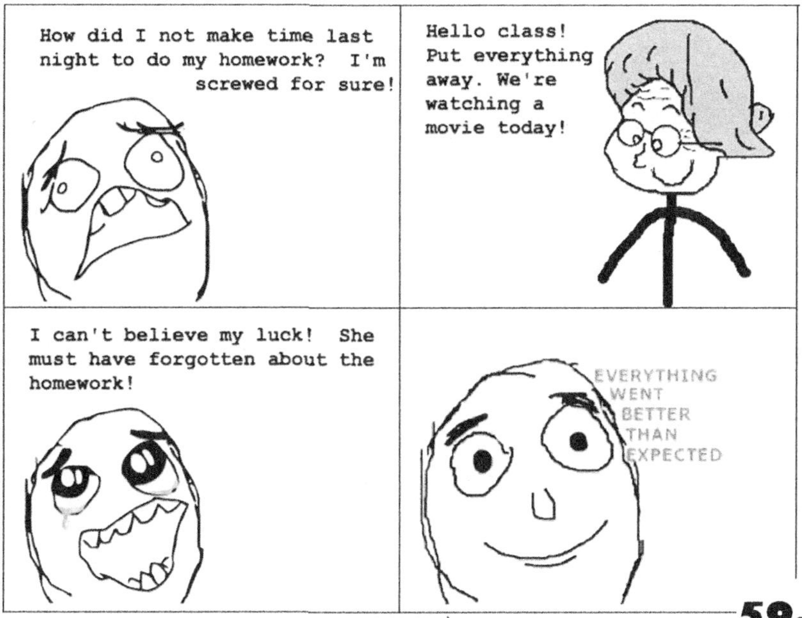
How did I not make time last night to do my homework? I'm screwed for sure!
Hello class! Put everything away. We're watching a movie today!
I can't believe my luck! She must have forgotten about the homework!
EVERYTHING WENT BETTER THAN EXPECTED

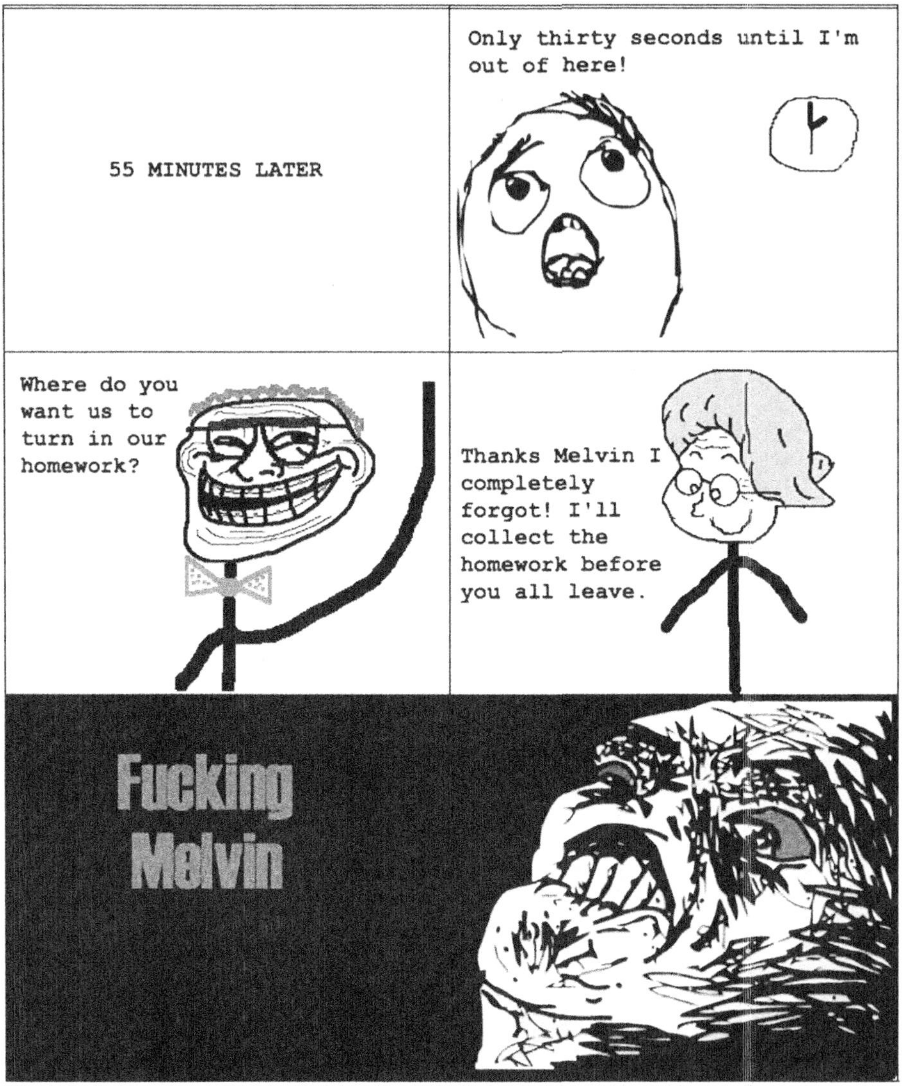
55 MINUTES LATER
Only thirty seconds until I'm out of here!
Where do you want us to turn in our homework?
Thanks Melvin I completely forgot! I'll collect the homework before you all leave.
Fucking Melvin

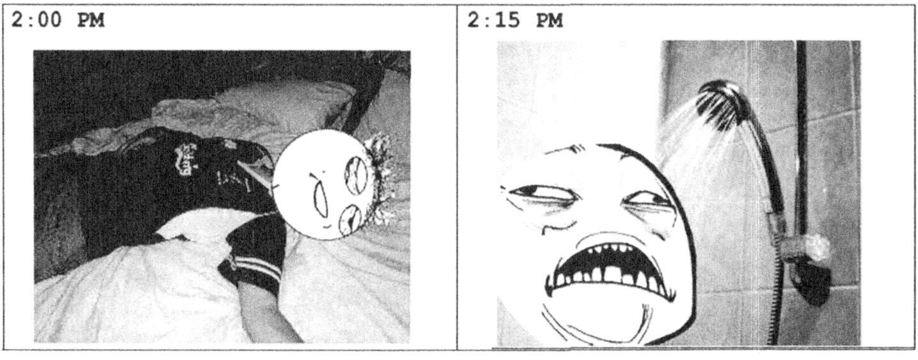
2:00 PM
2:15 PM

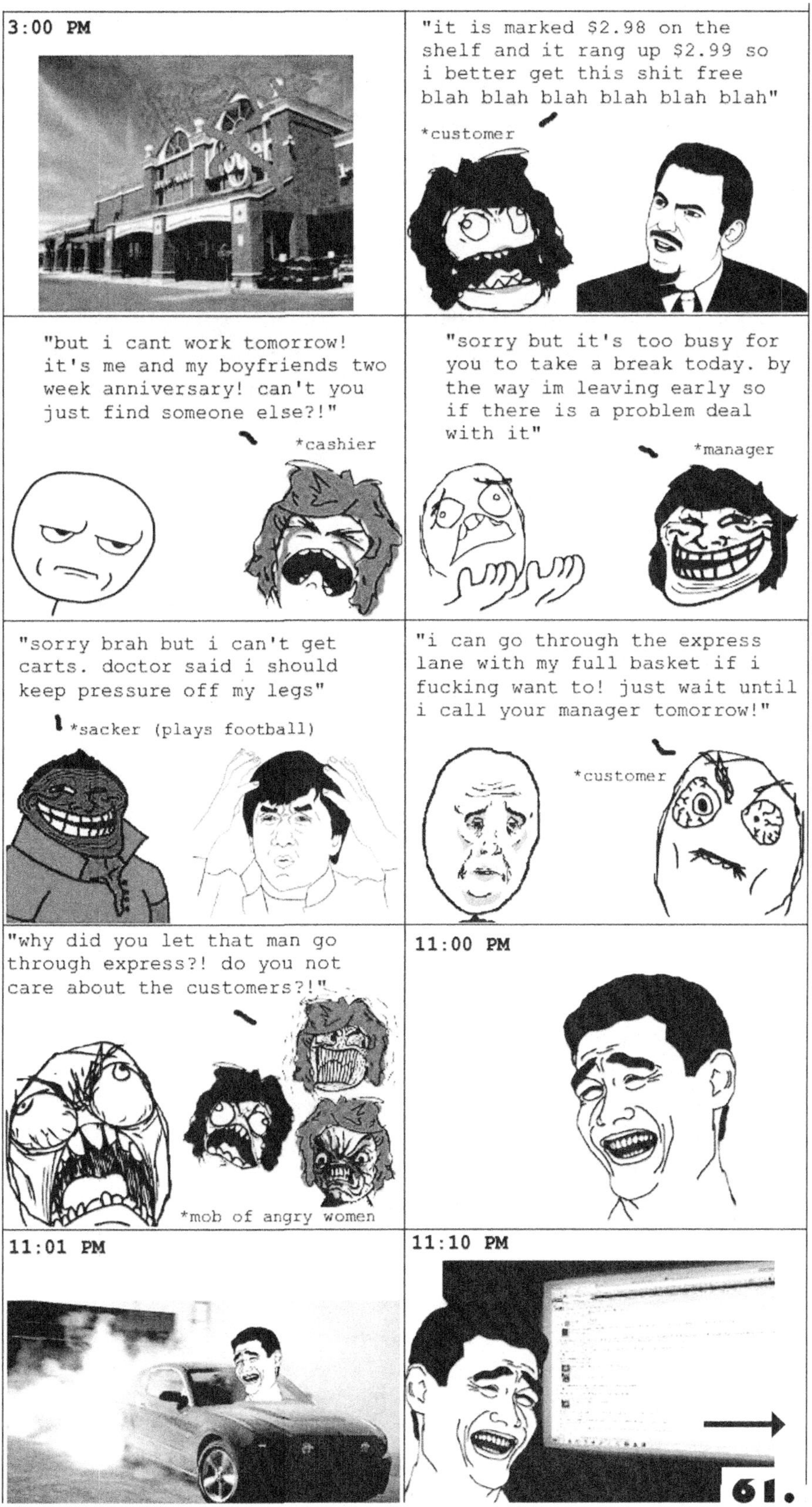
3:00 PM
"it is marked $2.98 on the shelf and it rang up $2.99 so i better get this shit free blah blah blah blah blah blah"
*customer
"but i cant work tomorrow! it's me and my boyfriends two week anniversary! can't you just find someone else?!"
*cashier
"sorry but it's too busy for you to take a break today. by the way im leaving early so if there is a problem deal with it"
*manager
"sorry brah but i can't get carts. doctor said i should keep pressure off my legs"
*sacker (plays football)
"i can go through the express lane with my full basket if i fucking want to! just wait until i call your manager tomorrow!"
*customer
"why did you let that man go through express?! do you not care about the customers?!"
*mob of angry women
11:00 PM
11:01 PM
11:10 PM

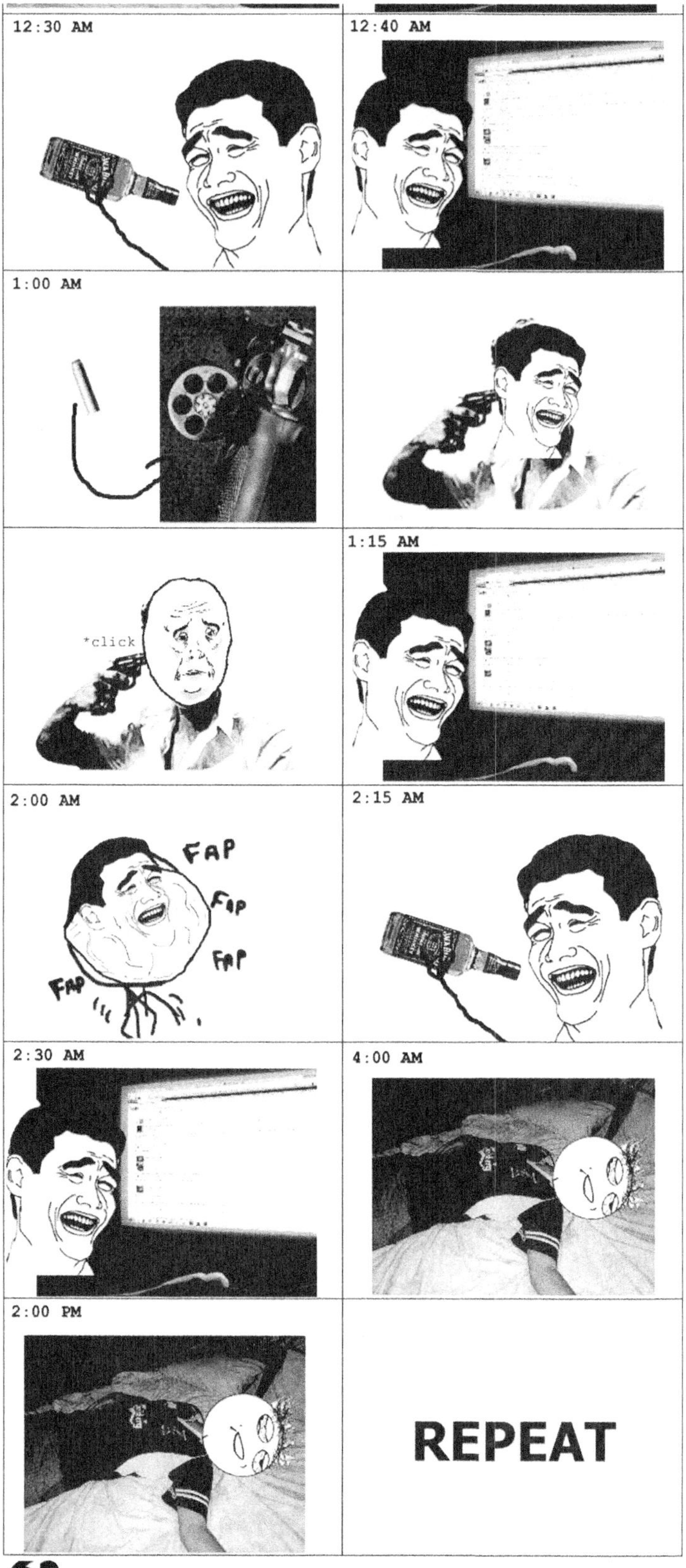
12:30 AM
12:40 AM
1:00 AM
*click
1:15 AM
2:00 AM
FAP
FAP
FAP
FAP
2:15 AM
2:30 AM
4:00 AM
2:00 PM
REPEAT

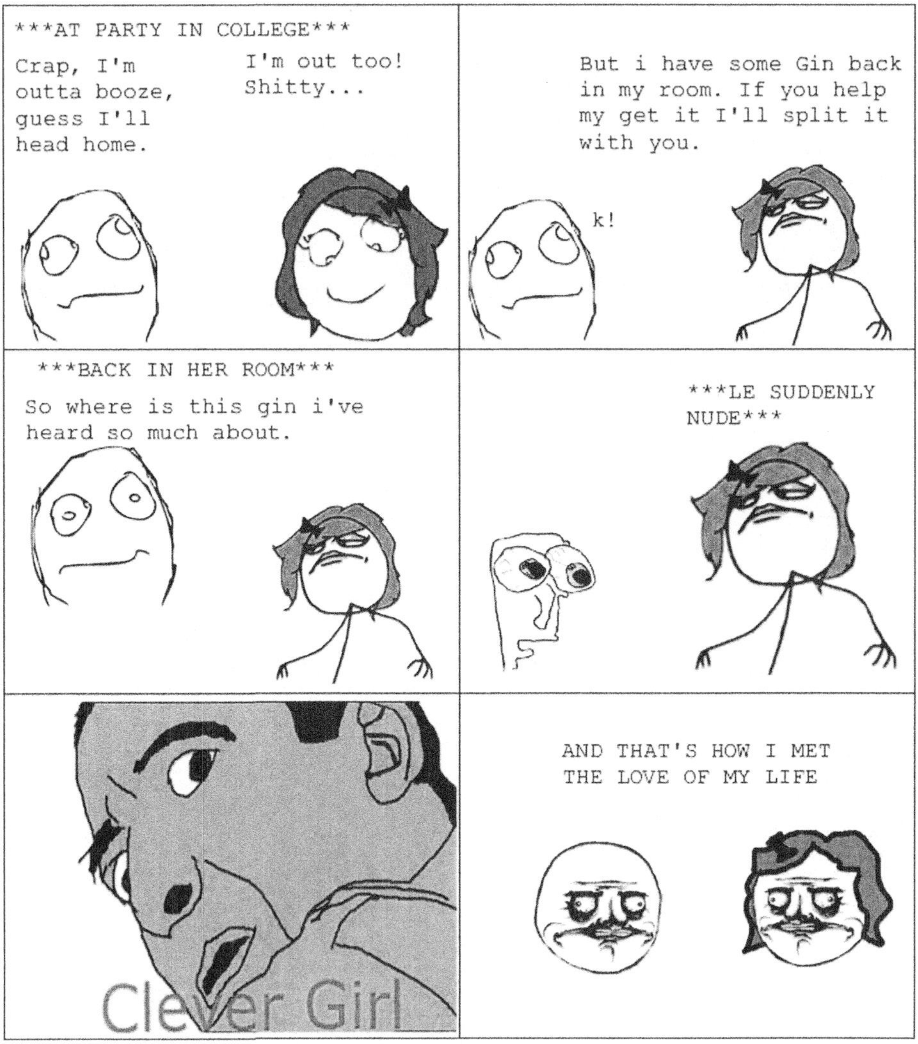
AT PARTY IN COLLEGE
Crap, I'm outta booze, guess I'll head home.
I'm out too! Shitty...
But i have some Gin back in my room. If you help my get it I'll split it with you.
k!
BACK IN HER ROOM
So where is this gin i've heard so much about.
LE SUDDENLY NUDE
Clever Girl
AND THAT'S HOW I MET THE LOVE OF MY LIFE

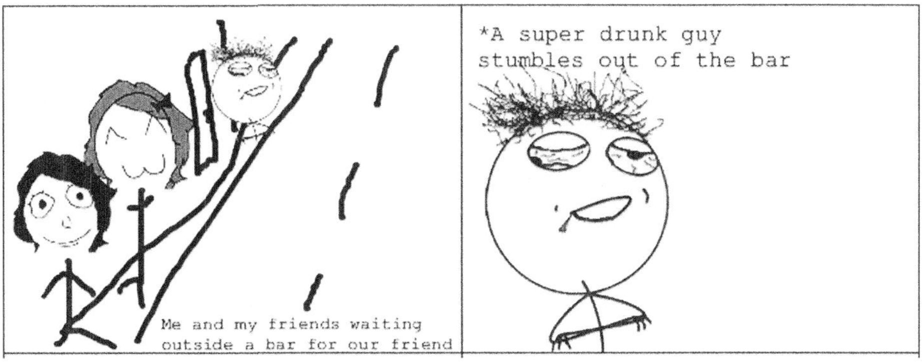
Me and my friends waiting outside a bar for our friend
*A super drunk guy stumbles out of the bar

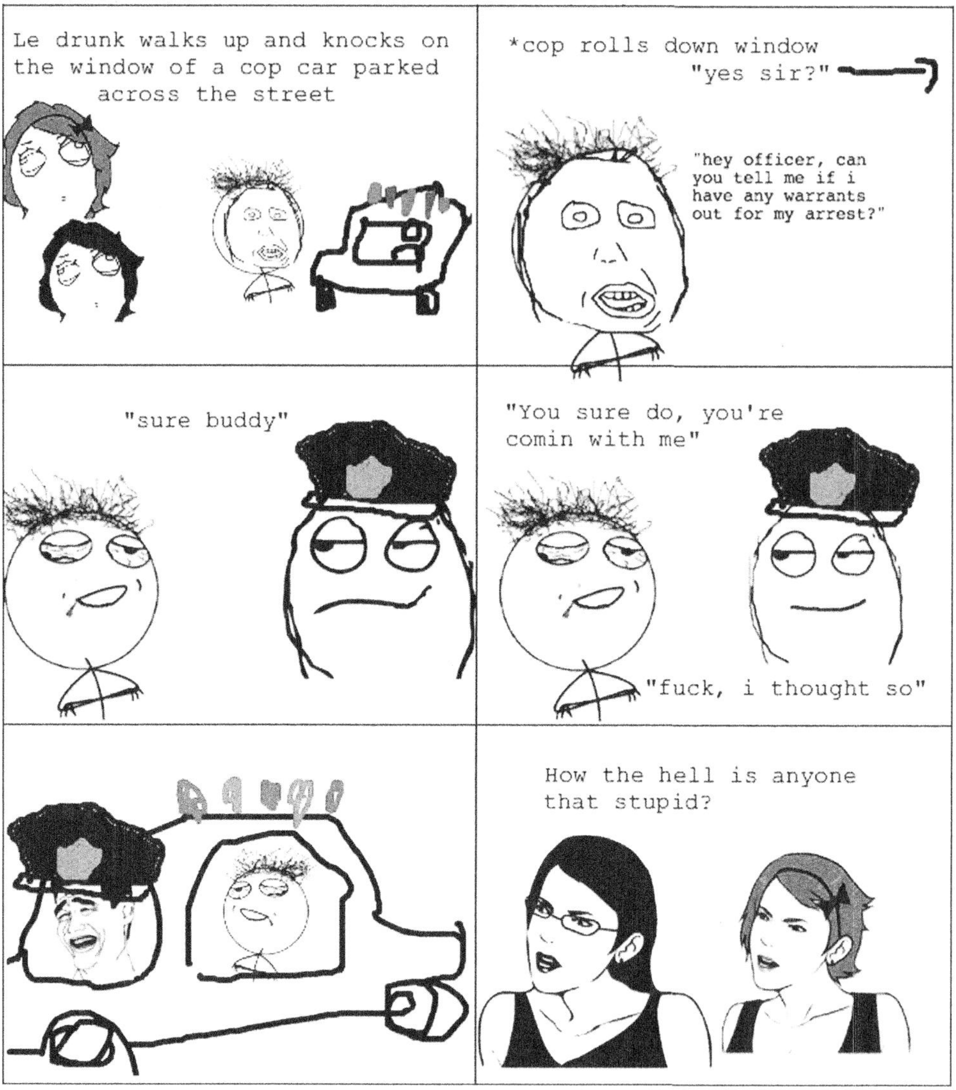

Le drunk walks up and knocks on the window of a cop car parked across the street
*cop rolls down window
"yes sir?"
"hey officer, can you tell me if i have any warrants out for my arrest?"
"sure buddy"
"You sure do, you're comin with me"
"fuck, i thought so"
How the hell is anyone that stupid?

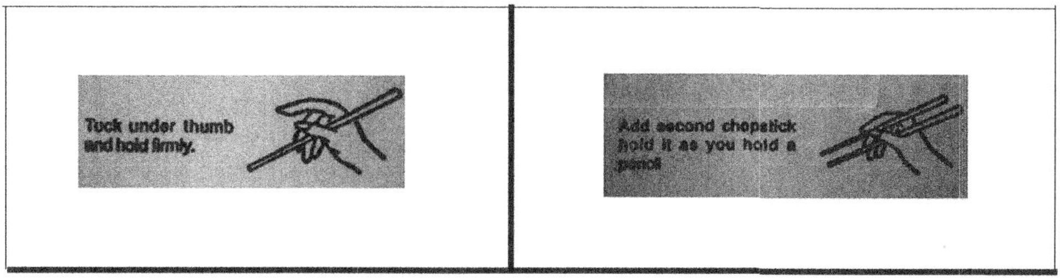

Tuck under thumb and hold firmly.
Add second chopstick hold it as you hold a pencil

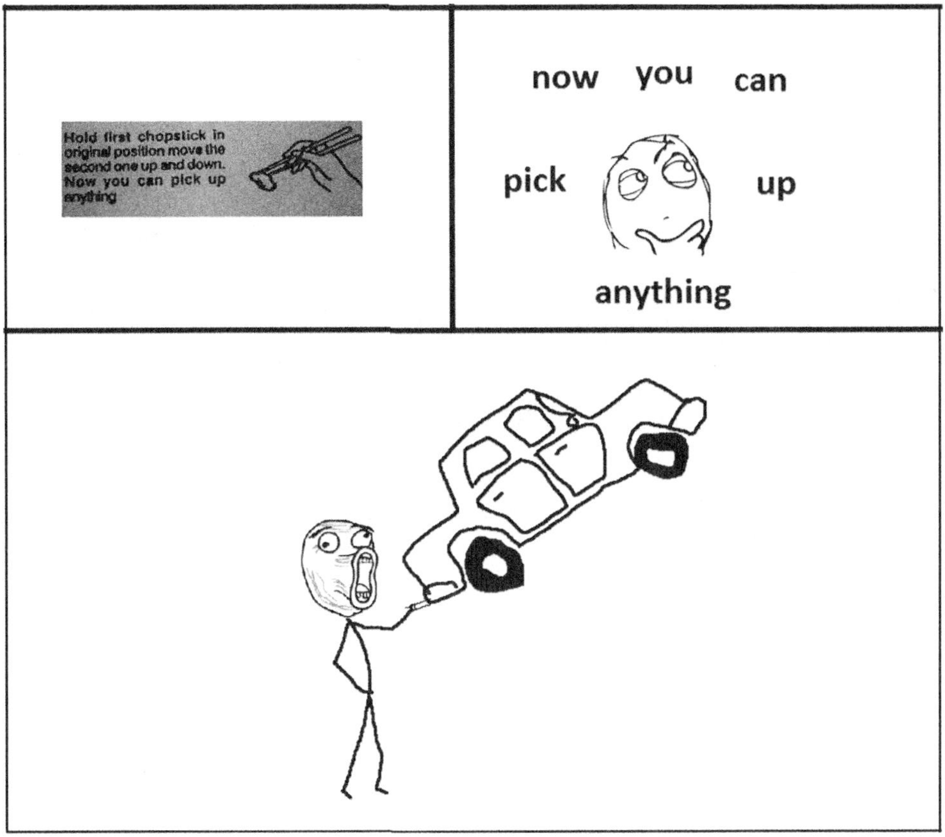
Hold first chopstick in original position move the second one up and down. Now you can pick up anything
now you can
pick
up
anything

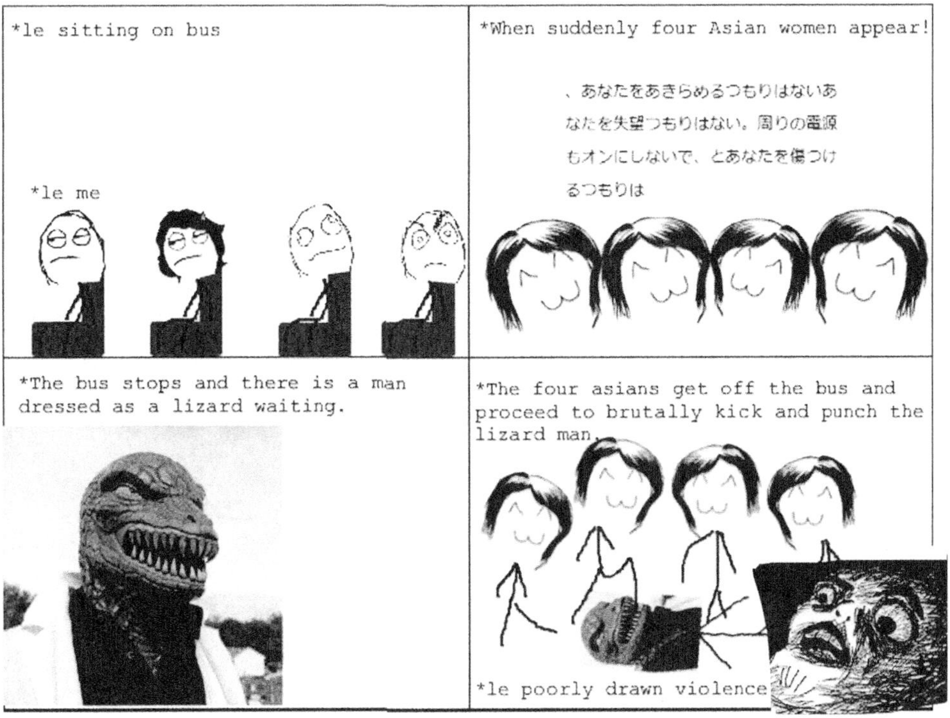
*le sitting on bus
*le me
*When suddenly four Asian women appear!
、あなたをあきらめるつもりはないあ
なたを失望つもりはない。周りの電源
もオンにしないで、とあなたを傷つけ
るつもりは
*The bus stops and there is a man dressed as a lizard waiting.
*The four asians get off the bus and proceed to brutally kick and punch the lizard man.
*le poorly drawn violence

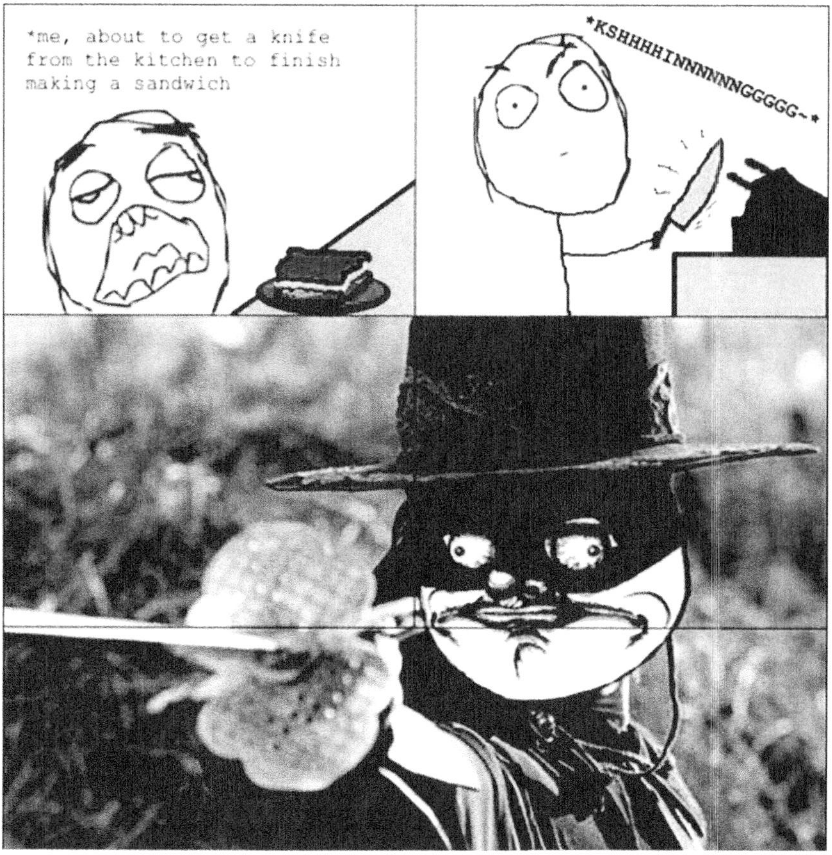
*me, about to get a knife from the kitchen to finish making a sandwich
KSHHHHINNNNNNNGGGGG~

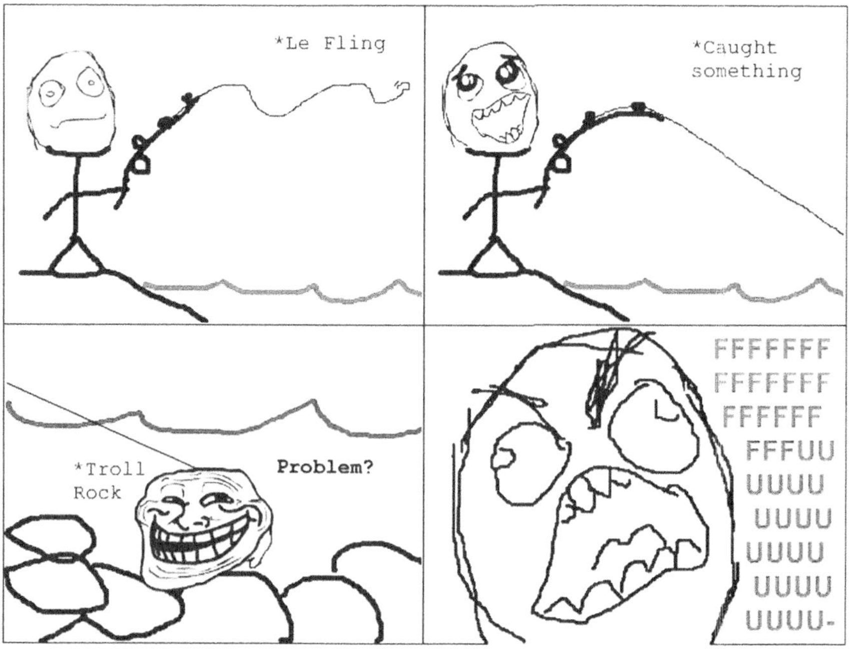
*Le Fling
*Caught something
*Troll Rock
Problem?
FFFFFFF FFFFFFF FFFFFF FFFUU UUUU UUUU UUUU UUUU UUUU-

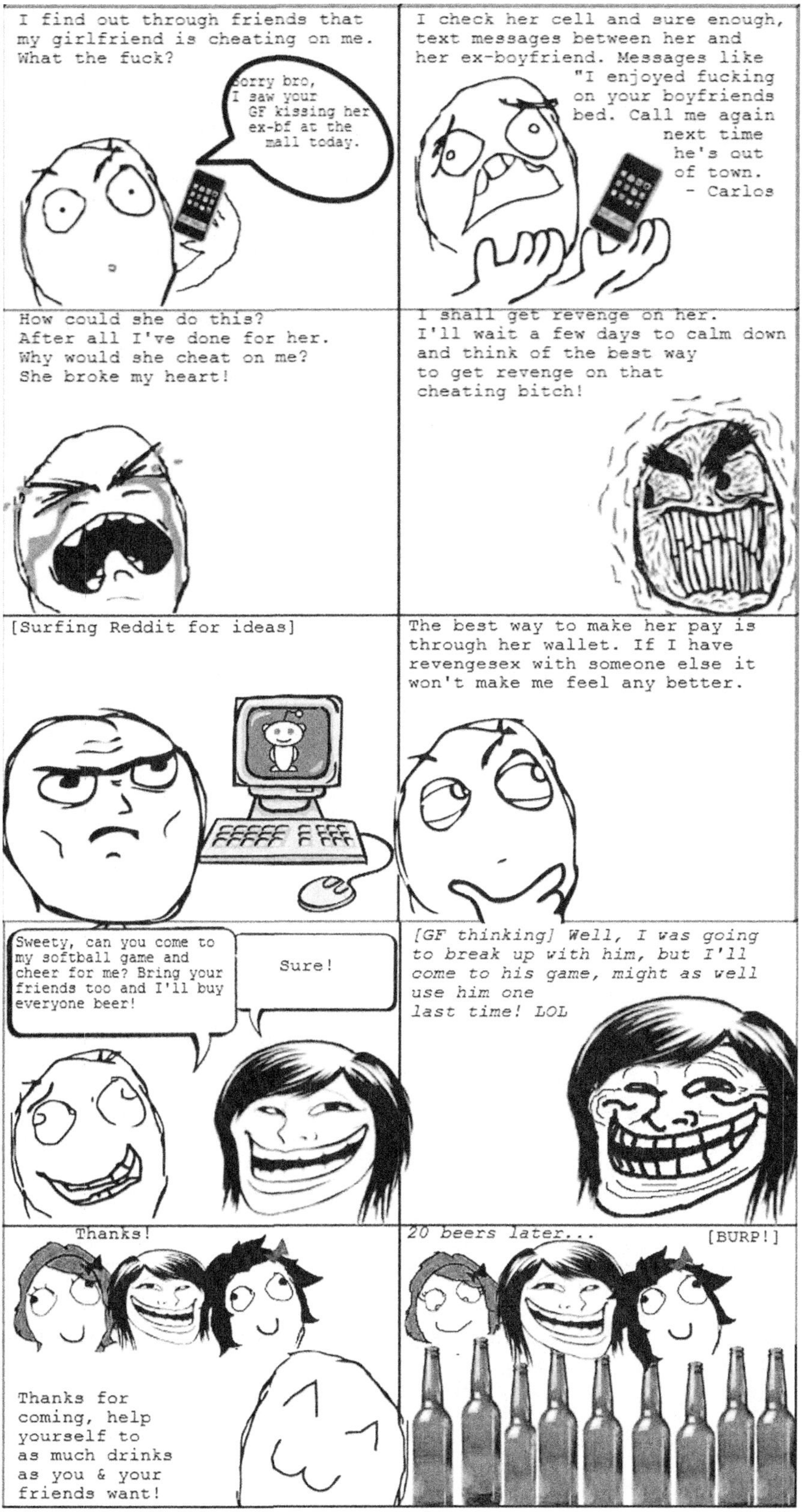

I find out through friends that my girlfriend is cheating on me. What the fuck?
Sorry bro, I saw your GF kissing her ex-bf at the mall today.
I check her cell and sure enough, text messages between her and her ex-boyfriend. Messages like "I enjoyed fucking on your boyfriends bed. Call me again next time he's out of town. - Carlos
How could she do this? After all I've done for her. Why would she cheat on me? She broke my heart!
I shall get revenge on her. I'll wait a few days to calm down and think of the best way to get revenge on that cheating bitch!
[Surfing Reddit for ideas]
The best way to make her pay is through her wallet. If I have revengesex with someone else it won't make me feel any better.
Sweety, can you come to my softball game and cheer for me? Bring your friends too and I'll buy everyone beer!
Sure!
[GF thinking] Well, I was going to break up with him, but I'll come to his game, might as well use him one last time! LOL
Thanks!
Thanks for coming, help yourself to as much drinks as you & your friends want!
20 beers later...
[BURP!]

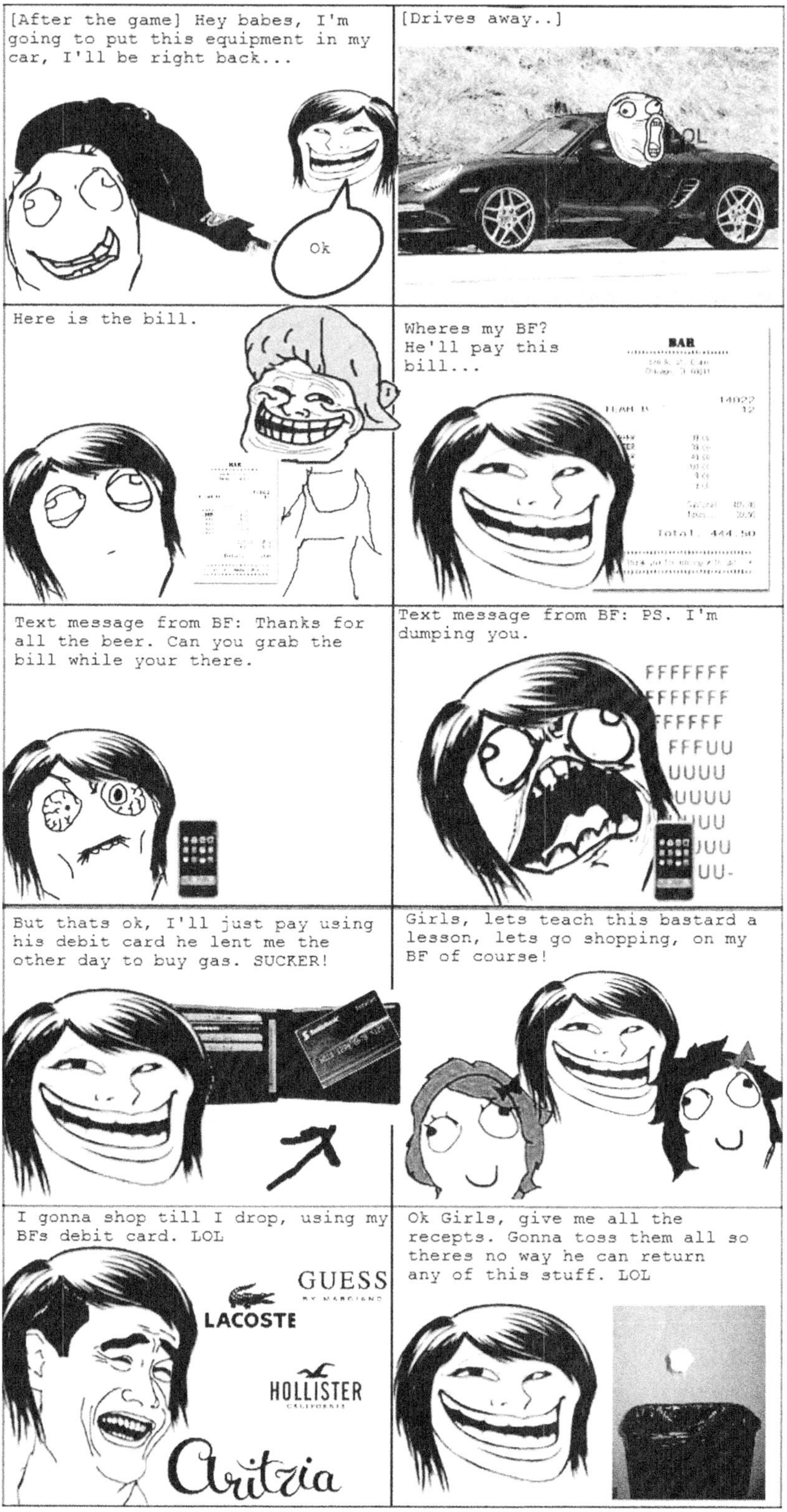

[After the game] Hey babes, I'm going to put this equipment in my car, I'll be right back...
Ok
[Drives away..]
LOL
Here is the bill.
Wheres my BF? He'll pay this bill...
BAR
Total: 444.50
Text message from BF: Thanks for all the beer. Can you grab the bill while your there.
Text message from BF: PS. I'm dumping you.
FFFFFFF FFFFFFF FFFFFF FFFUU UUUU UUUU UUU UUU UU-
But thats ok, I'll just pay using his debit card he lent me the other day to buy gas. SUCKER!
Girls, lets teach this bastard a lesson, lets go shopping, on my BF of course!
I gonna shop till I drop, using my BFs debit card. LOL
GUESS
BY MARCIANO
LACOSTE
HOLLISTER
CALIFORNIA
Aritzia
Ok Girls, give me all the recepts. Gonna toss them all so theres no way he can return any of this stuff. LOL

[But little did she know, that her boyfriend laughing his ass off..]

AAAAAAAAAAAWWWWWW

YYYYYYEEEEEEEEAAAAAAAAA

I knew she had my debit card, so I devised a plan that would really put revenge on the map!

LOL

[48 Hours ago]

Sweety Im going to the store to buy some milk, we are out.

ok

I took her debit and my debit card which looked the same (they were the same bank, and we did not sign the back)

I went to the ATM, I changed my GFs debit card to the same pin # as my debit card, and put a new pin # to my debit card

When I got home I secretly put both cards back in her wallet. She usually puts her card on the left side and mine on the right side. But I swapped them! So she would use hers thinking shes using mine. AWWW YEAH!!!!!!

LAAAAAAAWWWWWW

(YYEEEEEEEEAAAAAAAAA

[72 Hours later]

Asshole thinks he can dump me without consequences, I'll make him pay more. I'll shop 'till I drain his bank account dry!!!

HARRY ROSEN

TRUE RELIGION

[1 Week later]

Landlord: Sorry, your rent check bounced!

WTF? theres tons of money in my bank account?

She checks bank account on-line. Its empty. She checks the recent transactions and realizes that she used her own card instead of her boyfriends.

FFFFFFFFFFFF
FFFFFFFFFFFF
FUU UU
UU UU
UUU U-

69.

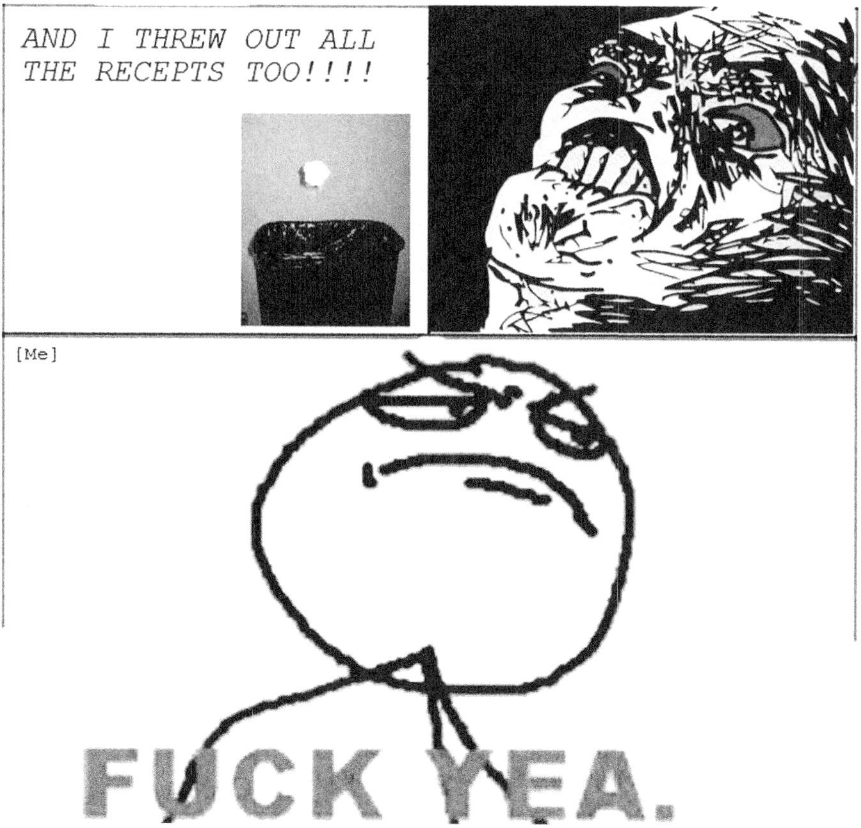

AND I THREW OUT ALL THE RECEPTS TOO!!!!
[Me]
FUCK YEA.

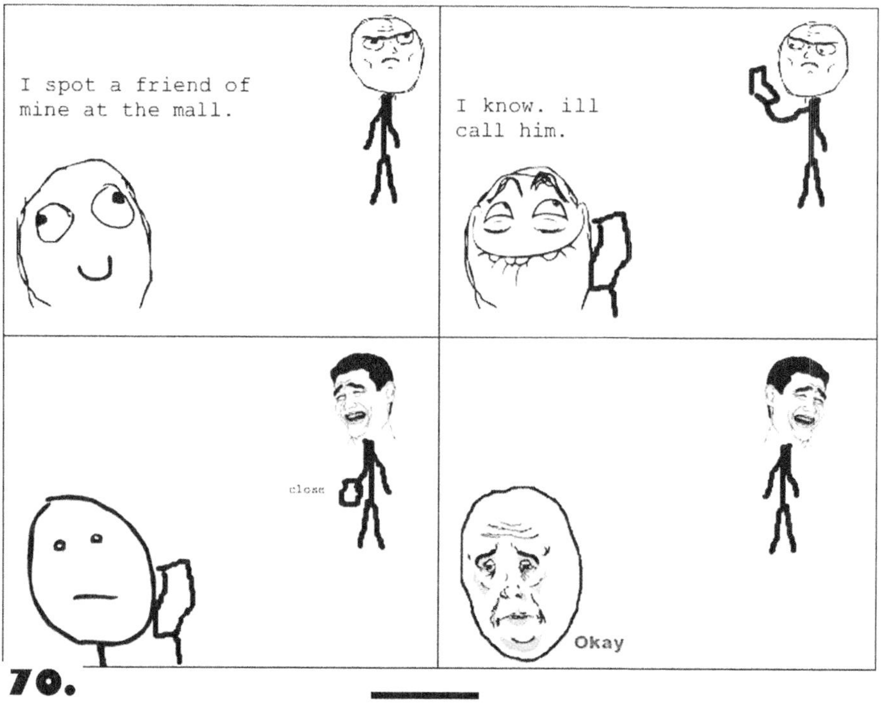

I spot a friend of mine at the mall.
I know. ill call him.
close
Okay

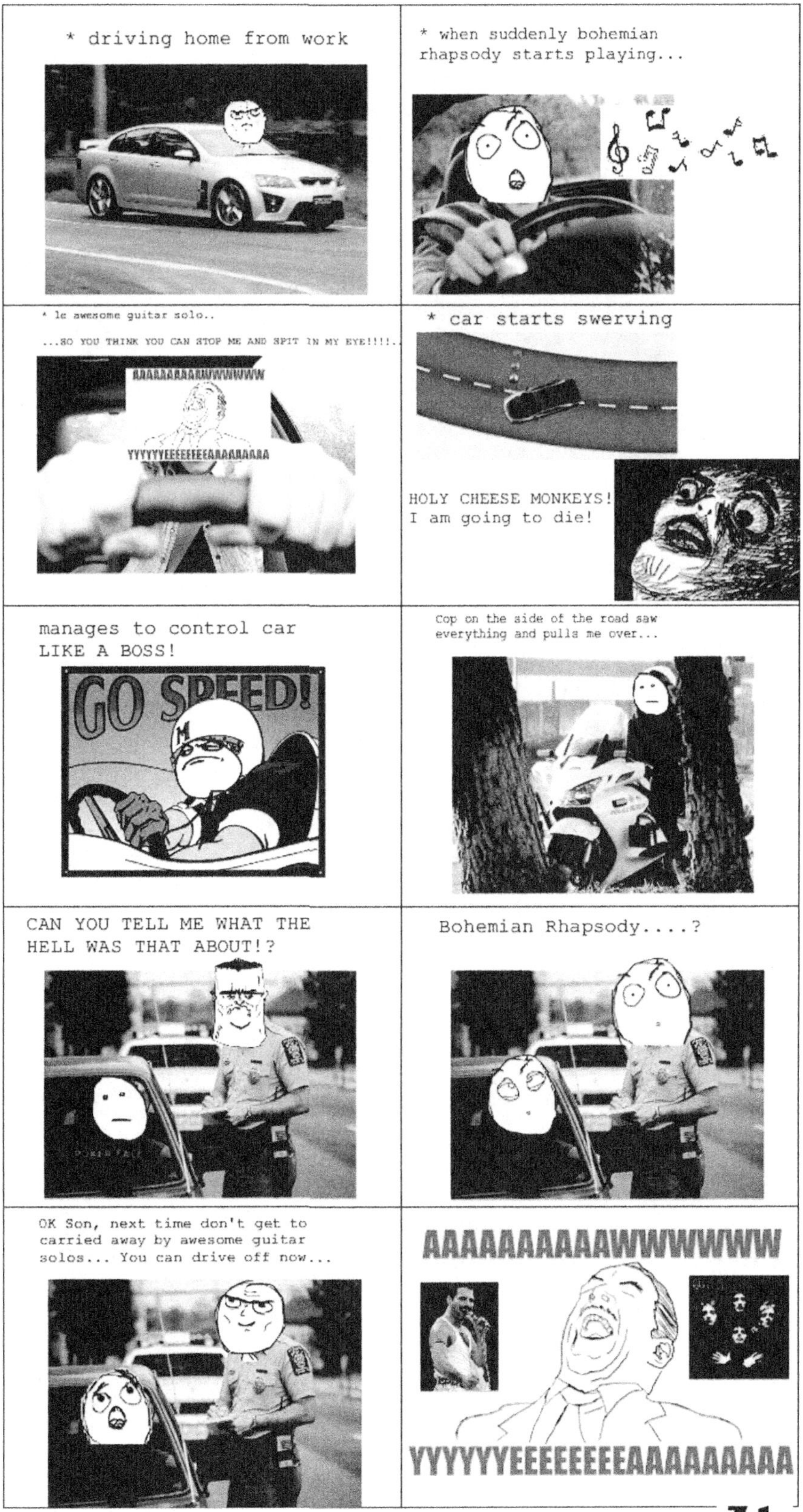
* driving home from work
* when suddenly bohemian rhapsody starts playing...
* le awesome guitar solo..
...SO YOU THINK YOU CAN STOP ME AND SPIT IN MY EYE!!!!..
AAAAAAAAAAWWWWWW
YYYYYYEEEEEEEEAAAAAAAAA
* car starts swerving
HOLY CHEESE MONKEYS! I am going to die!
manages to control car LIKE A BOSS!
GO SPEED!
Cop on the side of the road saw everything and pulls me over...
CAN YOU TELL ME WHAT THE HELL WAS THAT ABOUT!?
Bohemian Rhapsody....?
OK Son, next time don't get to carried away by awesome guitar solos... You can drive off now...
AAAAAAAAAAWWWWWW
YYYYYYEEEEEEEEAAAAAAAAA

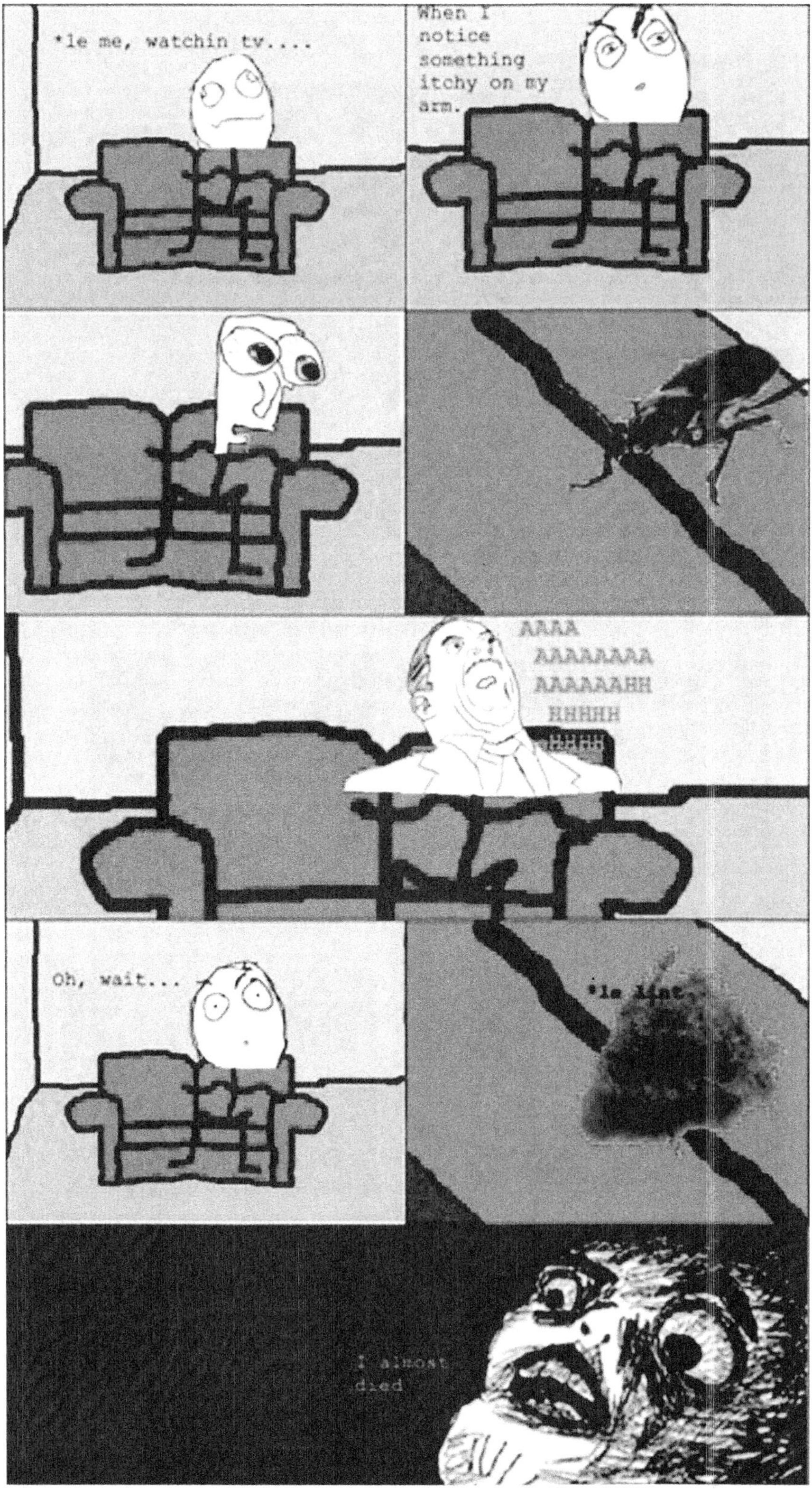
*le me, watchin tv....
When I notice something itchy on my arm.
AAAA
AAAAAAAA
AAAAAAHH
HHHHH
Oh, wait...
*le lint
I almost died

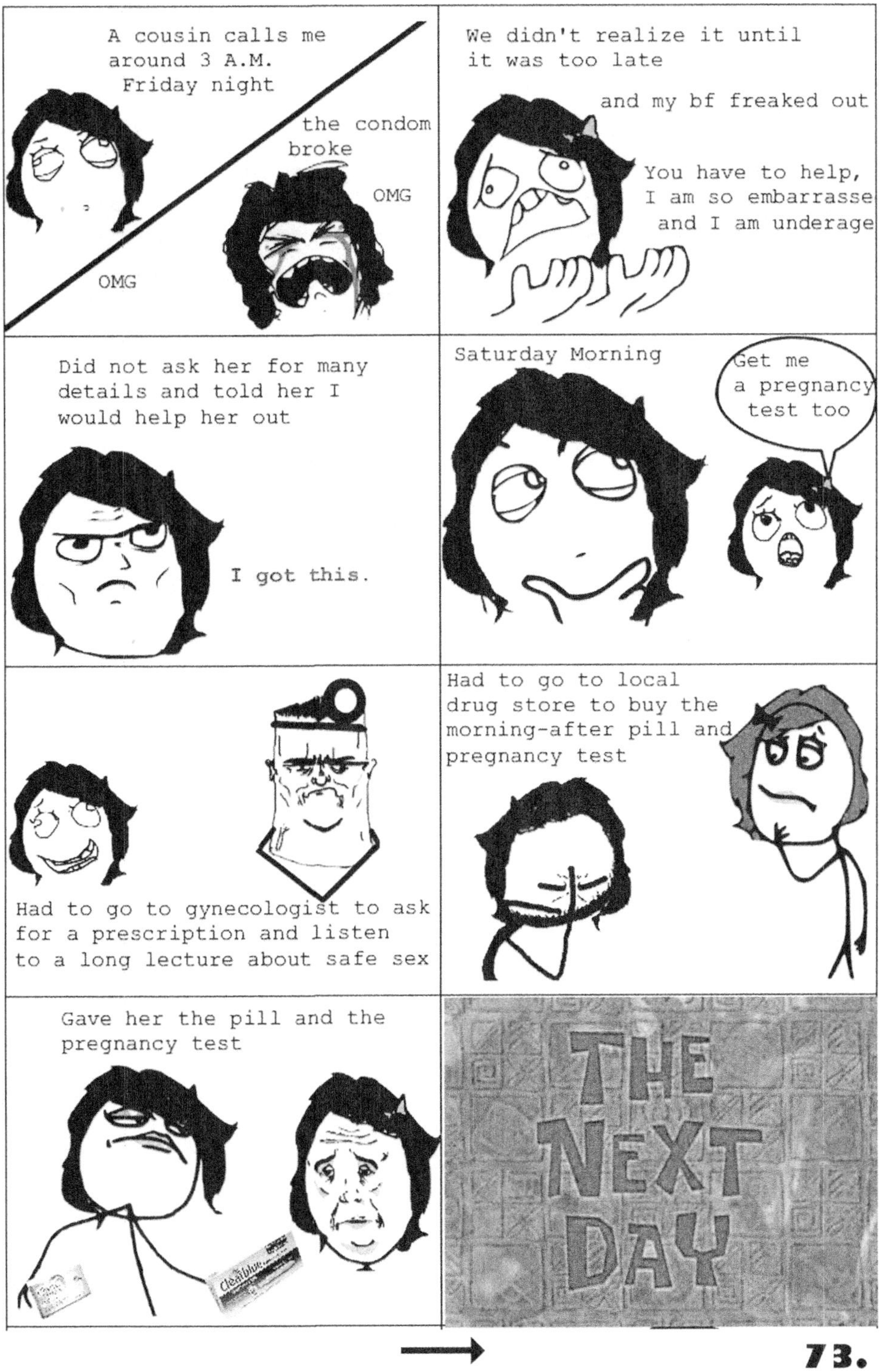

A cousin calls me
around 3 A.M.
Friday night
the condom
broke
OMG
OMG
We didn't realize it until
it was too late
and my bf freaked out
You have to help,
I am so embarrasse
and I am underage
Did not ask her for many
details and told her I
would help her out
I got this.
Saturday Morning
Get me
a pregnancy
test too
Had to go to gynecologist to ask
for a prescription and listen
to a long lecture about safe sex
Had to go to local
drug store to buy the
morning-after pill and
pregnancy test
Gave her the pill and the
pregnancy test
THE
NEXT
DAY

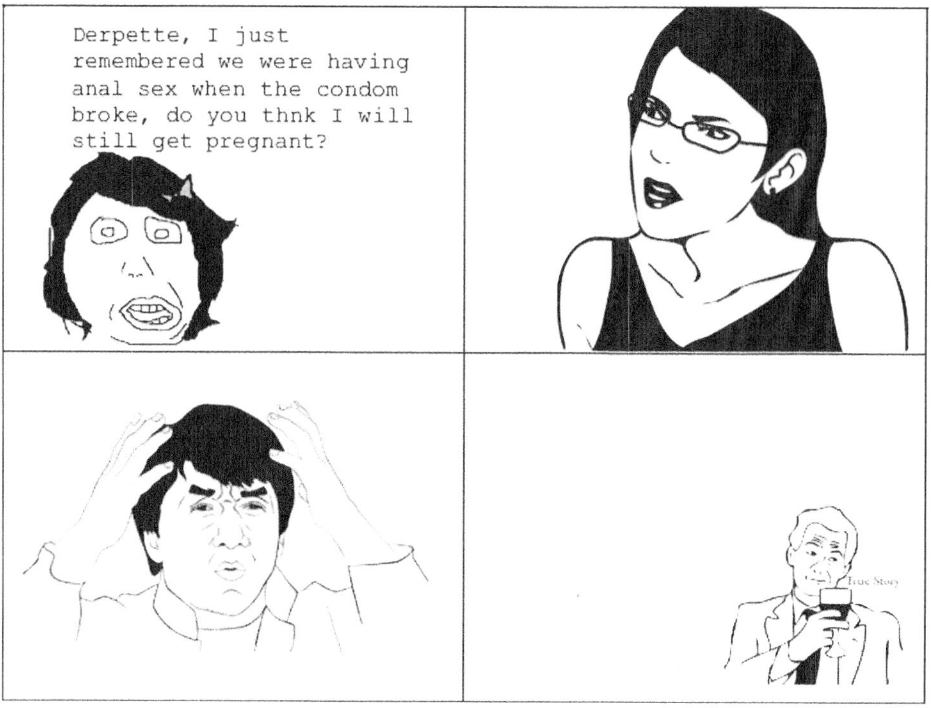
Derpette, I just remembered we were having anal sex when the condom broke, do you thnk I will still get pregnant?
True Story

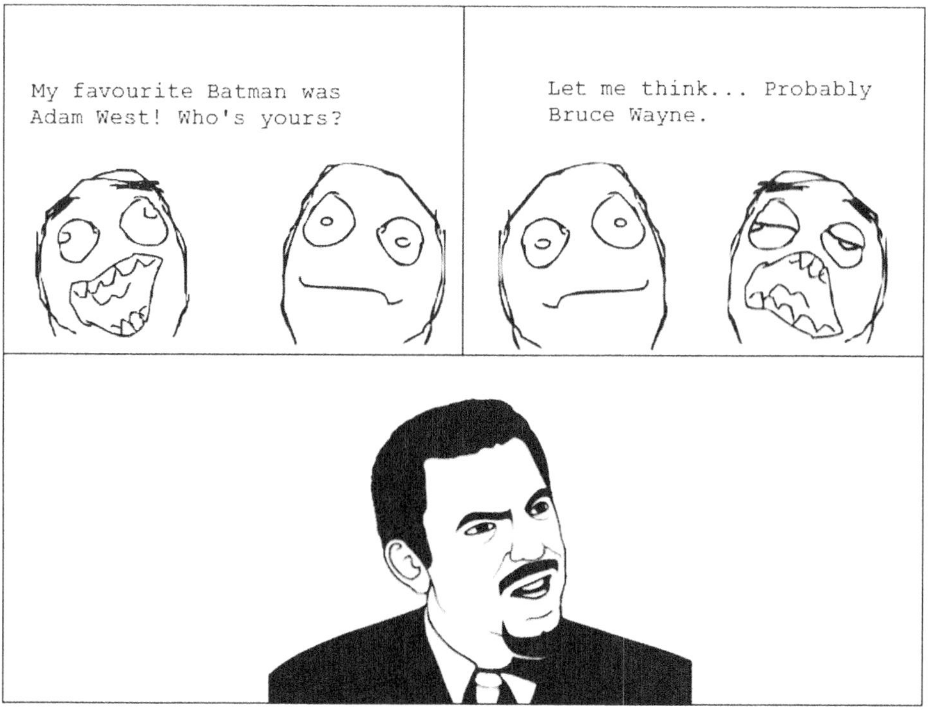
My favourite Batman was Adam West! Who's yours?
Let me think... Probably Bruce Wayne.

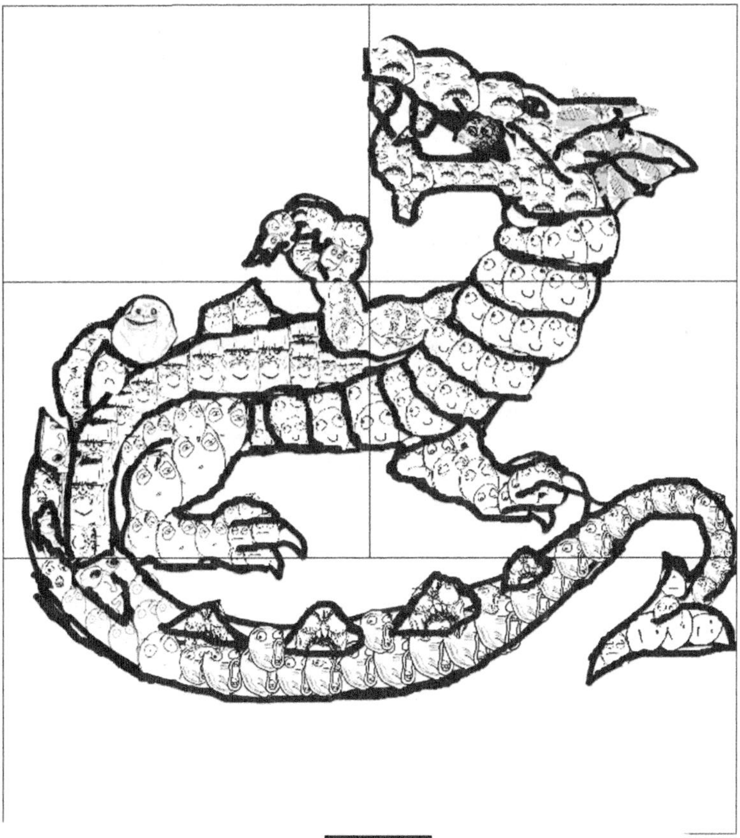

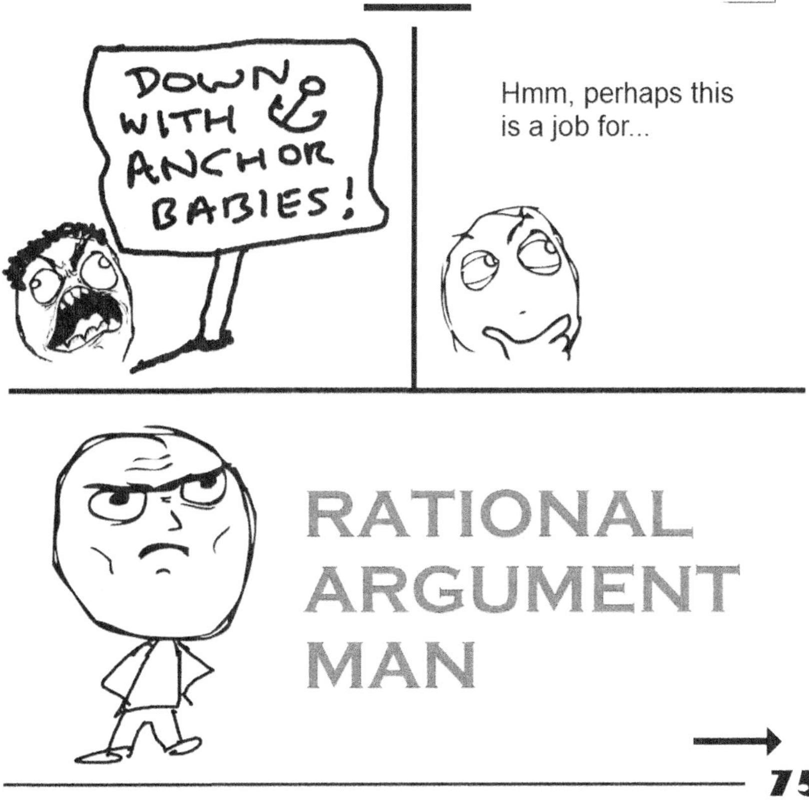
DOWN WITH ANCHOR BABIES!
Hmm, perhaps this is a job for...
RATIONAL ARGUMENT MAN

Pardon me, good citizen. Perhap you are laboring under a misconception. These so-called "anchor babies" can not sponsor citizenship applications for their parents until they are 21 years old.

Not exactly a short cut to citizenship, I dare say.

Wait, what? How did I not know that?

MY LIFE HAS BEEN A COMPLETE WASTE.

Thank you, Rational Argument Man.

AINT NO GAY MARRIAGE IN MY COPY OF THE CONSTITUTION!

Excuse me, friend, but I believe I have some information you have overlooked. In a free society such as ours, we need not justify making something legal.

Indeed, it is just the opposite. We must have compelling reason to make something illegal.

Have you such a reason, sir?

I have this book from my church.

And a fine book it is, sir.

However, how do we decide whose book to look to when deciding the law of the land? If you think the majority should be able to decide, are you comfortable with the fact that your brand of Christianity will one day no longer be the majority?

Will you be OK with, for example, Catholics or Mormons writing their religious practices into law?

Otherwise, if you solely want to make laws according to your version of the Bible, you're now talking about having some kind of

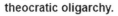

theocratic oligarchy.

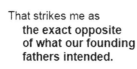

That strikes me as **the exact opposite of what our founding fathers intended.**

Gosh, I guess I never really thought about it that way.

Thank you, Rational Argument Man.

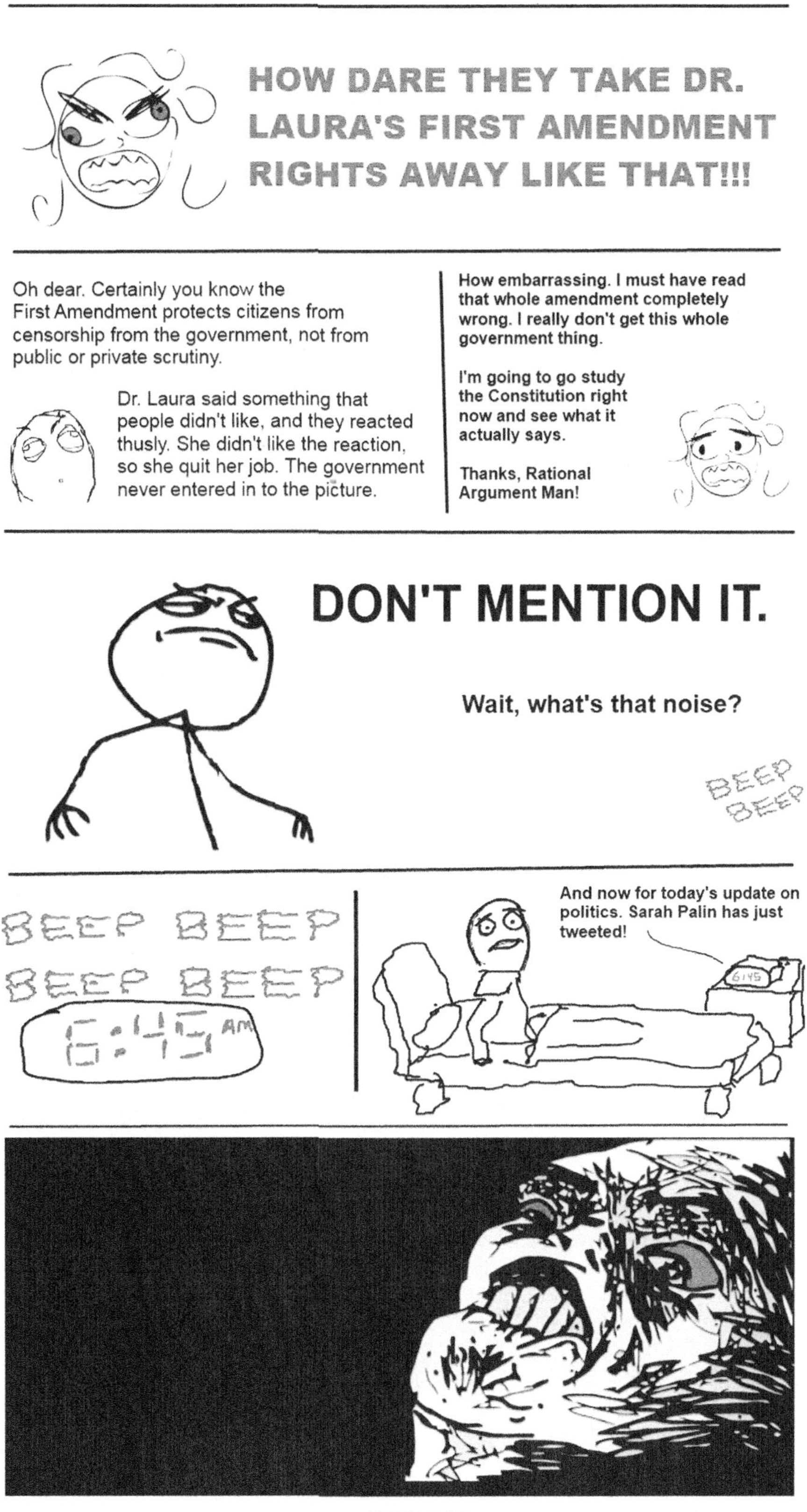
HOW DARE THEY TAKE DR. LAURA'S FIRST AMENDMENT RIGHTS AWAY LIKE THAT!!!
Oh dear. Certainly you know the First Amendment protects citizens from censorship from the government, not from public or private scrutiny.
Dr. Laura said something that people didn't like, and they reacted thusly. She didn't like the reaction, so she quit her job. The government never entered in to the picture.
How embarrassing. I must have read that whole amendment completely wrong. I really don't get this whole government thing.
I'm going to go study the Constitution right now and see what it actually says.
Thanks, Rational Argument Man!
DON'T MENTION IT.
Wait, what's that noise?
BEEP BEEP
BEEP BEEP BEEP BEEP
6:45 AM
And now for today's update on politics. Sarah Palin has just tweeted!
6:45

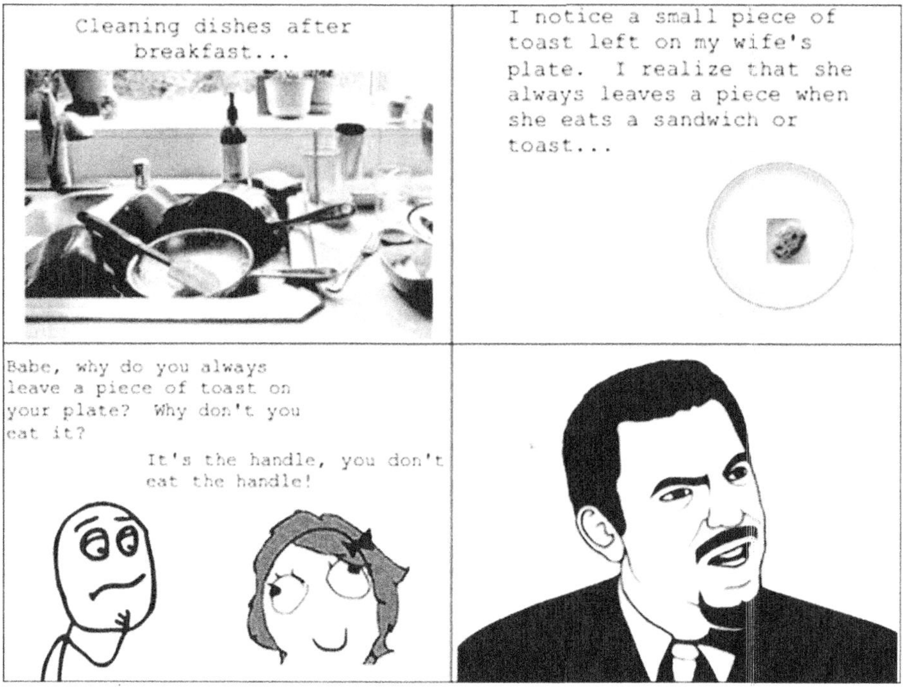
Cleaning dishes after breakfast...
I notice a small piece of toast left on my wife's plate. I realize that she always leaves a piece when she eats a sandwich or toast...
Babe, why do you always leave a piece of toast on your plate? Why don't you eat it?
It's the handle, you don't eat the handle!

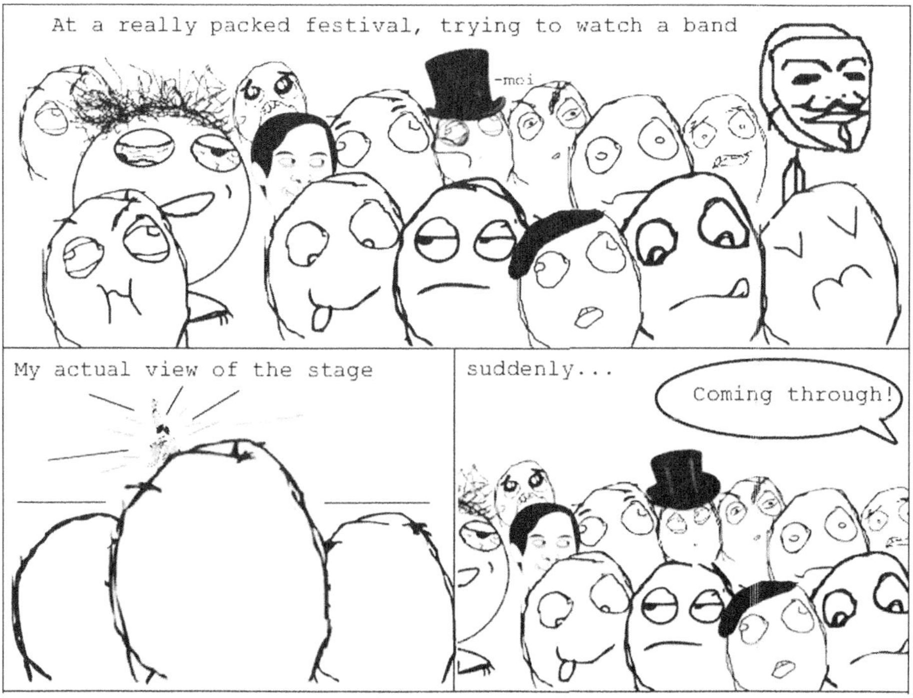
At a really packed festival, trying to watch a band
-moi
My actual view of the stage
suddenly...
Coming through!

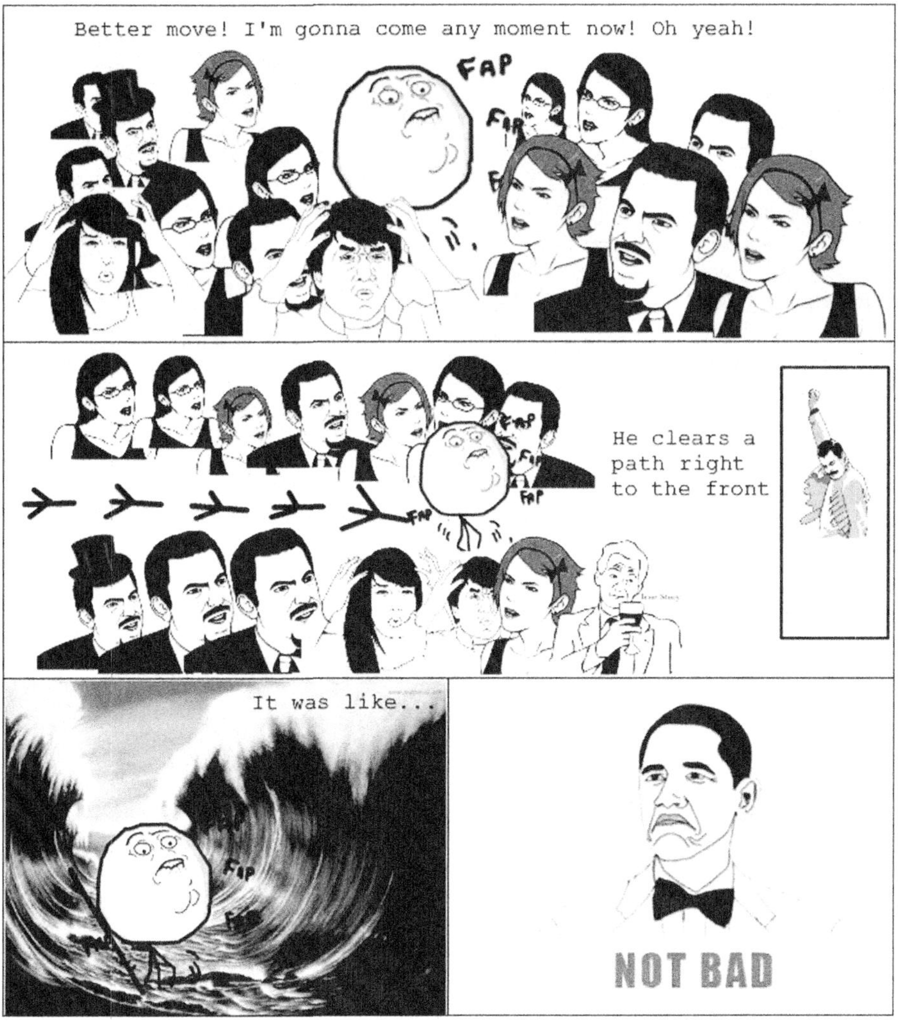
Better move! I'm gonna come any moment now! Oh yeah!
FAP
He clears a path right to the front
It was like...
NOT BAD

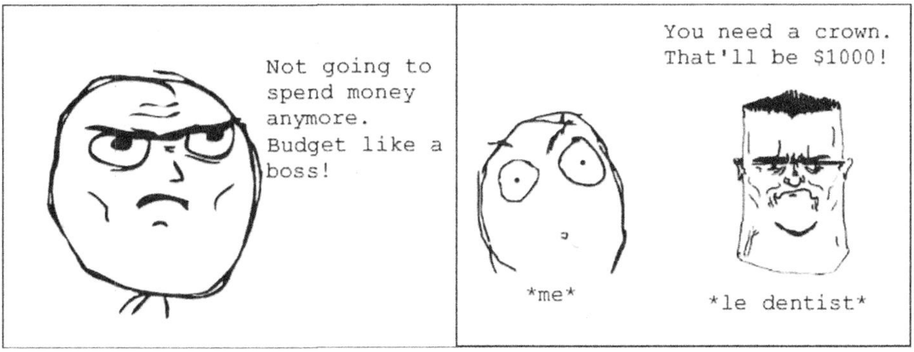
Not going to spend money anymore. Budget like a boss!
You need a crown. That'll be $1000!
me
le dentist

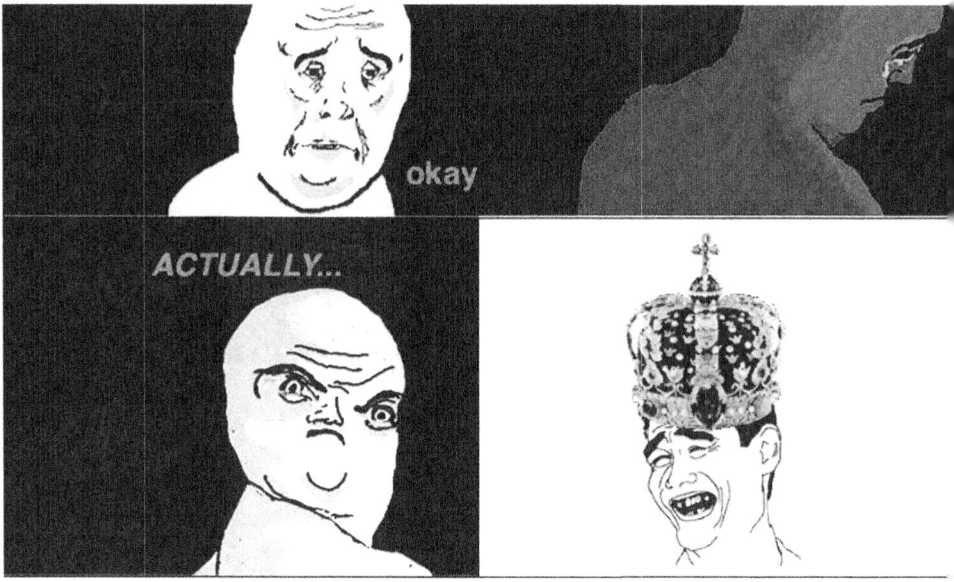
okay
ACTUALLY...

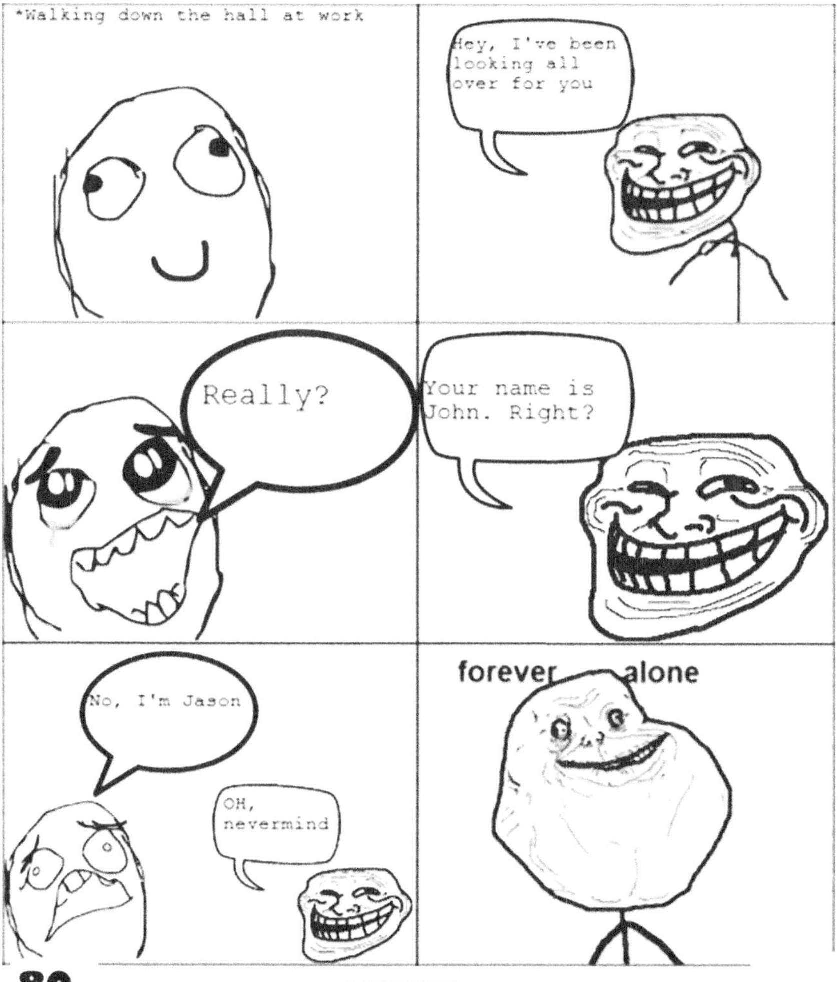
*Walking down the hall at work
Hey, I've been looking all over for you
Really?
Your name is John. Right?
No, I'm Jason
OH, nevermind
forever alone

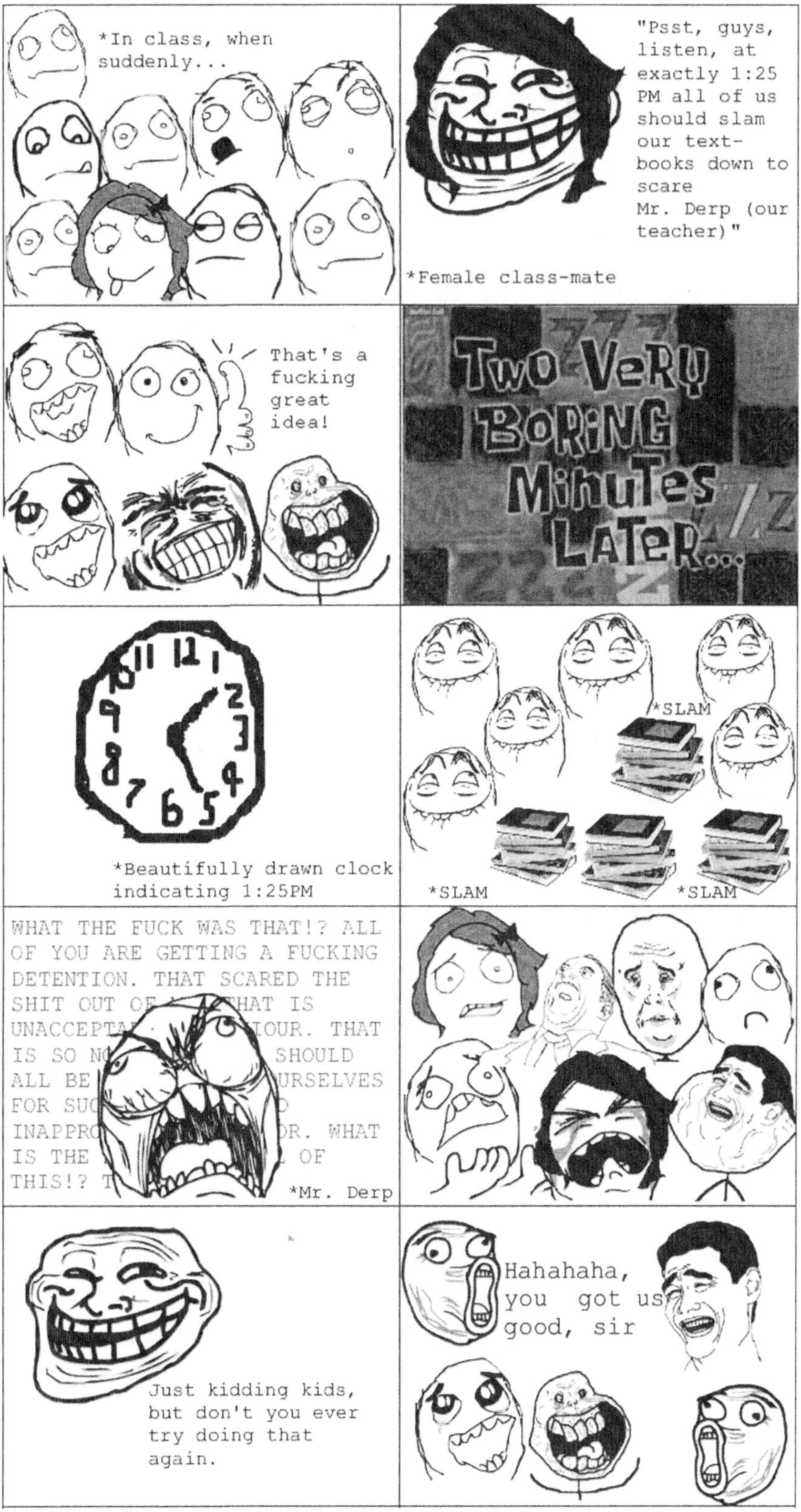
*In class, when suddenly...
"Psst, guys, listen, at exactly 1:25 PM all of us should slam our text-books down to scare Mr. Derp (our teacher)"
*Female class-mate
That's a fucking great idea!
Two Very Boring Minutes Later...
*Beautifully drawn clock indicating 1:25PM
*SLAM
*SLAM
*SLAM
WHAT THE FUCK WAS THAT!? ALL OF YOU ARE GETTING A FUCKING DETENTION. THAT SCARED THE SHIT OUT OF
HAT IS
UNACCEPTA
IOUR. THAT
IS SO N
SHOULD
ALL BE
URSELVES
FOR SU
INAPPR
R. WHAT
IS THE
OF
THIS!? T
*Mr. Derp
Just kidding kids, but don't you ever try doing that again.
Hahahaha, you got us good, sir

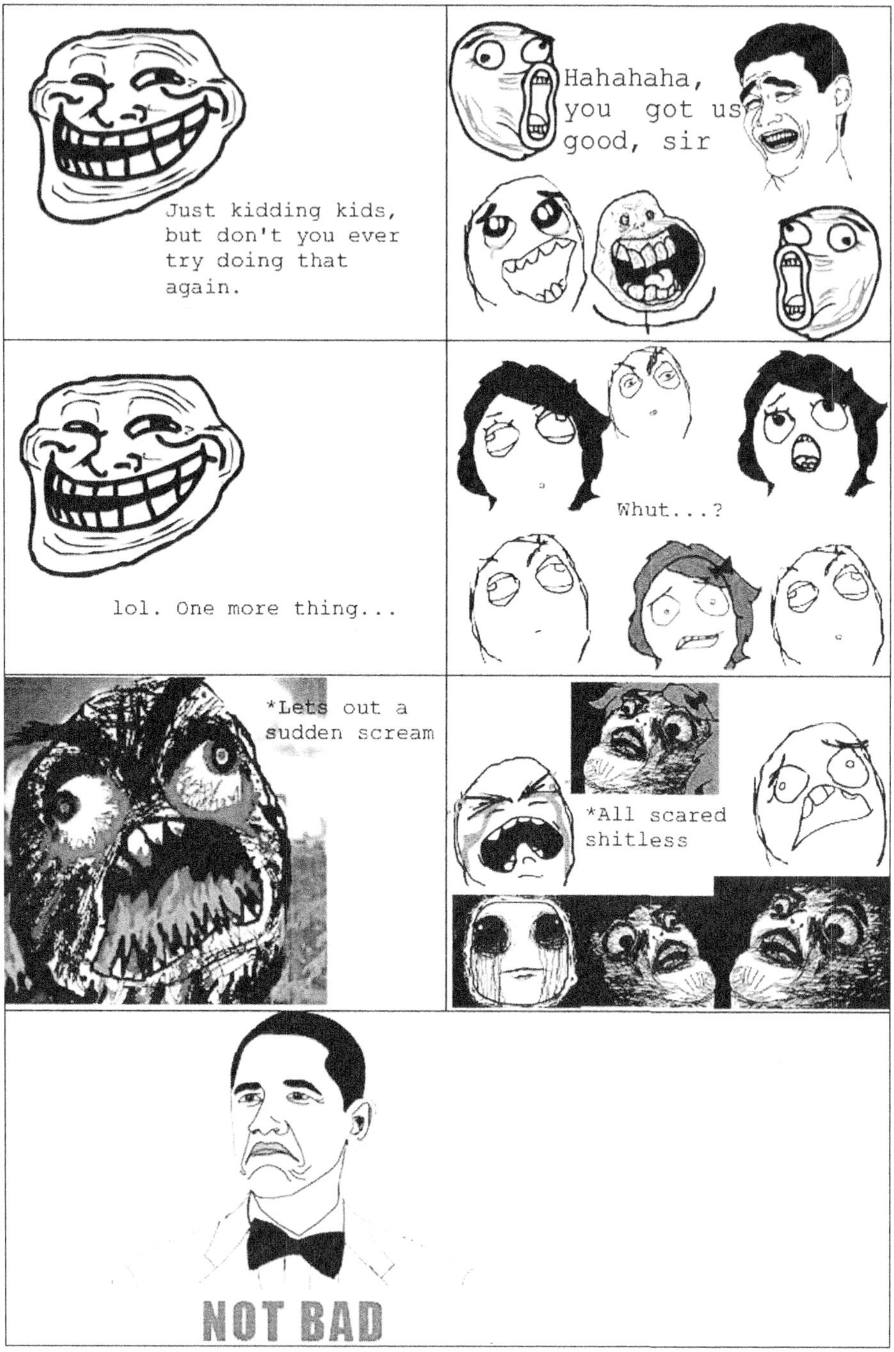
Just kidding kids, but don't you ever try doing that again.
Hahahaha, you got us good, sir
lol. One more thing...
Whut...?
*Lets out a sudden scream
*All scared shitless
NOT BAD

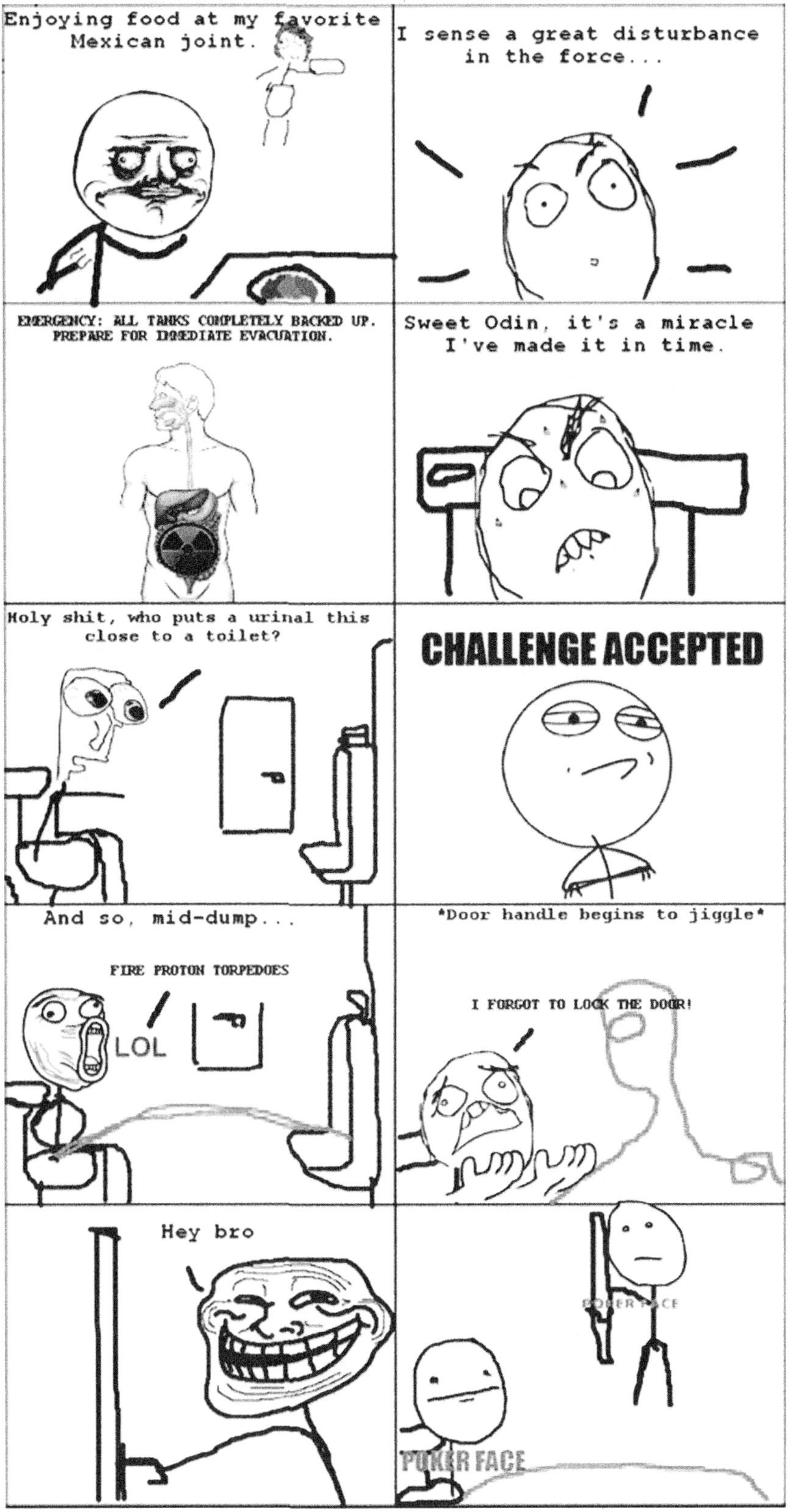

Enjoying food at my favorite Mexican joint.
I sense a great disturbance in the force...
EMERGENCY: ALL TANKS COMPLETELY BACKED UP. PREPARE FOR IMMEDIATE EVACUATION.
Sweet Odin, it's a miracle I've made it in time.
Holy shit, who puts a urinal this close to a toilet?
CHALLENGE ACCEPTED
And so, mid-dump...
FIRE PROTON TORPEDOES
LOL
Door handle begins to jiggle
I FORGOT TO LOCK THE DOOR!
Hey bro
POKER FACE

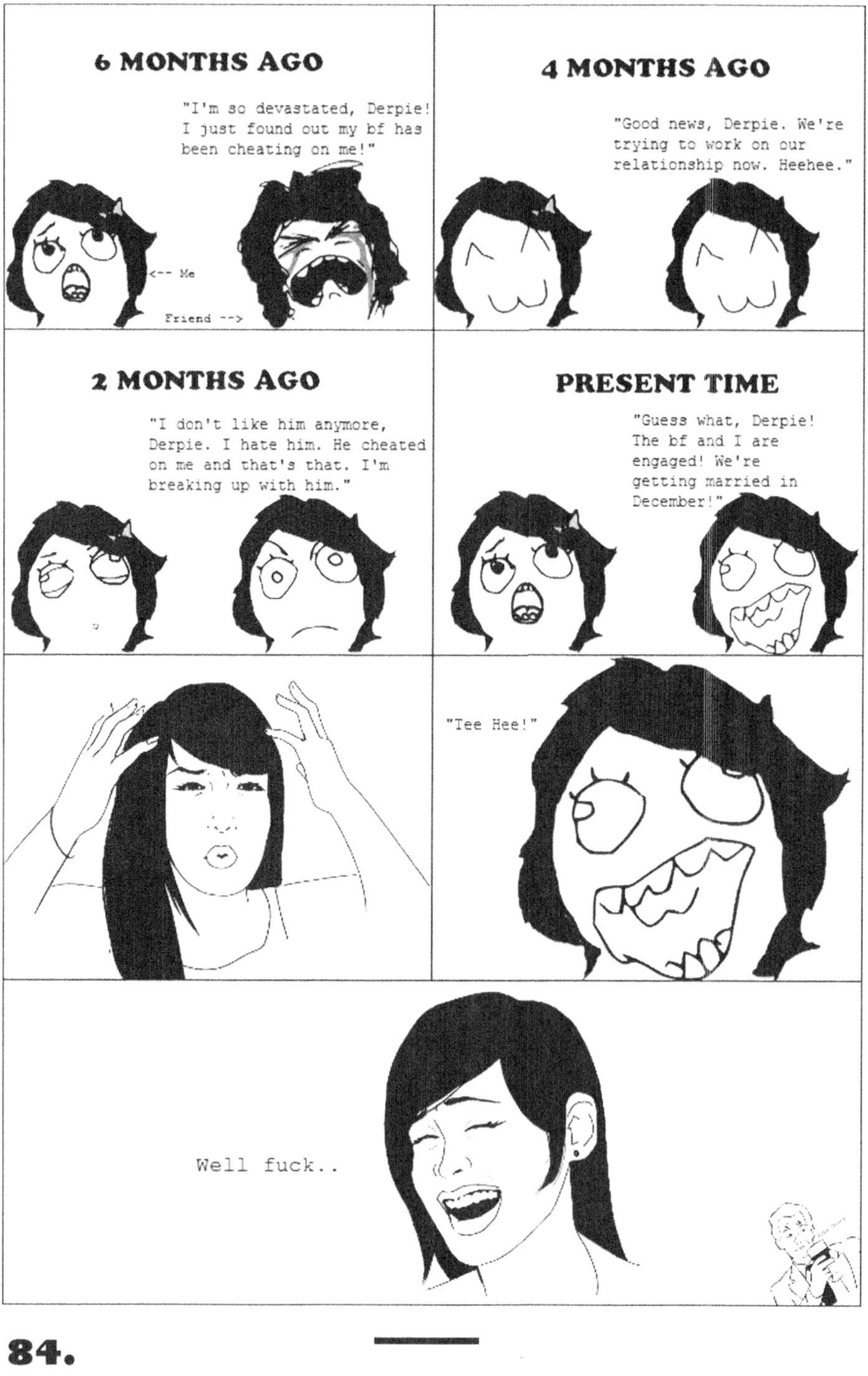
6 MONTHS AGO
"I'm so devastated, Derpie! I just found out my bf has been cheating on me!"
<-- Me
Friend -->
4 MONTHS AGO
"Good news, Derpie. We're trying to work on our relationship now. Heehee."
2 MONTHS AGO
"I don't like him anymore, Derpie. I hate him. He cheated on me and that's that. I'm breaking up with him."
PRESENT TIME
"Guess what, Derpie! The bf and I are engaged! We're getting married in December!"
"Tee Hee!"
Well fuck..

WE GOT A BILLION REPORTS DUE
BY TOMORROW AND YOU NEED TO
DO THEM ALL IF NOT I WILL
FIRE YOU BLAH BLAH

*le boss

*le me

OK I WILL DO THIS AND
I WILL NOT GET FIRED

except im
already
quitting
tomorrow

*what i do instead.
browse reddit...

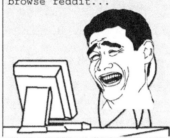

*playing video games in
break room

*wishing my co-worker a
happy birthday

*at home, going to bed

THE NEXT DAY

WHERE THE HELL IS DERP?!
THOSE REPORTS ARE MISSING!!
HE B⬛⬛ER BETTER HAVE DONE
TH⬛⬛⬛⬛OR HE'S FIRED!!!

yesterday was his
last day. didnt he
tell you?

85.

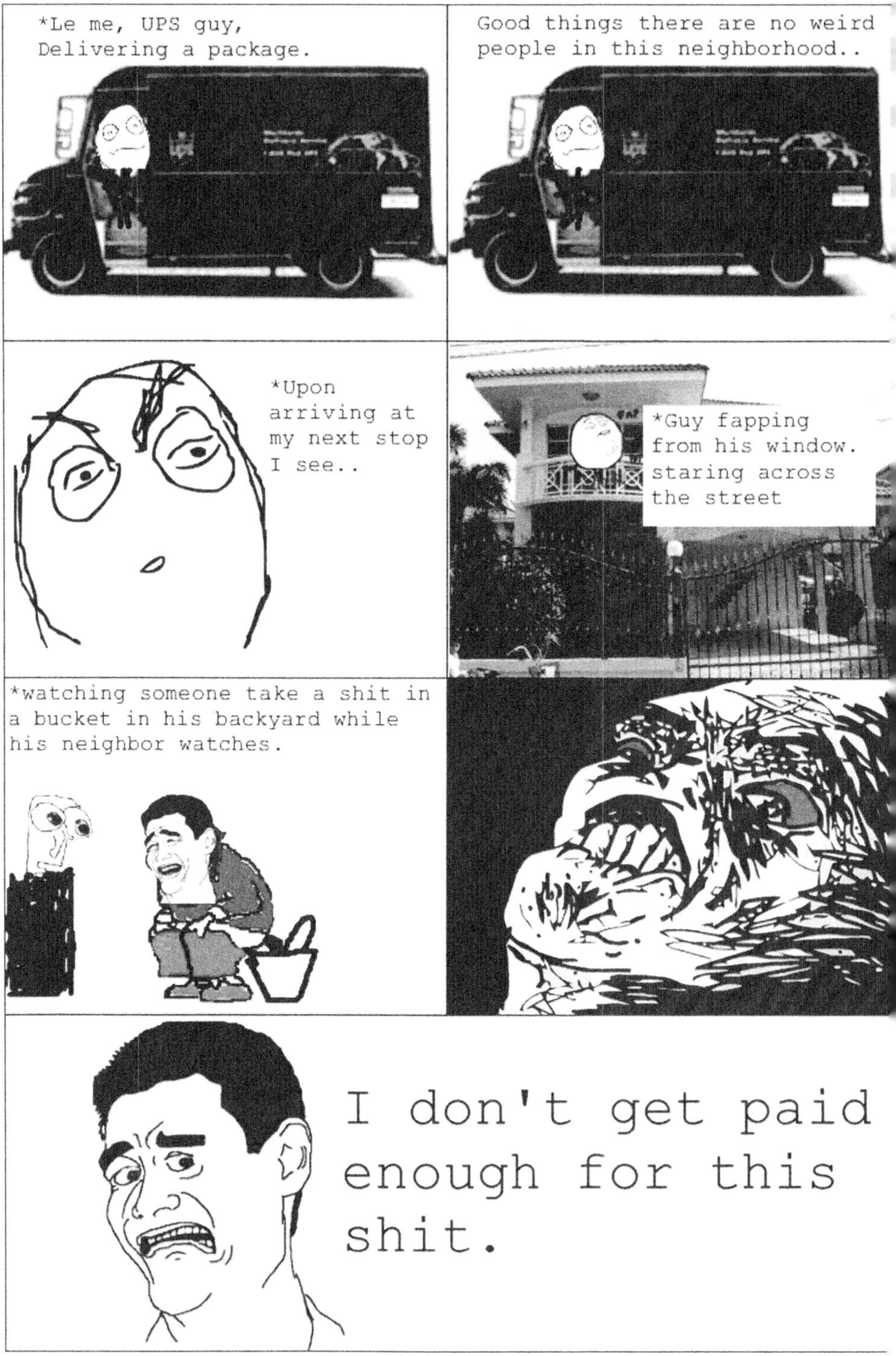
*Le me, UPS guy,
Delivering a package.
Good things there are no weird
people in this neighborhood..
*Upon
arriving at
my next stop
I see..
*Guy fapping
from his window.
staring across
the street
*watching someone take a shit in
a bucket in his backyard while
his neighbor watches.
I don't get paid
enough for this
shit.

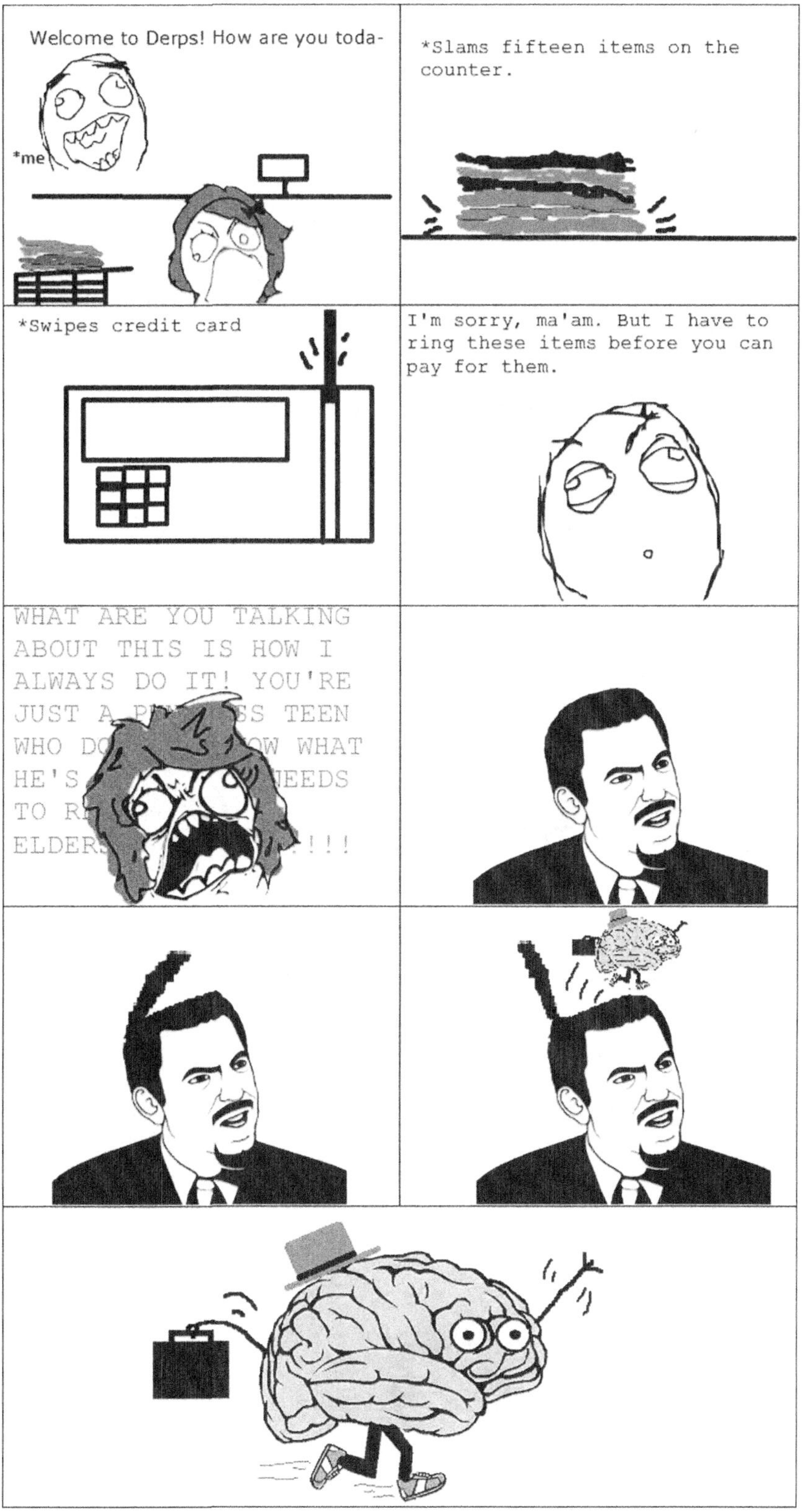
Welcome to Derps! How are you toda-
*me
*Slams fifteen items on the counter.
*Swipes credit card
I'm sorry, ma'am. But I have to ring these items before you can pay for them.
WHAT ARE YOU TALKING
ABOUT THIS IS HOW I
ALWAYS DO IT! YOU'RE
JUST A
TEEN
WHO
WHAT
HE'S
NEEDS
TO
ELDER
!!!

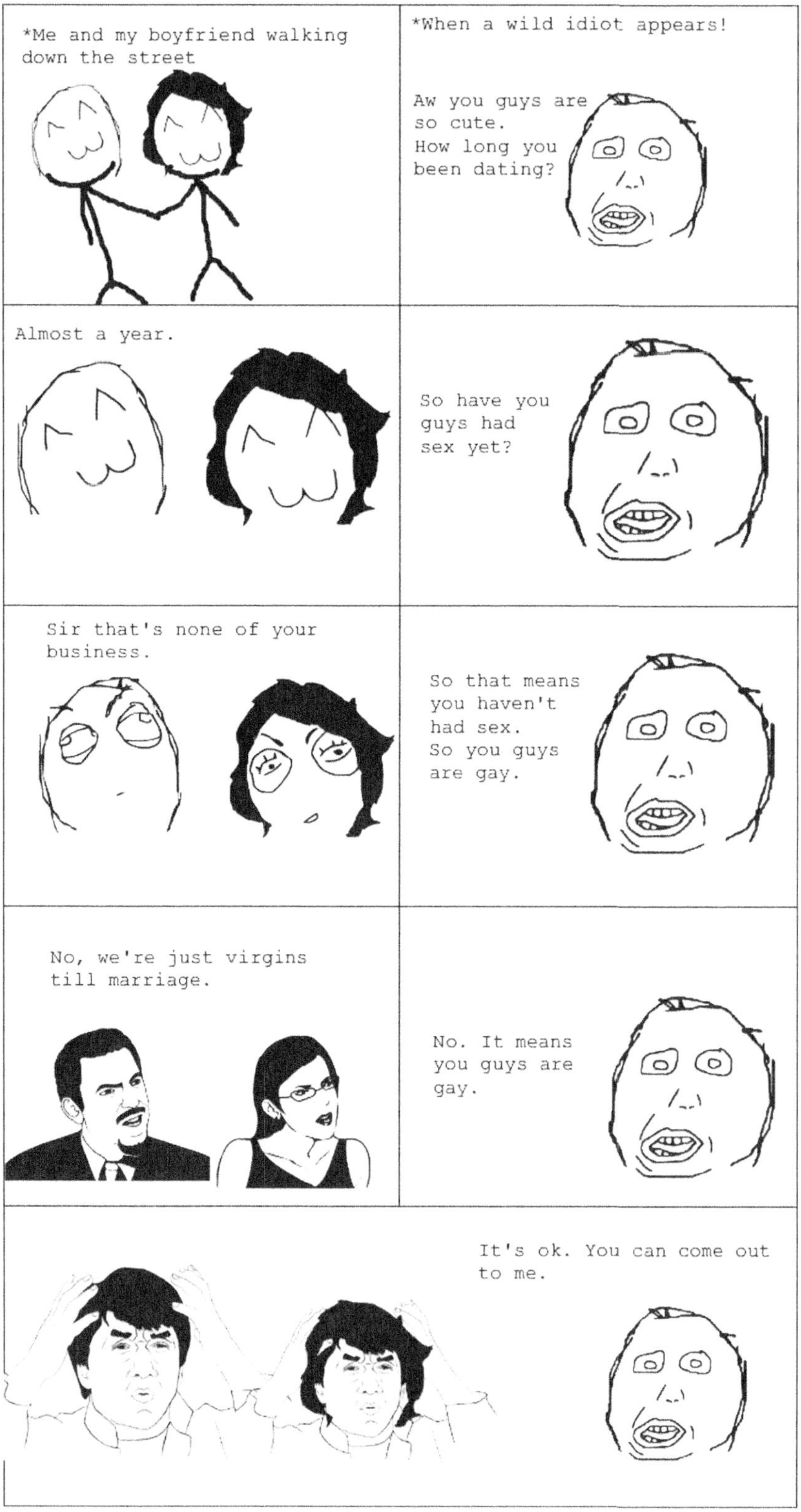
*Me and my boyfriend walking down the street
*When a wild idiot appears!
Aw you guys are so cute. How long you been dating?
Almost a year.
So have you guys had sex yet?
Sir that's none of your business.
So that means you haven't had sex. So you guys are gay.
No, we're just virgins till marriage.
No. It means you guys are gay.
It's ok. You can come out to me.

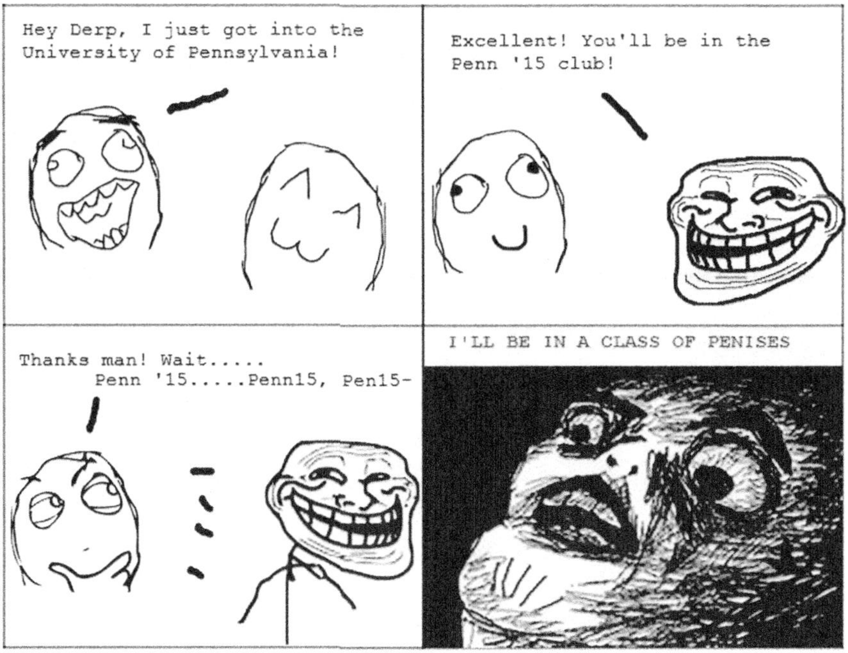
Hey Derp, I just got into the University of Pennsylvania!
Excellent! You'll be in the Penn '15 club!
Thanks man! Wait.....
Penn '15.....Penn15, Pen15-
I'LL BE IN A CLASS OF PENISES

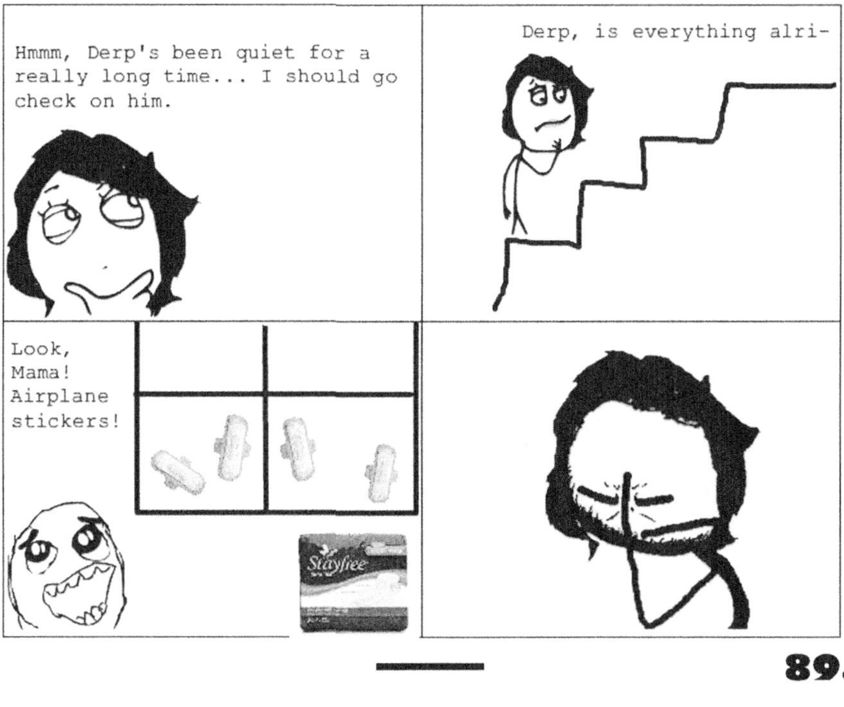
Hmmm, Derp's been quiet for a really long time... I should go check on him.
Derp, is everything alri-
Look, Mama! Airplane stickers!
Stayfree

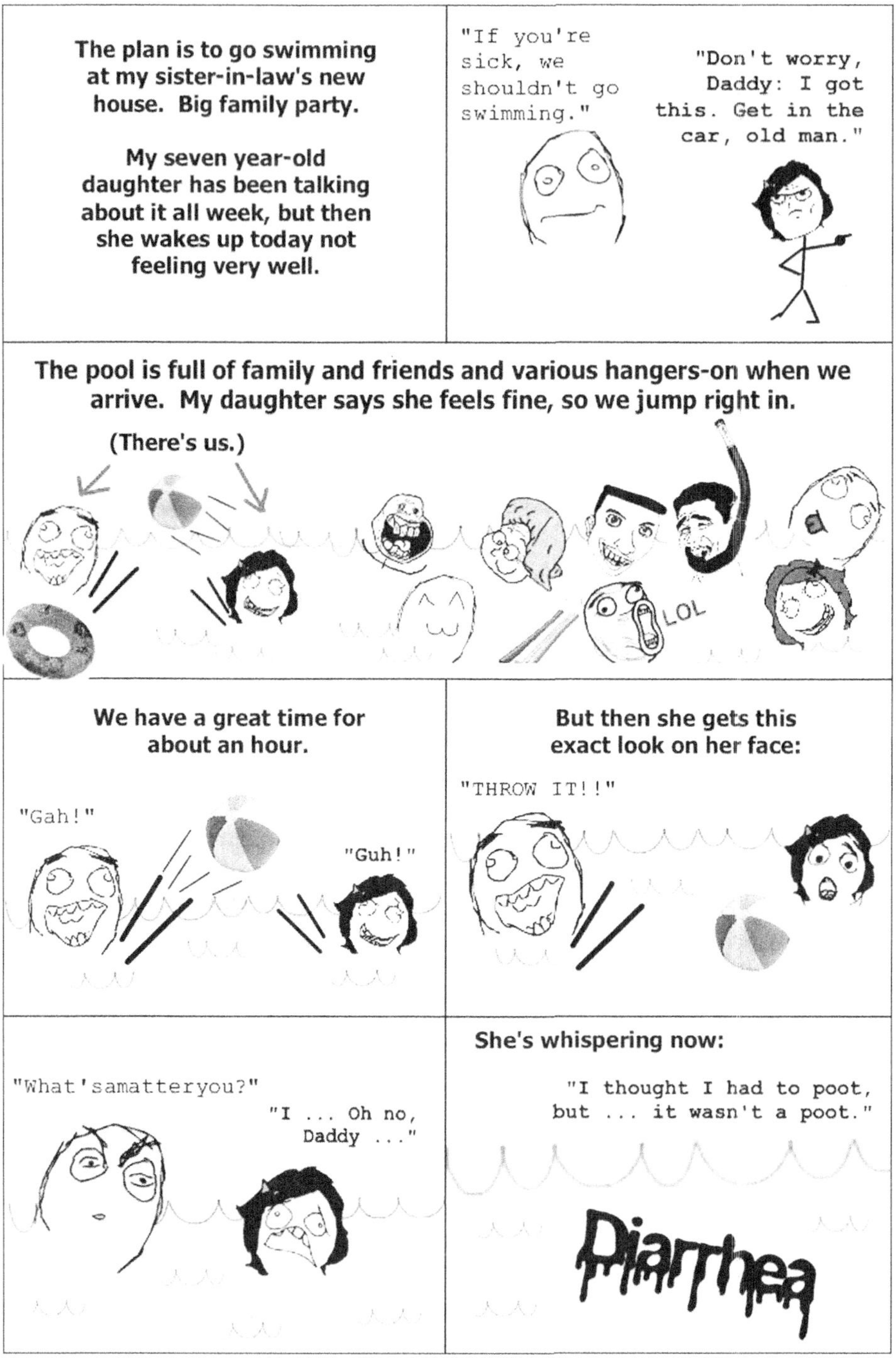
The plan is to go swimming at my sister-in-law's new house. Big family party.
My seven year-old daughter has been talking about it all week, but then she wakes up today not feeling very well.
"If you're sick, we shouldn't go swimming."
"Don't worry, Daddy: I got this. Get in the car, old man."
The pool is full of family and friends and various hangers-on when we arrive. My daughter says she feels fine, so we jump right in.
(There's us.)
LOL
We have a great time for about an hour.
"Gah!"
"Guh!"
But then she gets this exact look on her face:
"THROW IT!!"
"What'samatteryou?"
"I ... Oh no, Daddy ..."
She's whispering now:
"I thought I had to poot, but ... it wasn't a poot."
Diarrhea

"Everyone's gonna be mad at me and everyone's gonna laugh at me all day."

Diarrhea

"They won't laugh at you."

"Yes, they will."

"No. They won't. I got this."

Diarrhea

"ATTENTION EVERYONE IN THE POOL. WE ALL HAVE TO GET OUT RIGHT NOW."

"Oh God."

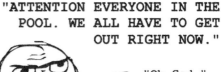

Diarrhea

"I'M NOT FEELING WELL, AND I'M AFRAID I HAD A DIARRHEA ATTACK IN THE POOL. I'M VERY SORRY. PLEASE GET OUT NOW."

"WTF, man?"

"Nasty!"

"YUCK!"

"Jezzus!"

Diarrhea

(Eventually, we're the last ones out.)

"They're mad at you. They'll tease you. Mommy is going to kill you."

"Eh, no big whoop. Lets go get cleaned up."

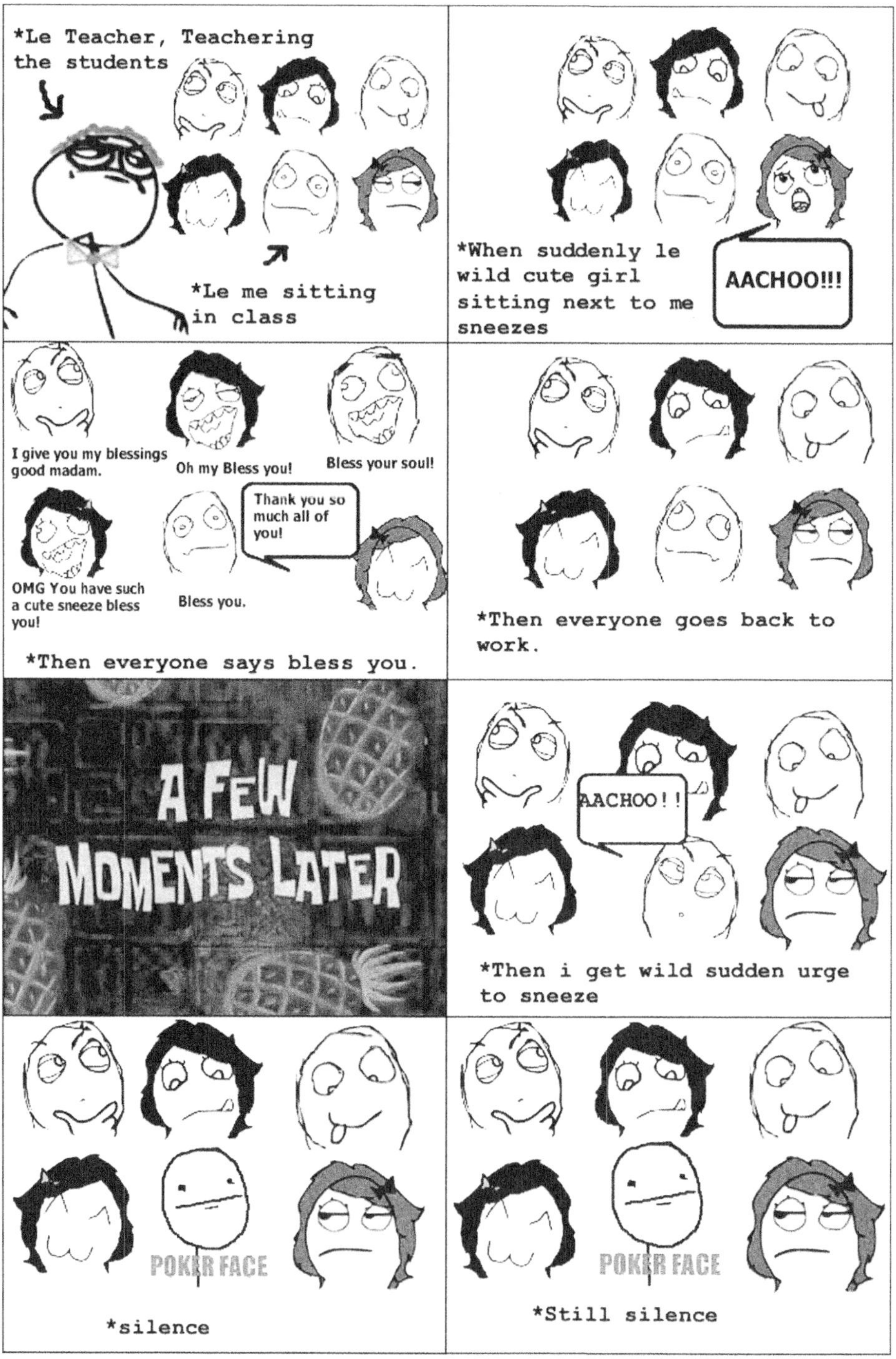
*Le Teacher, Teachering the students
*Le me sitting in class
*When suddenly le wild cute girl sitting next to me sneezes
AACHOO!!!
I give you my blessings good madam.
Oh my Bless you!
Bless your soul!
OMG You have such a cute sneeze bless you!
Bless you.
Thank you so much all of you!
*Then everyone says bless you.
*Then everyone goes back to work.
A FEW MOMENTS LATER
AACHOO!!
*Then i get wild sudden urge to sneeze
POKER FACE
*silence
POKER FACE
*Still silence

92.

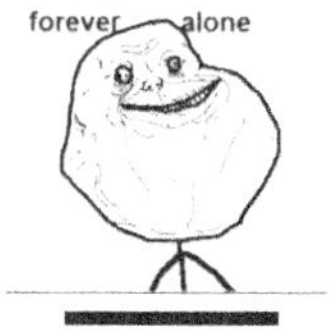
forever alone

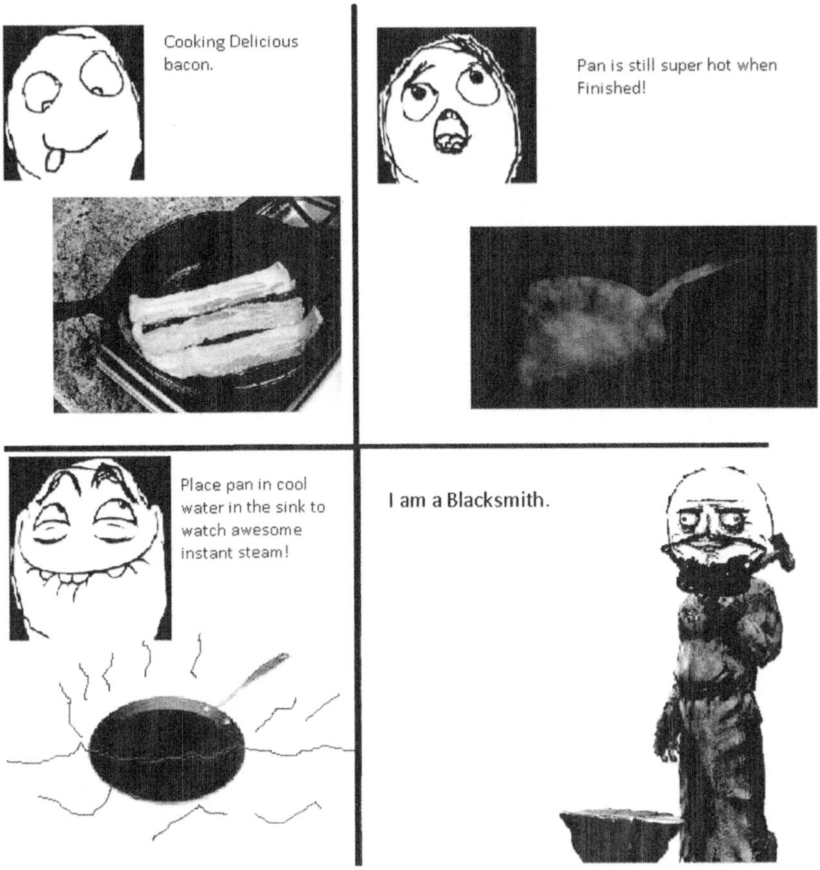

Cooking Delicious bacon.
Pan is still super hot when Finished!
Place pan in cool water in the sink to watch awesome instant steam!
I am a Blacksmith.

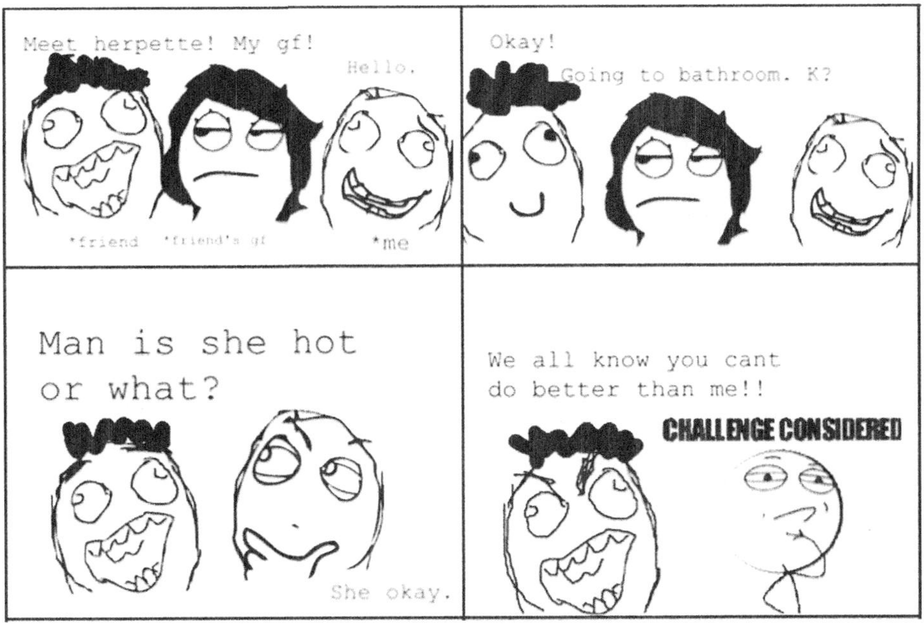

Meet herpette! My gf!
Hello.
*friend
*friend's gf
*me
Okay!
Going to bathroom. K?
Man is she hot or what?
She okay.
We all know you cant do better than me!!
CHALLENGE CONSIDERED

CHALLENGE ACCEPTED

Derping around
zharmony.com

Derpette.

She looks interesting...
Set date...

At date....

Hmm.. When is she
coming...

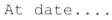

Derp?

Yes.

Hallelujah!!!

Turns out we have A
LOT in common.

Blah blah
Blah
Blahhh.

Should i ask her if
she does reddit??

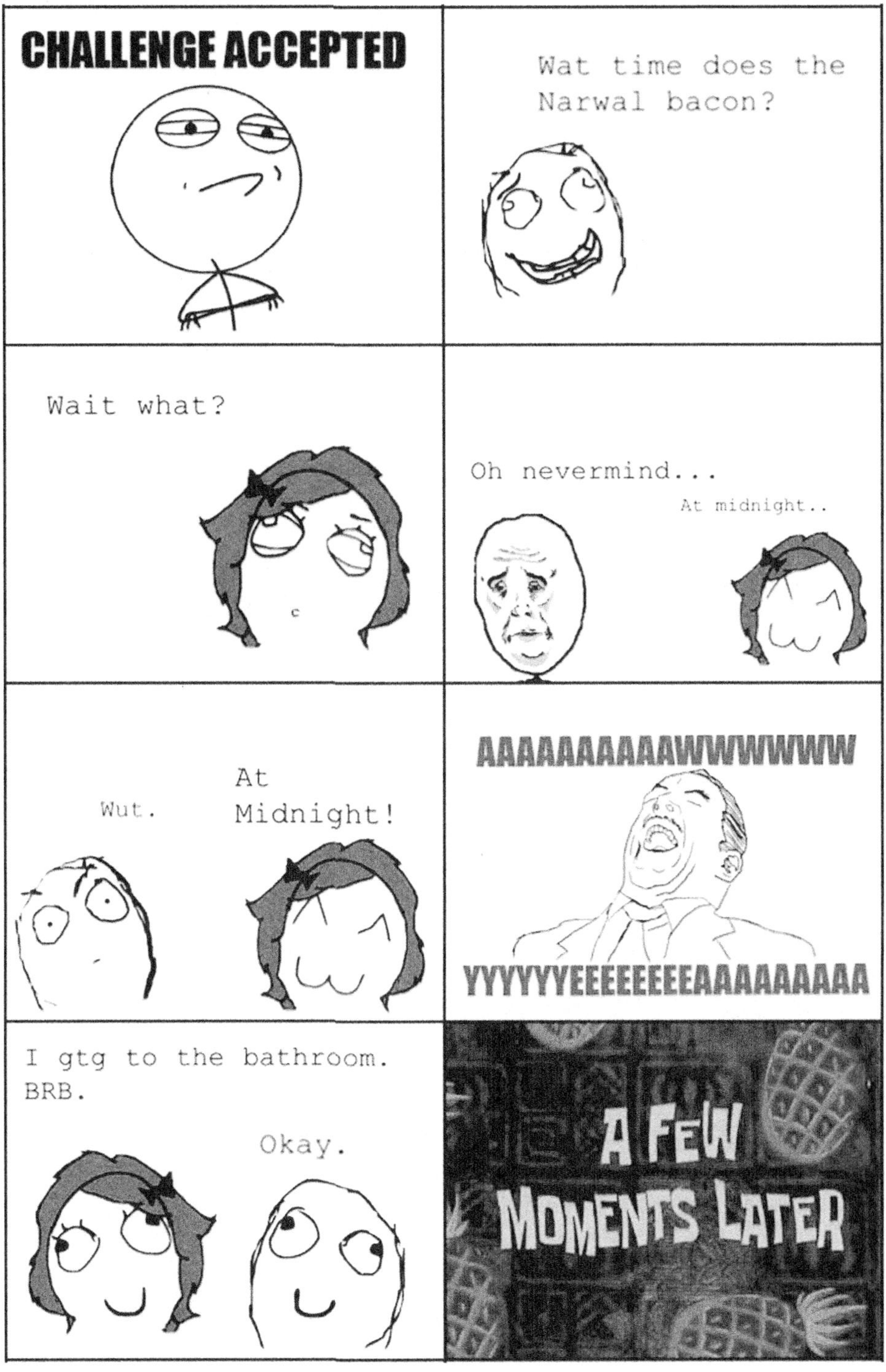
CHALLENGE ACCEPTED
Wat time does the Narwal bacon?
Wait what?
Oh nevermind...
At midnight..
Wut.
At Midnight!
AAAAAAAAAAWWWWWW
YYYYYYEEEEEEEEAAAAAAAAA
I gtg to the bathroom. BRB.
Okay.
A FEW MOMENTS LATER

I have to go the bathroom too...

Walks out of bathroom.

I see her making out with another guy.

Snaps pic for proof.

Click!

Sorry i took so long..

Problem?

How could you?!?!? On a first date! Well i took a pic! And you go off kissing some random guys!!! Seriously... What kind of person..

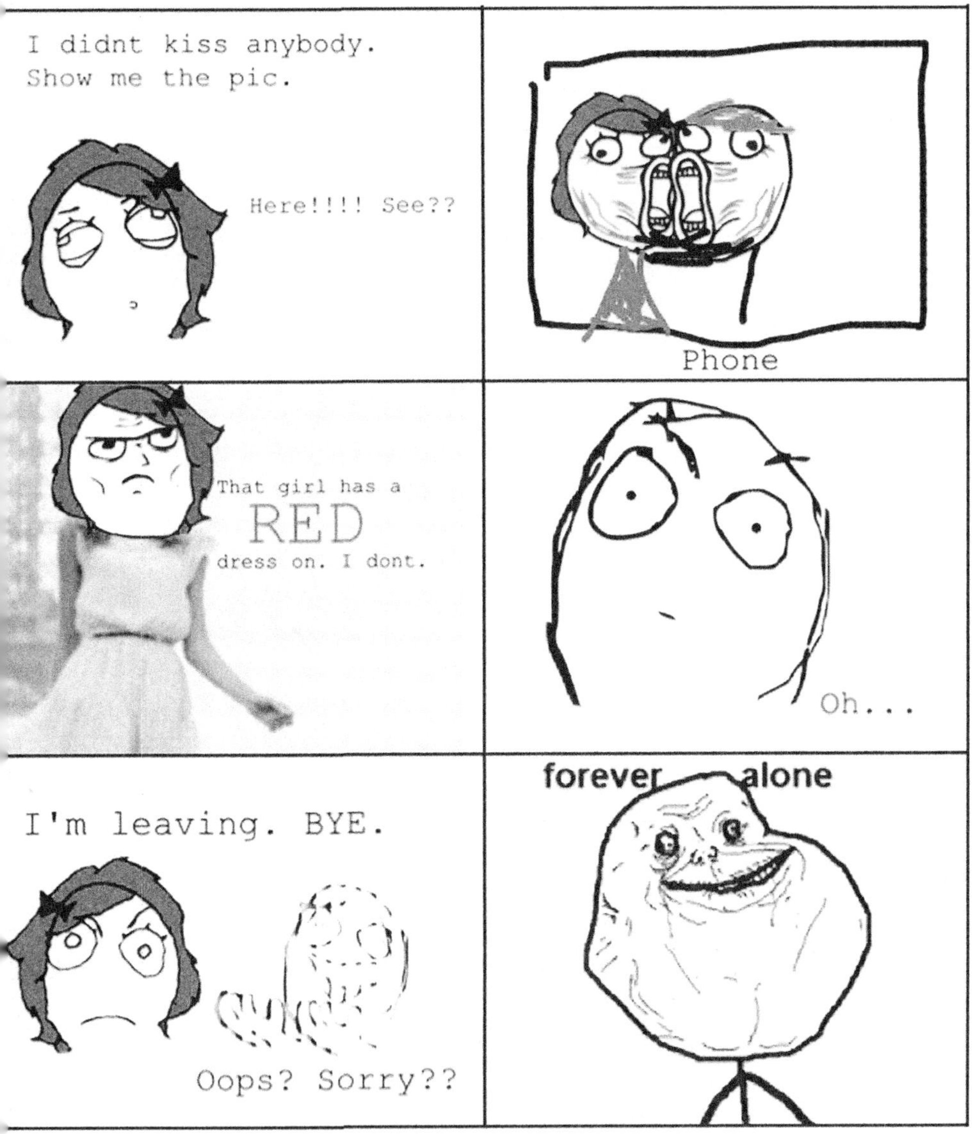
I didnt kiss anybody.
Show me the pic.
Here!!!! See??
Phone
That girl has a
RED
dress on. I dont.
Oh...
I'm leaving. BYE.
Oops? Sorry??
forever alone

97.

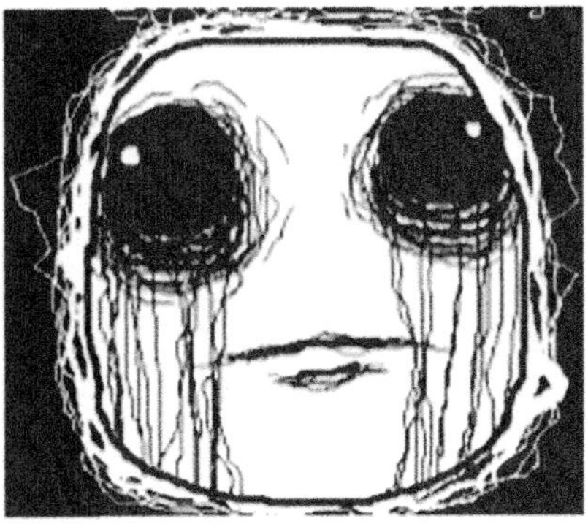

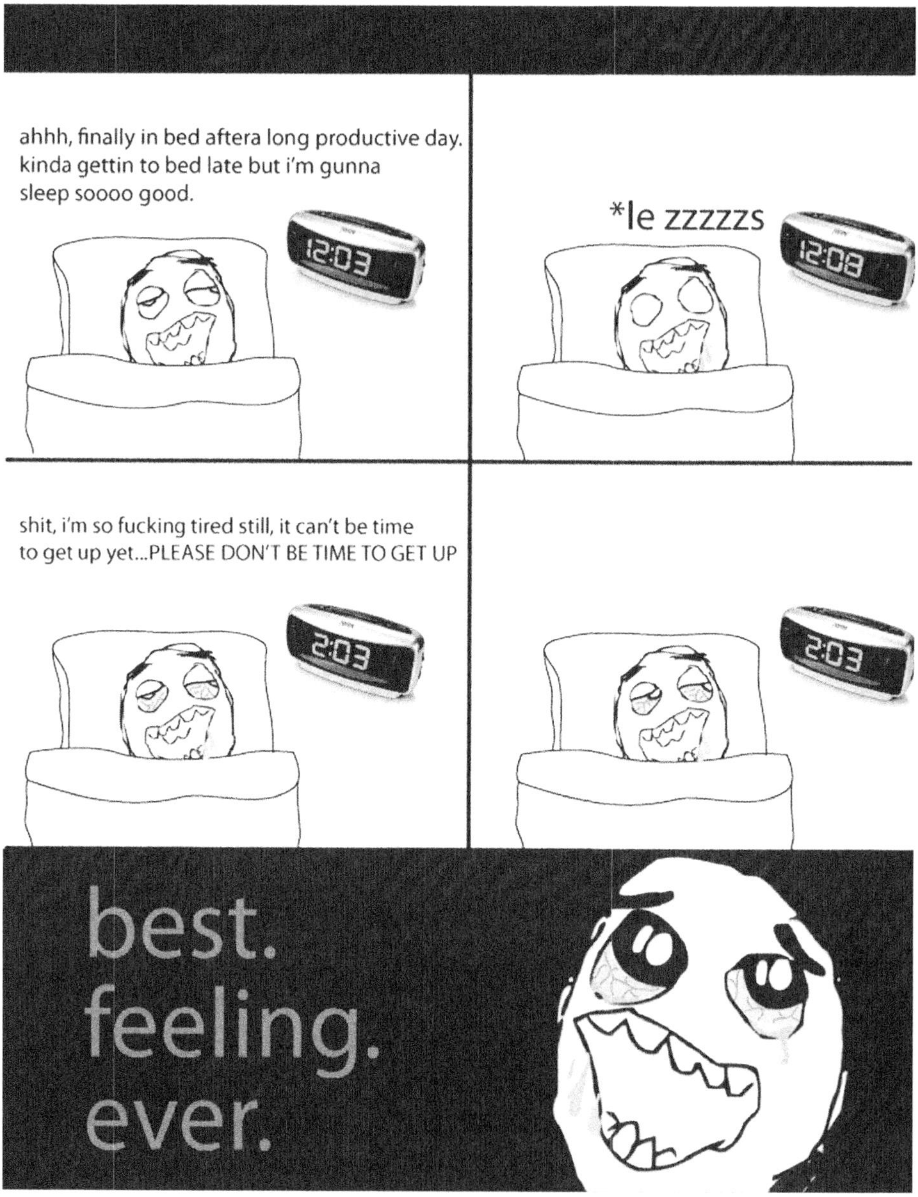
ahhh, finally in bed aftera long productive day. kinda gettin to bed late but i'm gunna sleep soooo good.
12:03
*le zzzzzs
12:08
shit, i'm so fucking tired still, it can't be time to get up yet...PLEASE DON'T BE TIME TO GET UP
2:03
2:03
best.
feeling.
ever.

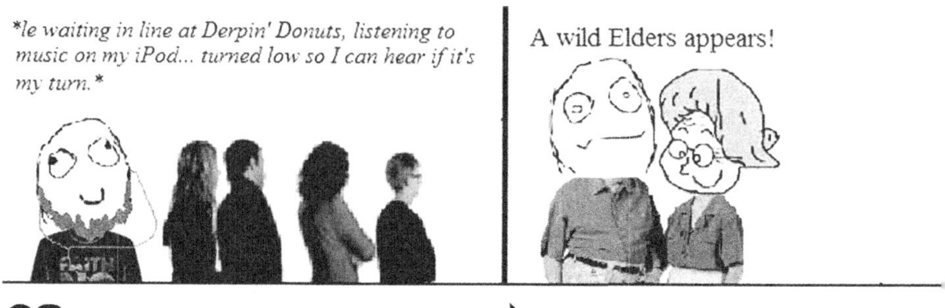
le waiting in line at Derpin' Donuts, listening to music on my iPod... turned low so I can hear if it's my turn.
A wild Elders appears!

→

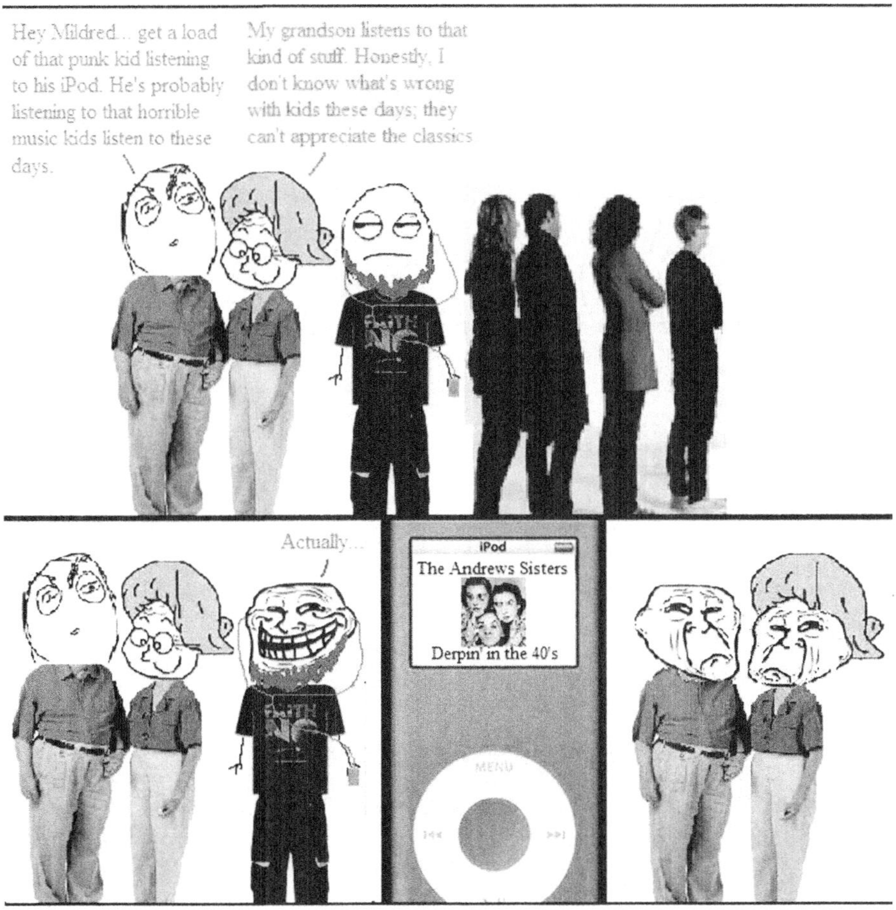
Hey Mildred... get a load of that punk kid listening to his iPod. He's probably listening to that horrible music kids listen to these days.
My grandson listens to that kind of stuff. Honestly, I don't know what's wrong with kids these days; they can't appreciate the classics
Actually...
iPod
The Andrews Sisters
Derpin' in the 40's
MENU

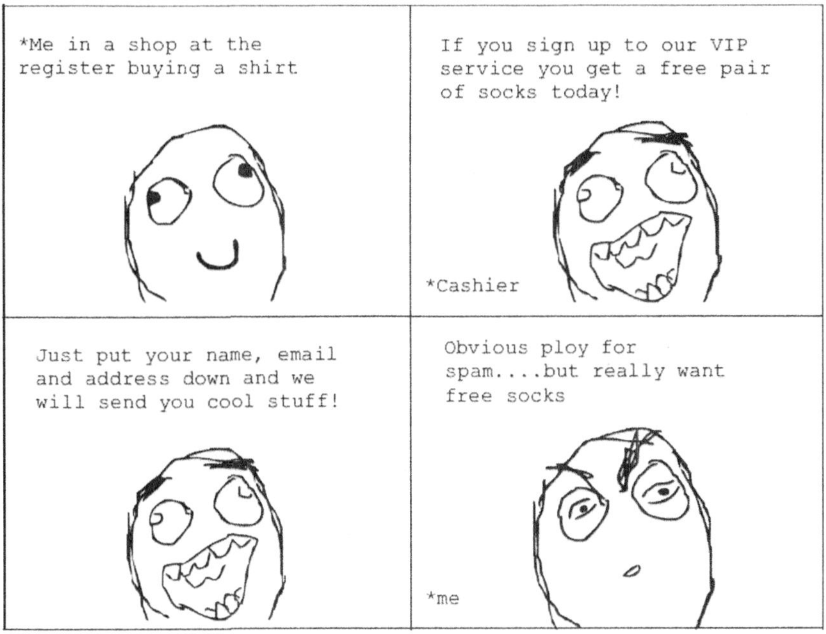
*Me in a shop at the register buying a shirt
If you sign up to our VIP service you get a free pair of socks today!
*Cashier
Just put your name, email and address down and we will send you cool stuff!
Obvious ploy for spam....but really want free socks
*me

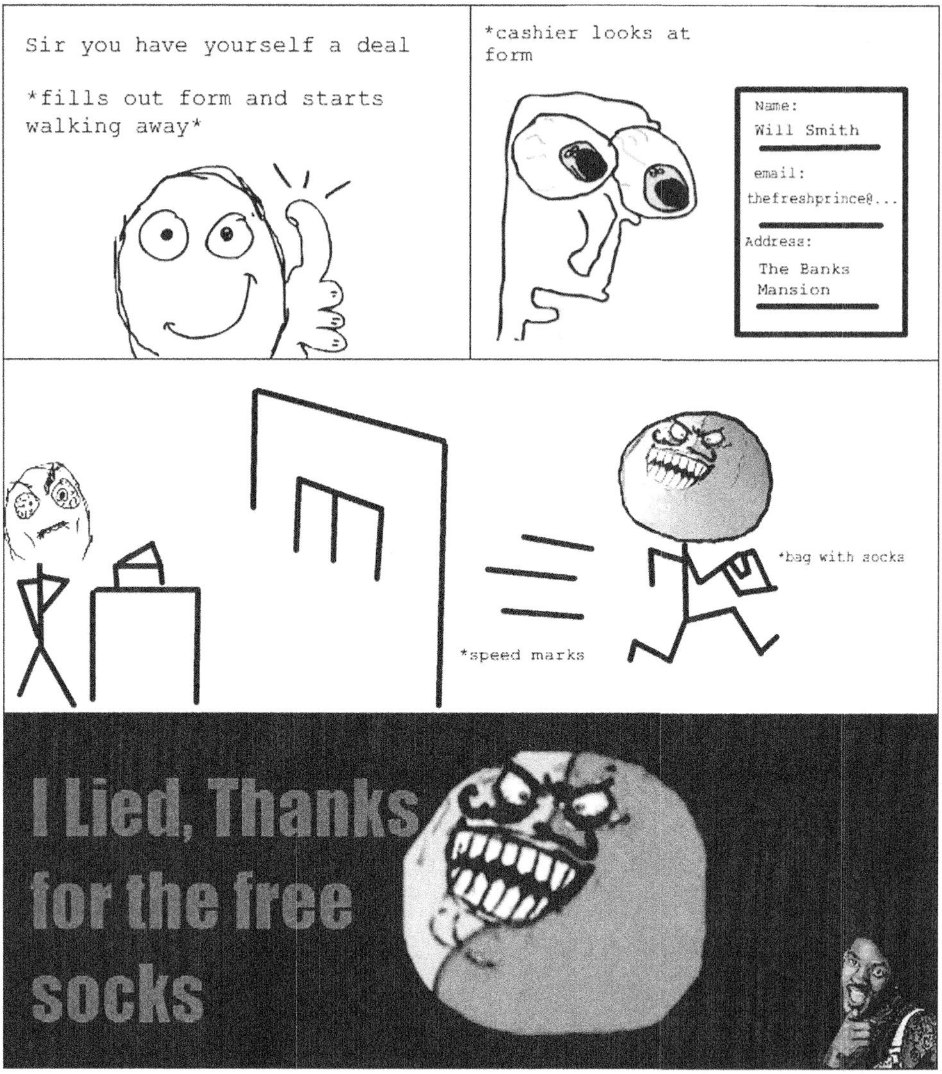
Sir you have yourself a deal
fills out form and starts walking away
*cashier looks at form
Name:
Will Smith
email:
thefreshprince@...
Address:
The Banks Mansion
*bag with socks
*speed marks
I Lied, Thanks for the free socks

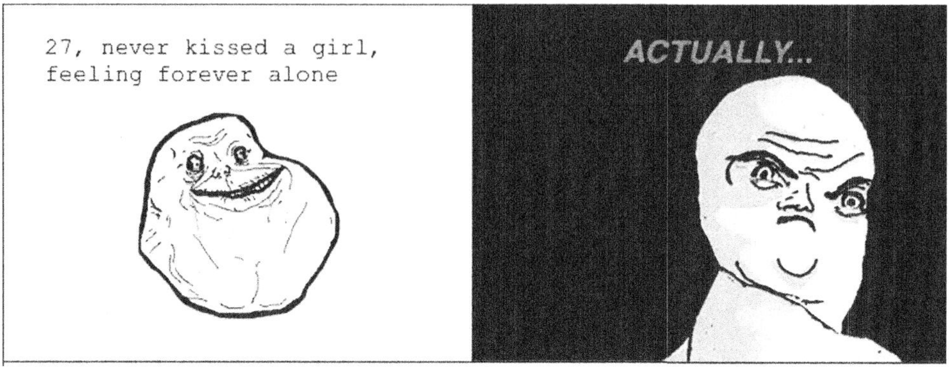
27, never kissed a girl, feeling forever alone
ACTUALLY...

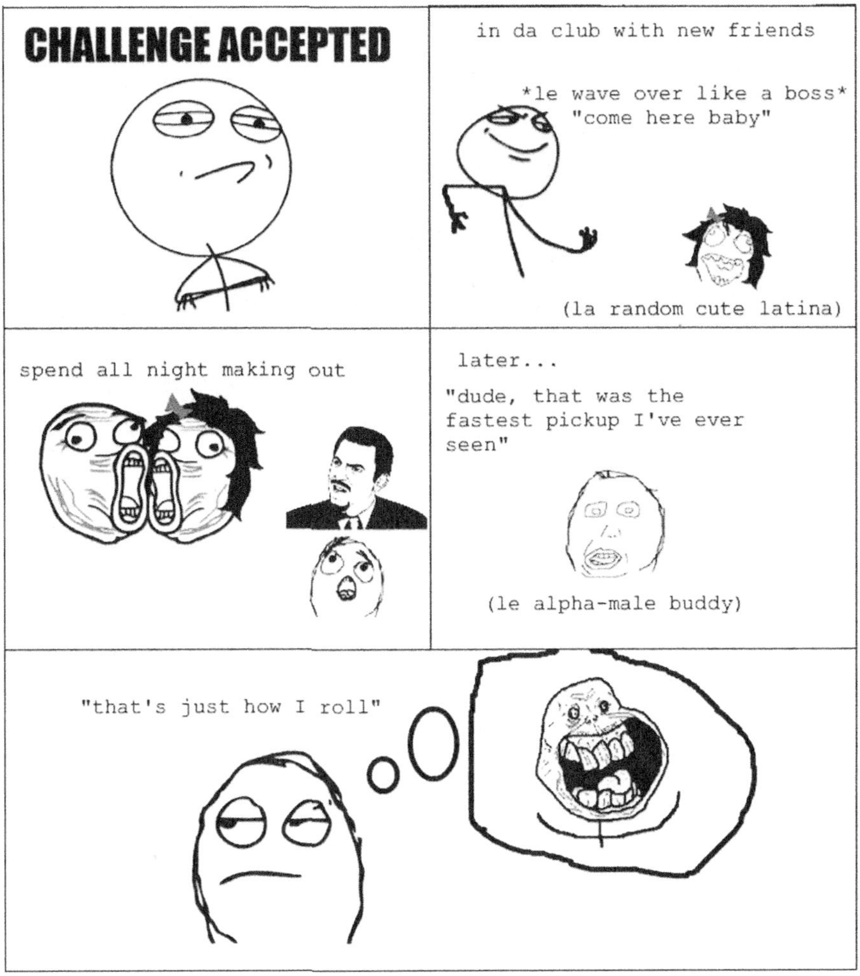
CHALLENGE ACCEPTED
in da club with new friends
le wave over like a boss
"come here baby"
(la random cute latina)
spend all night making out
later...
"dude, that was the fastest pickup I've ever seen"
(le alpha-male buddy)
"that's just how I roll"

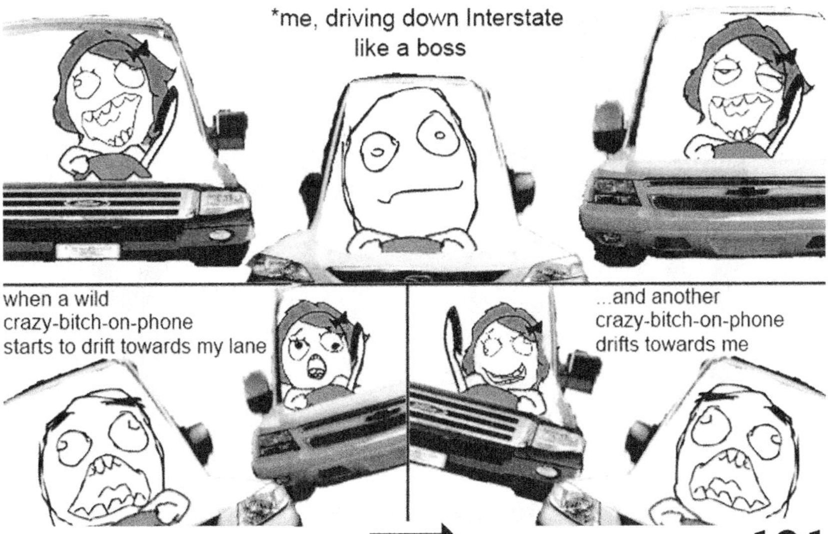
*me, driving down Interstate like a boss
when a wild crazy-bitch-on-phone starts to drift towards my lane
...and another crazy-bitch-on-phone drifts towards me

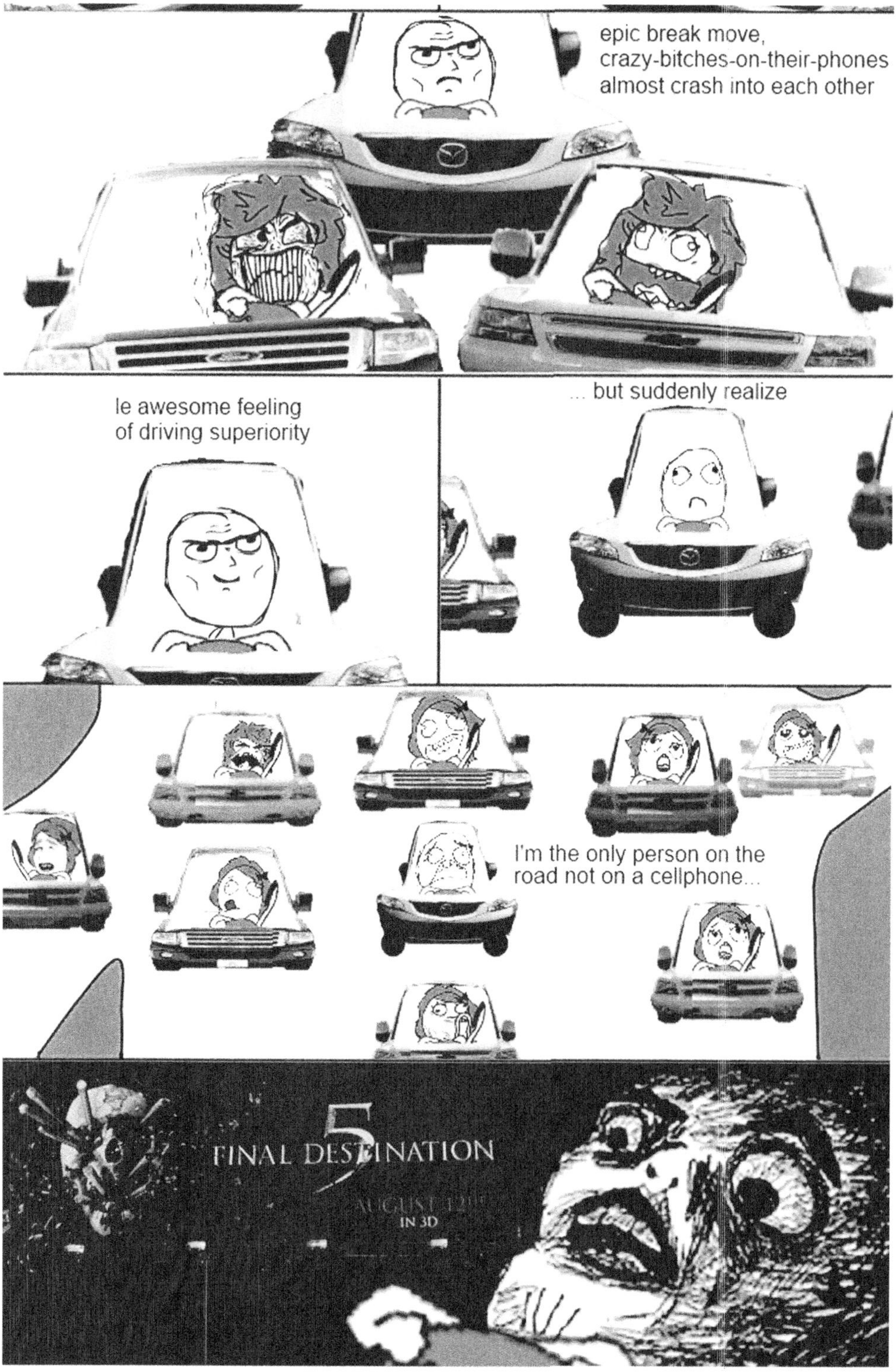
epic break move, crazy-bitches-on-their-phones almost crash into each other
le awesome feeling of driving superiority
... but suddenly realize
I'm the only person on the road not on a cellphone...
5
FINAL DESTINATION
IN 3D

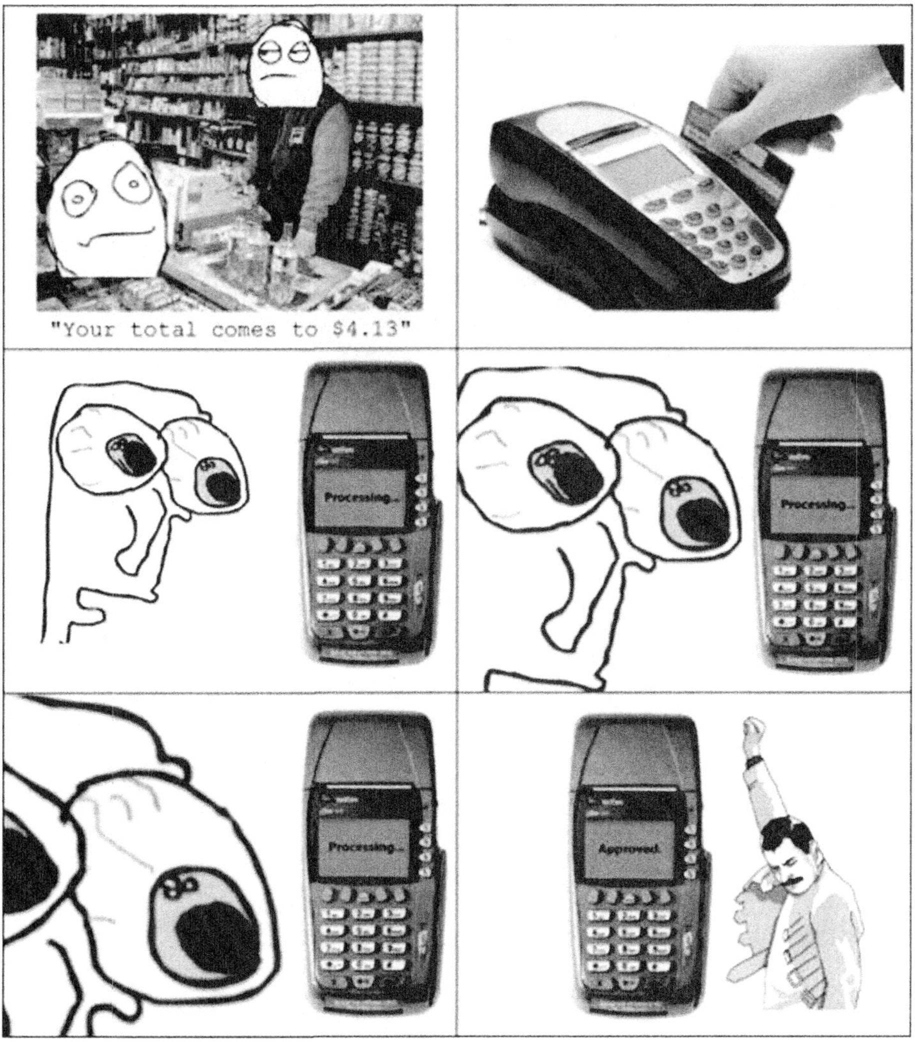
"Your total comes to $4.13"
Processing...
Processing...
Processing...
Approved.

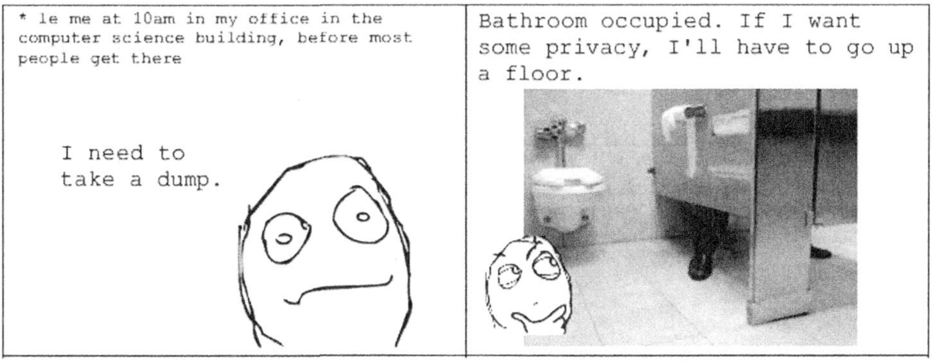
* le me at 10am in my office in the computer science building, before most people get there
I need to take a dump.
Bathroom occupied. If I want some privacy, I'll have to go up a floor.

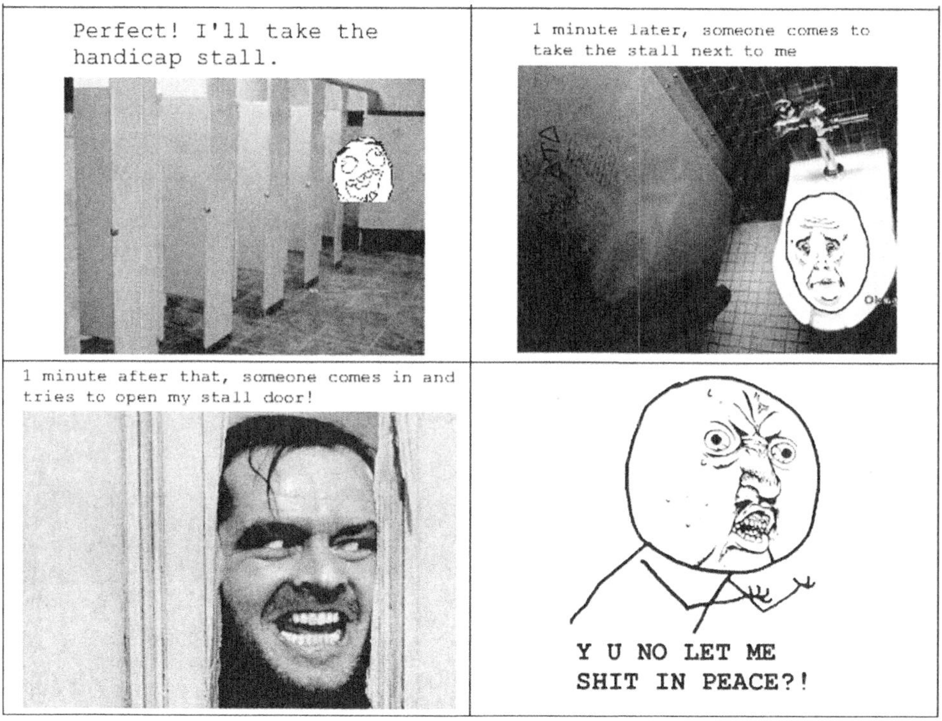
Perfect! I'll take the handicap stall.
1 minute later, someone comes to take the stall next to me
1 minute after that, someone comes in and tries to open my stall door!
Y U NO LET ME SHIT IN PEACE?!

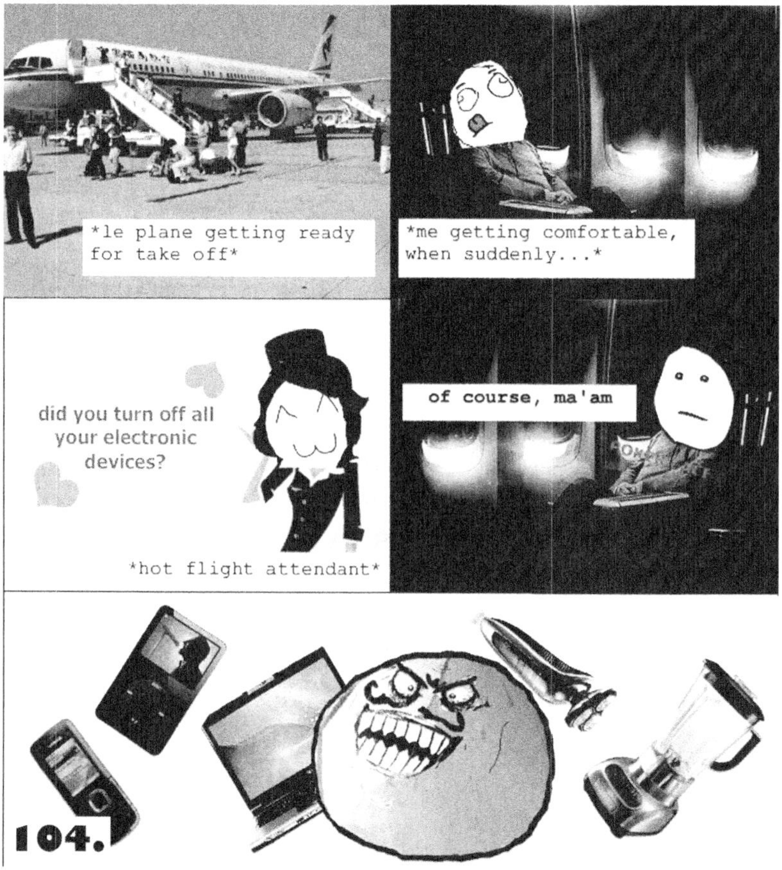
le plane getting ready for take off
me getting comfortable, when suddenly...
did you turn off all your electronic devices?
hot flight attendant
of course, ma'am

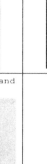

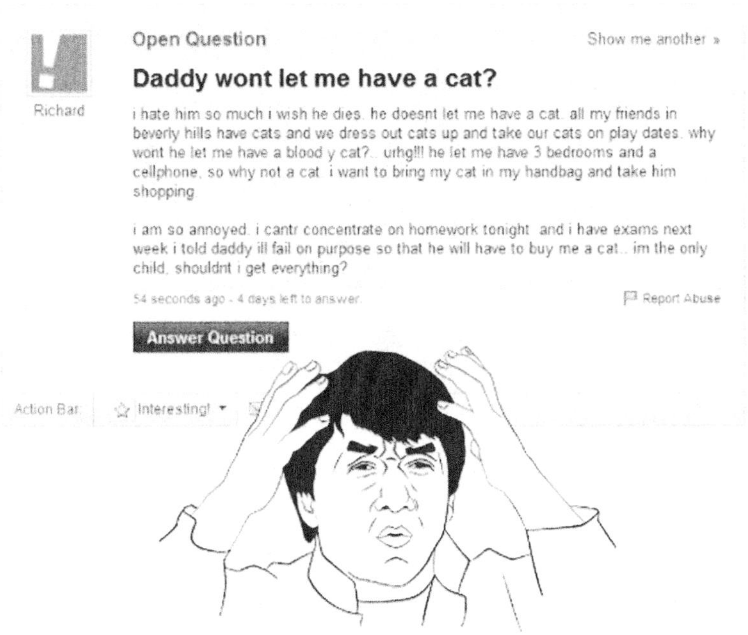
Open Question
Show me another »
Daddy wont let me have a cat?
Richard
i hate him so much i wish he dies. he doesnt let me have a cat. all my friends in beverly hills have cats and we dress out cats up and take our cats on play dates. why wont he let me have a blood y cat?.. urhg!!! he let me have 3 bedrooms and a cellphone. so why not a cat. i want to bring my cat in my handbag and take him shopping
i am so annoyed. i cantr concentrate on homework tonight. and i have exams next week i told daddy ill fail on purpose so that he will have to buy me a cat.. im the only child. shouldnt i get everything?
54 seconds ago - 4 days left to answer.
Report Abuse
Answer Question
Action Bar
Interesting!

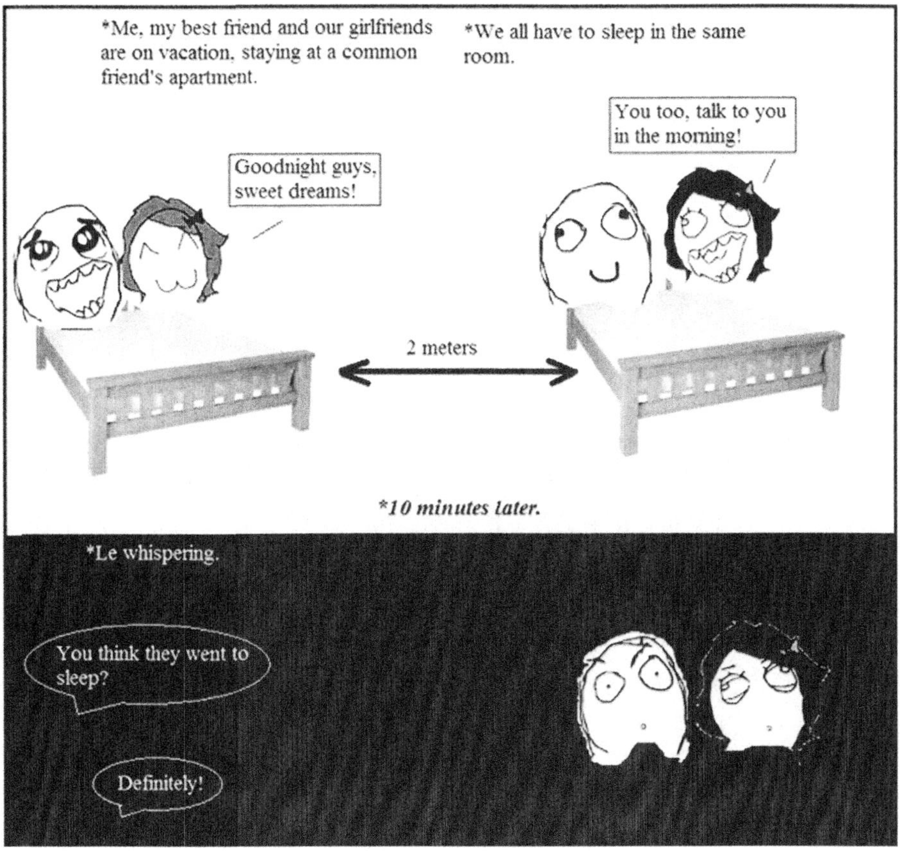
*Me, my best friend and our girlfriends are on vacation, staying at a common friend's apartment.
*We all have to sleep in the same room.
Goodnight guys, sweet dreams!
You too, talk to you in the morning!
2 meters
*10 minutes later.
*Le whispering.
You think they went to sleep?
Definitely!

*slick slick slick slick
oh god oh god oh god ah yeah!
ah ah ah ah oh oh oh oh!
*slick slick slick slick
*slick slick slick slick
*25 very, VERY long minutes later...
OH SWEET JESUS HERE I CUUUUUMMM!!!
*om nom nom nom
*10 more minutes of cuddling and giggling pass...
hihihihihi
hihihihihi
*When...
*slick slick slick slick
ah ah ah ah oh oh oh oh!
ROUND 2!!!
*slick slick slick slick

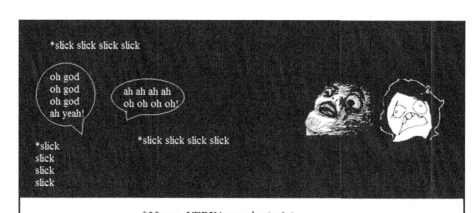

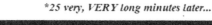

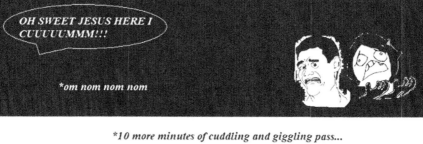

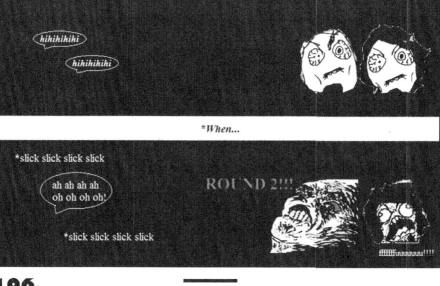

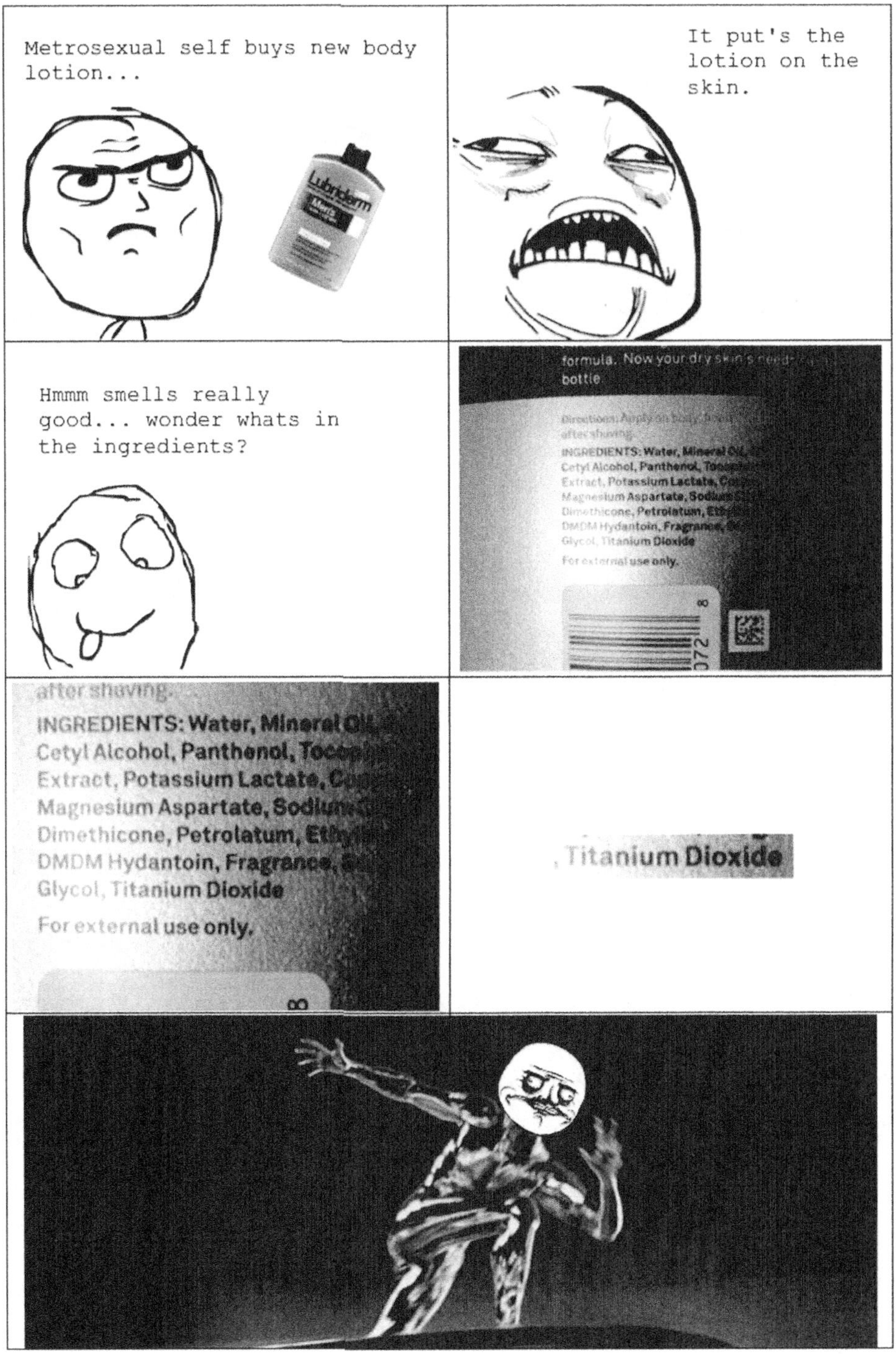

Metrosexual self buys new body lotion...

It put's the lotion on the skin.

Hmmm smells really good... wonder whats in the ingredients?

formula. Now your dry skin's need
bottle

Directions: Apply on body
after shaving.

INGREDIENTS: Water, Mineral Oil,
Cetyl Alcohol, Panthenol, Tocoph
Extract, Potassium Lactate, Co
Magnesium Aspartate, Sodium
Dimethicone, Petrolatum, Eth
DMDM Hydantoin, Fragrance,
Glycol, Titanium Dioxide

For external use only.

072 8

after shaving.

INGREDIENTS: Water, Mineral Oil
Cetyl Alcohol, Panthenol, Tocop
Extract, Potassium Lactate, Co
Magnesium Aspartate, Sodium
Dimethicone, Petrolatum, Eth
DMDM Hydantoin, Fragrance,
Glycol, Titanium Dioxide

For external use only.

8

, Titanium Dioxide

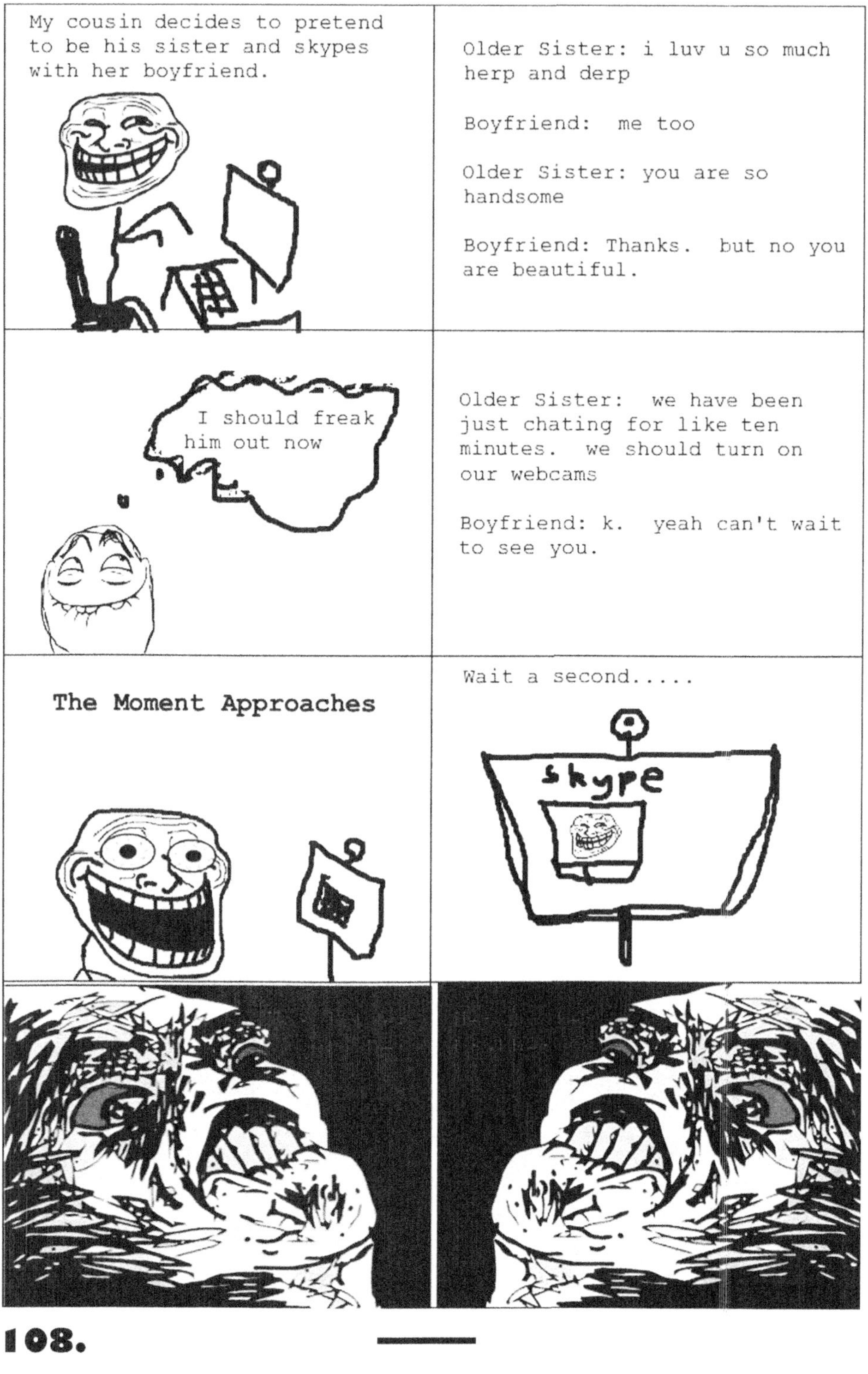

My cousin decides to pretend to be his sister and skypes with her boyfriend.
Older Sister: i luv u so much herp and derp
Boyfriend: me too
Older Sister: you are so handsome
Boyfriend: Thanks. but no you are beautiful.
I should freak him out now
Older Sister: we have been just chating for like ten minutes. we should turn on our webcams
Boyfriend: k. yeah can't wait to see you.
The Moment Approaches
Wait a second.....
skype

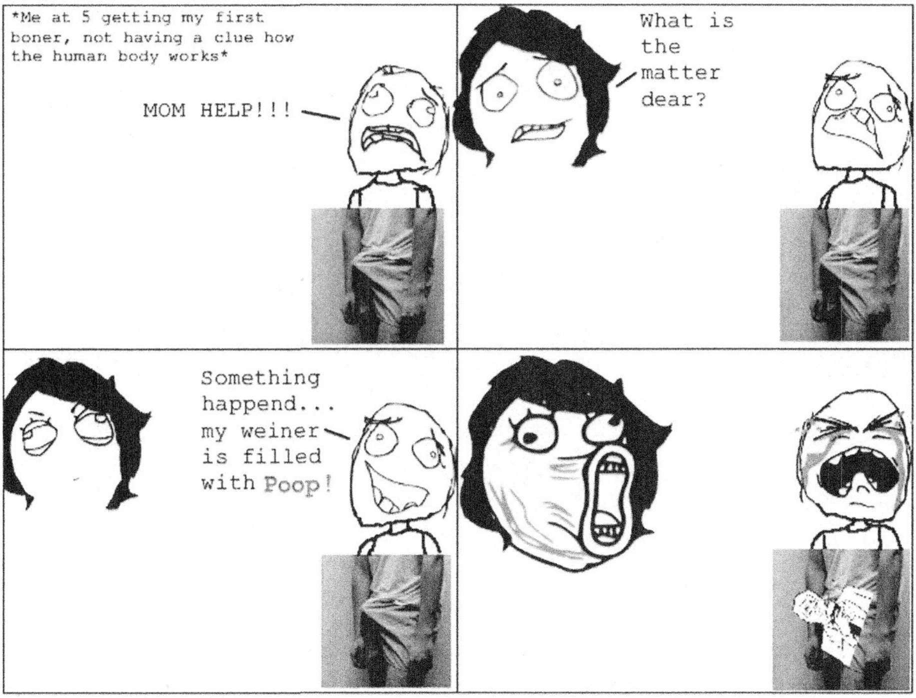
Me at 5 getting my first boner, not having a clue how the human body works
MOM HELP!!!
What is the matter dear?
Something happend... my weiner is filled with Poop!

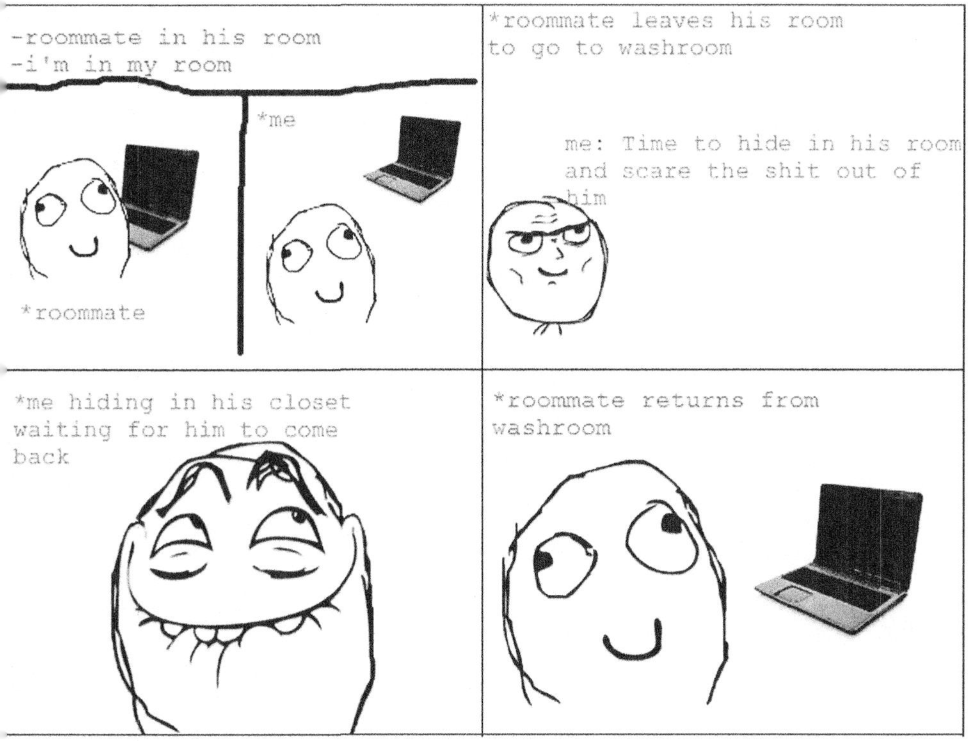
-roommate in his room
-i'm in my room
*me
*roommate
*roommate leaves his room to go to washroom
me: Time to hide in his room and scare the shit out of him
*me hiding in his closet waiting for him to come back
*roommate returns from washroom

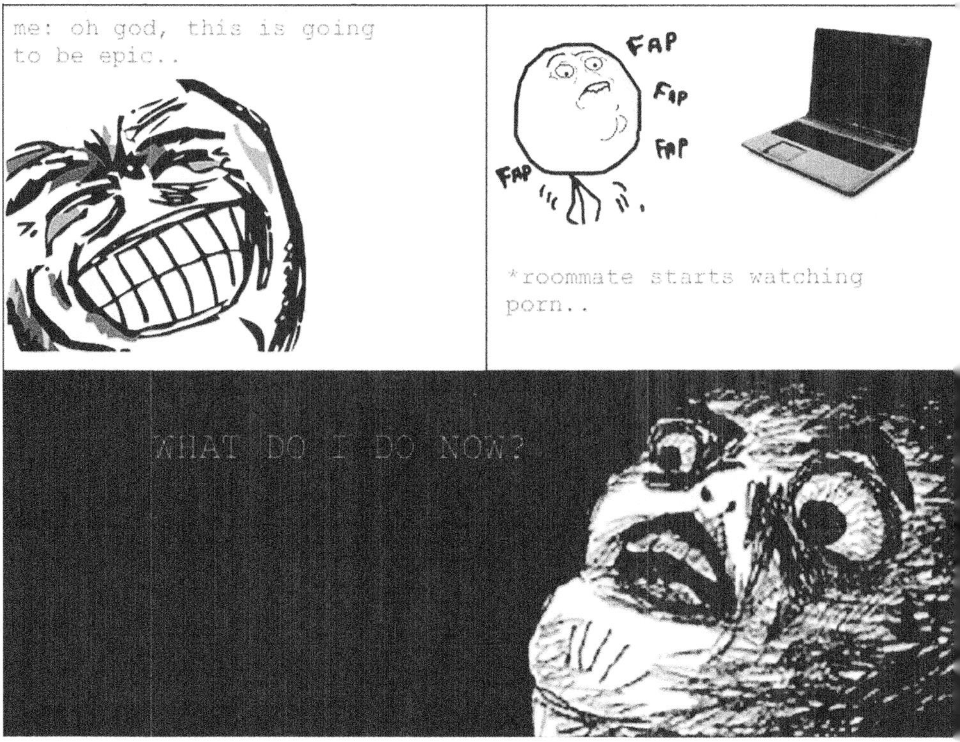
me: oh god, this is going to be epic..
FAP
FAP
FAP
FAP
*roommate starts watching porn..
WHAT DO I DO NOW?

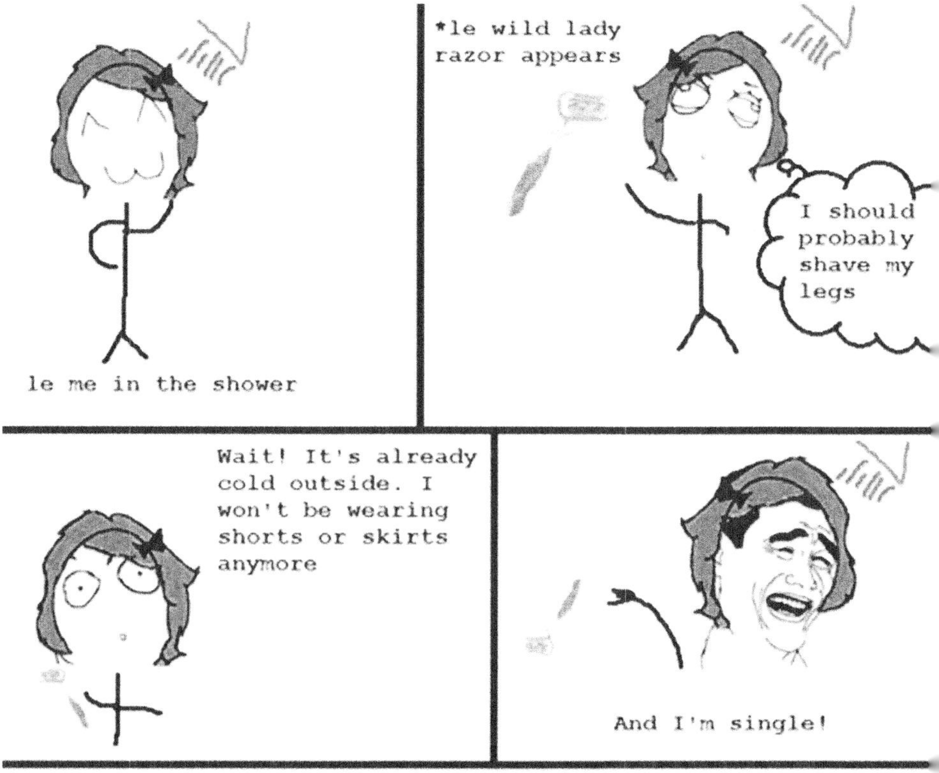
le me in the shower
*le wild lady razor appears
I should probably shave my legs
Wait! It's already cold outside. I won't be wearing shorts or skirts anymore
And I'm single!

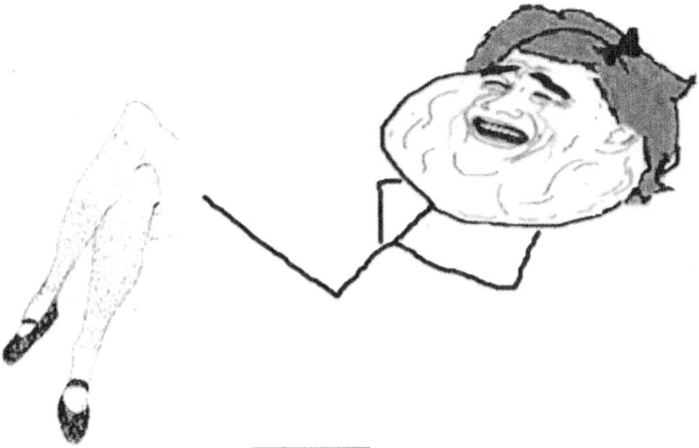

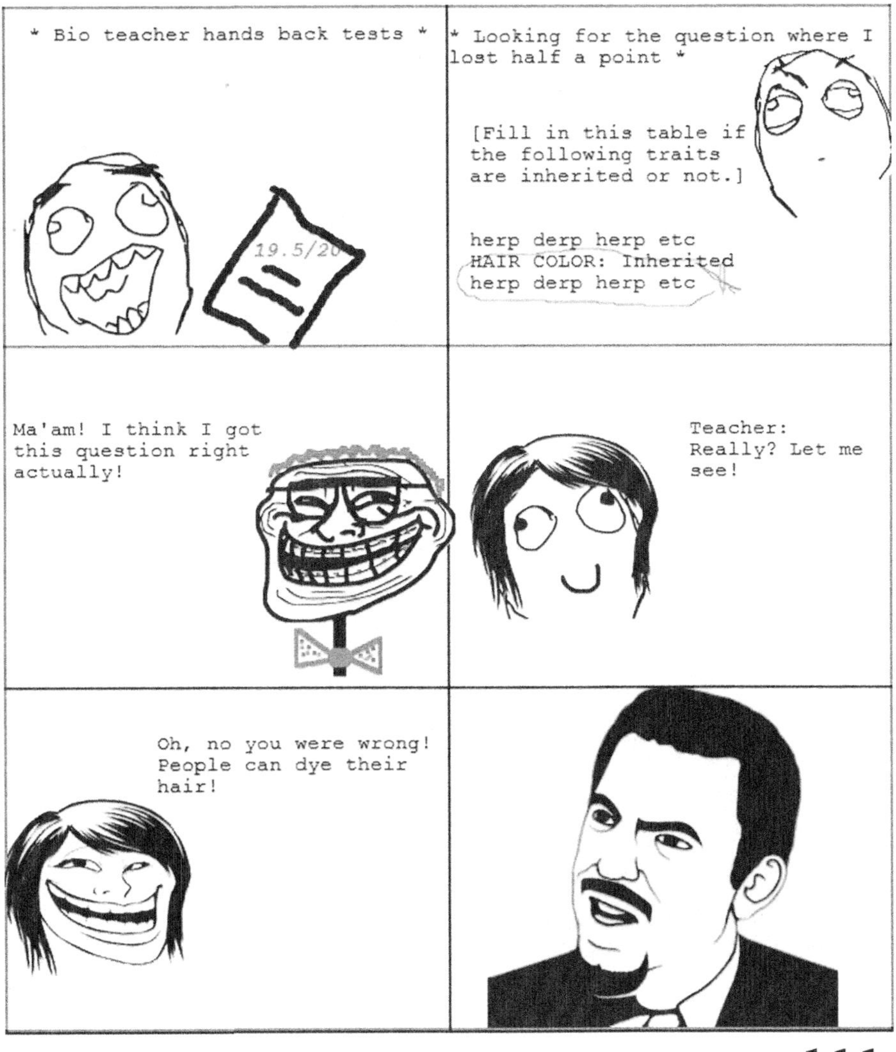

* Bio teacher hands back tests *
19.5/20
* Looking for the question where I lost half a point *
[Fill in this table if the following traits are inherited or not.]
herp derp herp etc
HAIR COLOR: Inherited
herp derp herp etc
Ma'am! I think I got this question right actually!
Teacher: Really? Let me see!
Oh, no you were wrong! People can dye their hair!

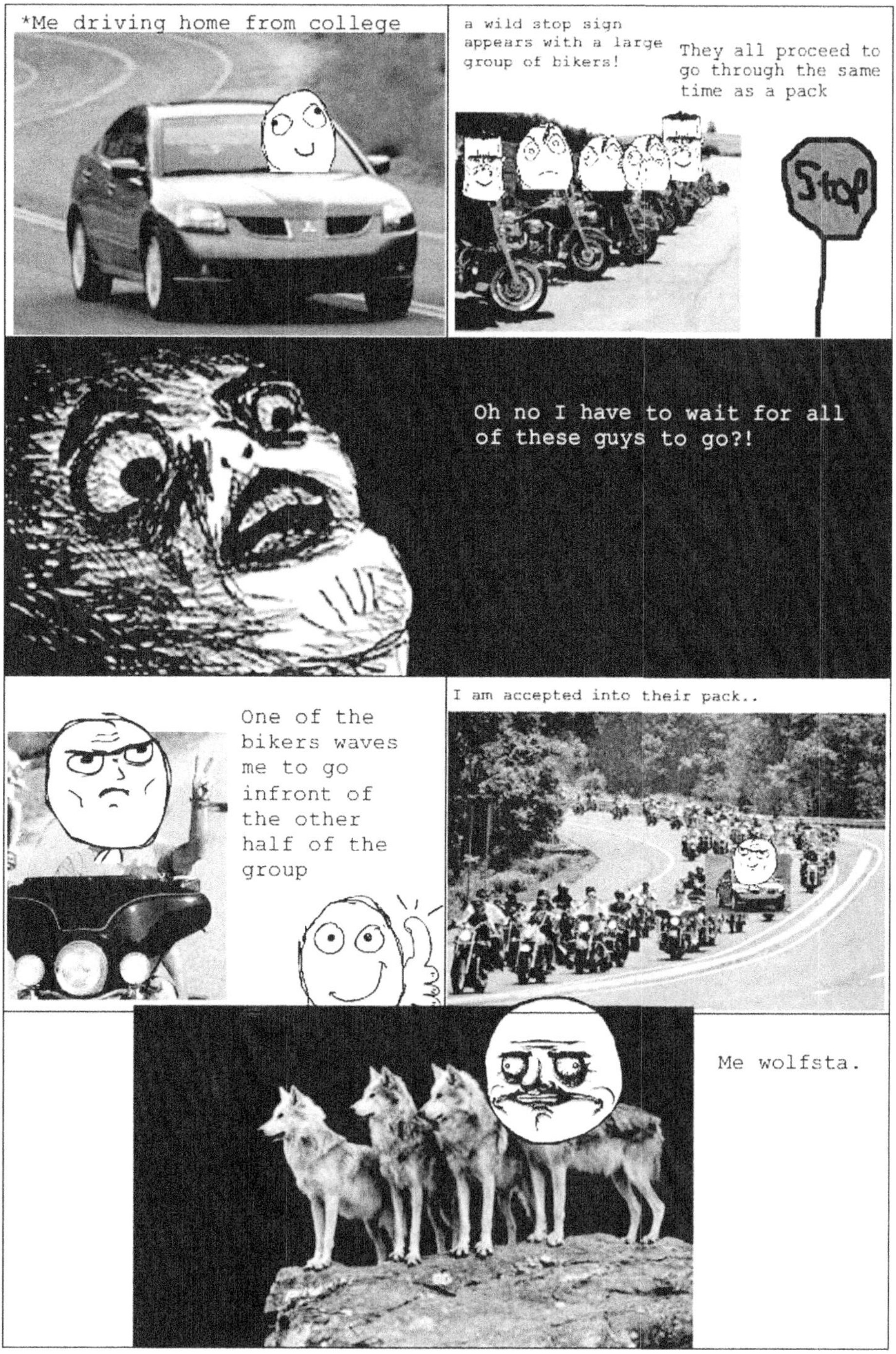
*Me driving home from college
a wild stop sign appears with a large group of bikers!
They all proceed to go through the same time as a pack
Stop
Oh no I have to wait for all of these guys to go?!
One of the bikers waves me to go infront of the other half of the group
I am accepted into their pack..
Me wolfsta.

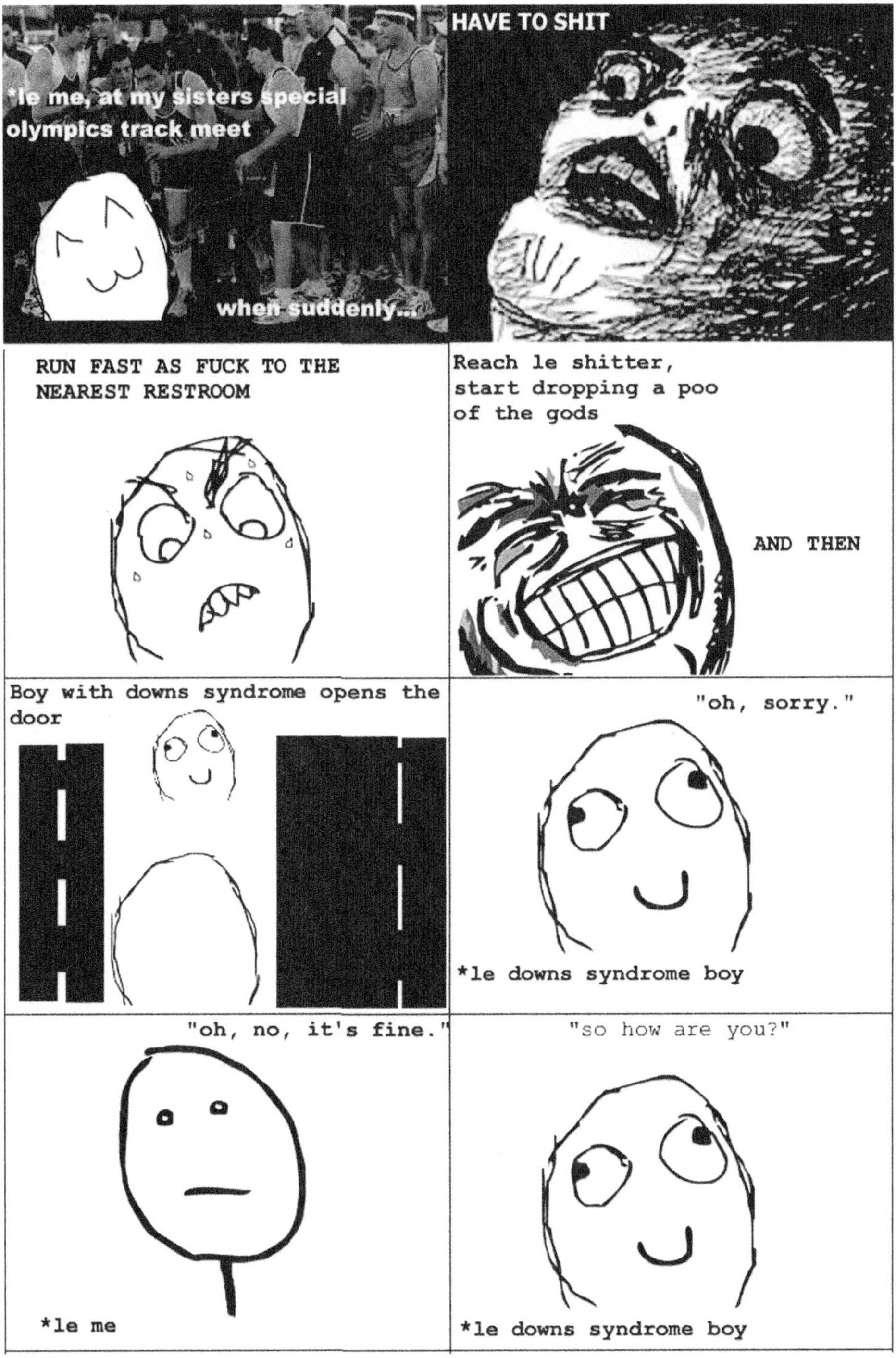
*le me, at my sisters special
olympics track meet
when suddenly...
HAVE TO SHIT
RUN FAST AS FUCK TO THE
NEAREST RESTROOM
Reach le shitter,
start dropping a poo
of the gods
AND THEN
Boy with downs syndrome opens the
door
"oh, sorry."
*le downs syndrome boy
"oh, no, it's fine."
*le me
"so how are you?"
*le downs syndrome boy

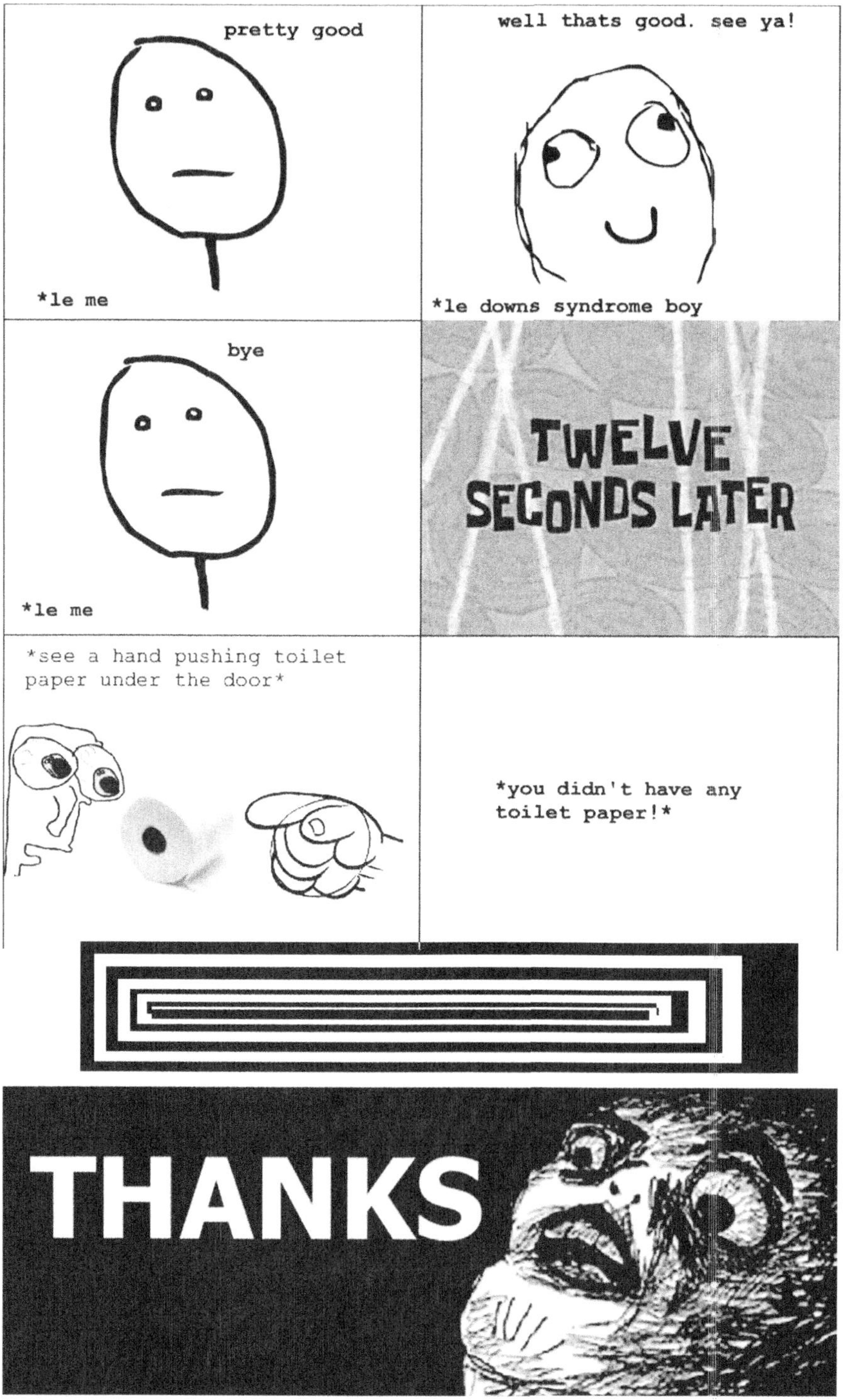
pretty good
*le me
well thats good. see ya!
*le downs syndrome boy
bye
*le me
TWELVE SECONDS LATER
see a hand pushing toilet paper under the door
you didn't have any toilet paper!
THANKS

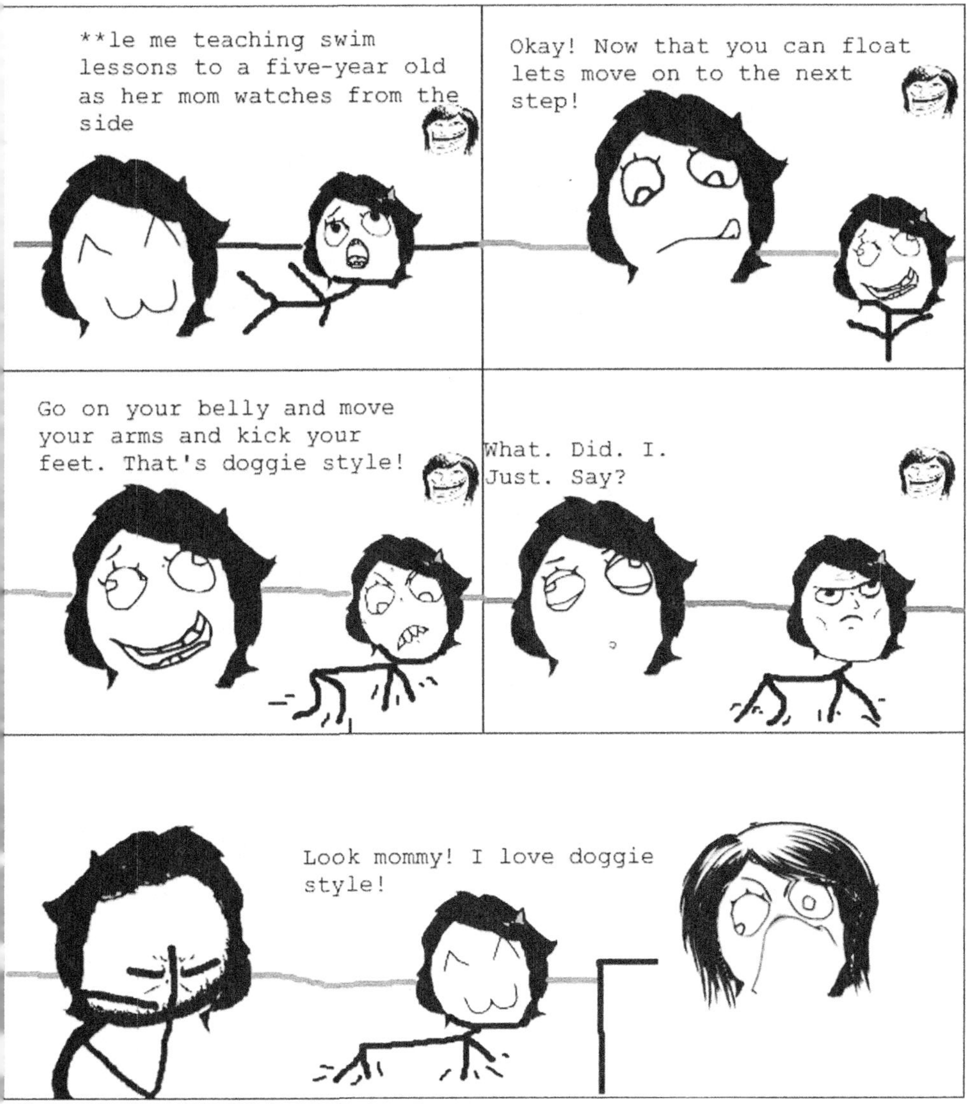
**le me teaching swim lessons to a five-year old as her mom watches from the side
Okay! Now that you can float lets move on to the next step!
Go on your belly and move your arms and kick your feet. That's doggie style!
What. Did. I. Just. Say?
Look mommy! I love doggie style!

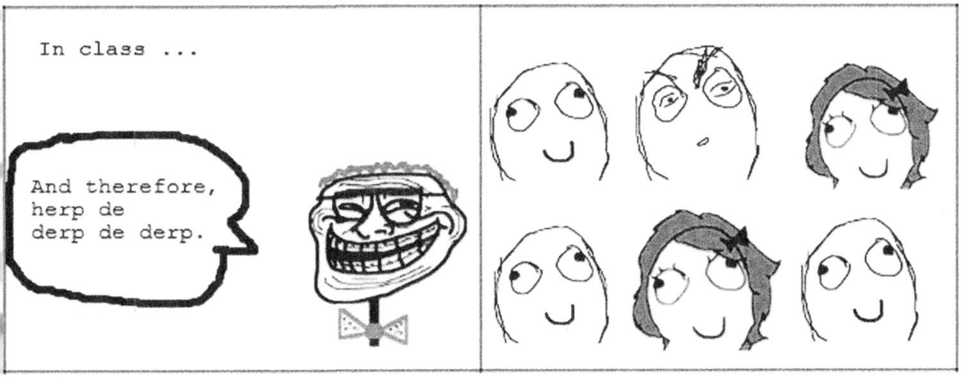
In class ...
And therefore, herp de derp de derp.

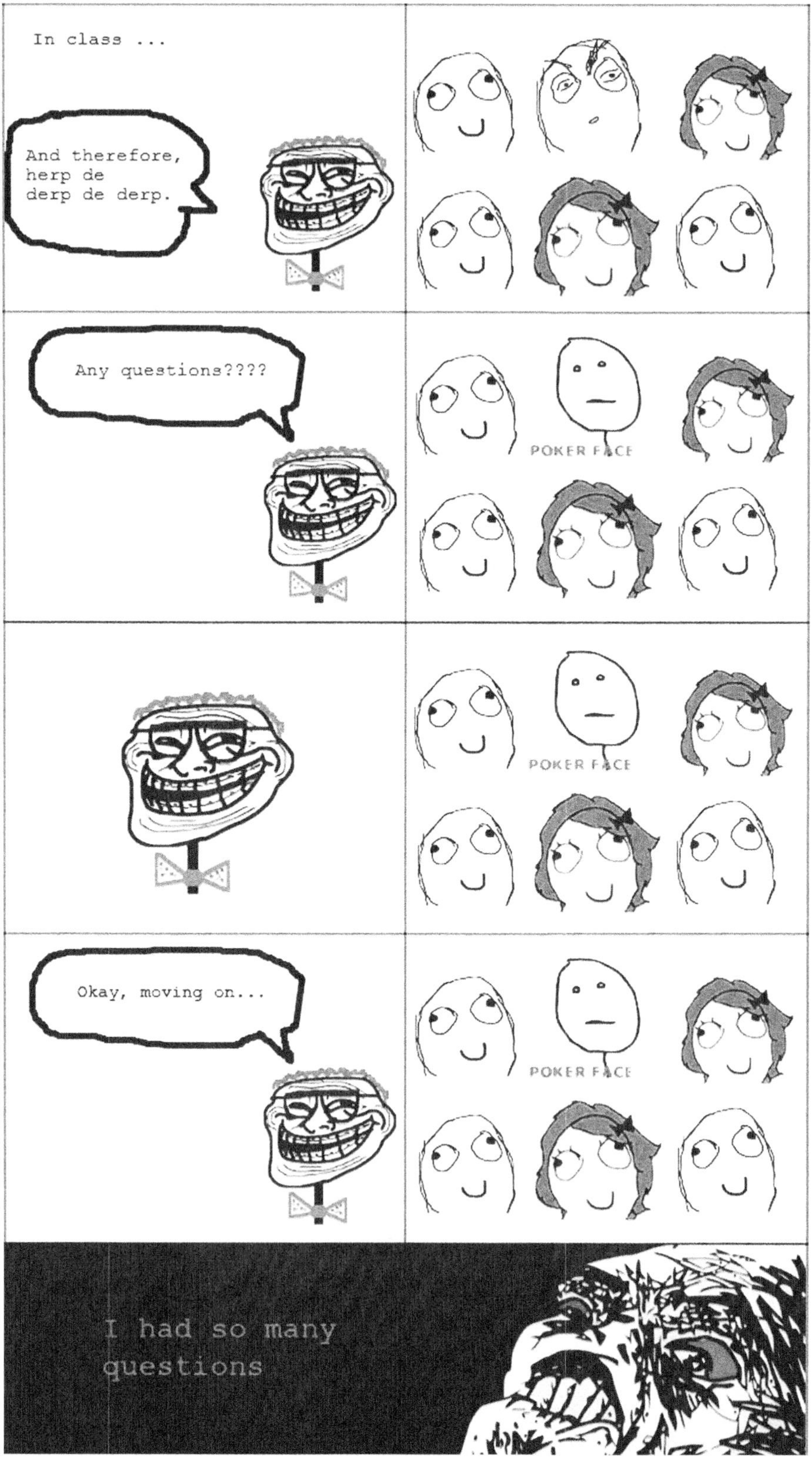
In class ...
And therefore, herp de derp de derp.
Any questions????
POKER FACE
POKER FACE
Okay, moving on...
POKER FACE
I had so many questions

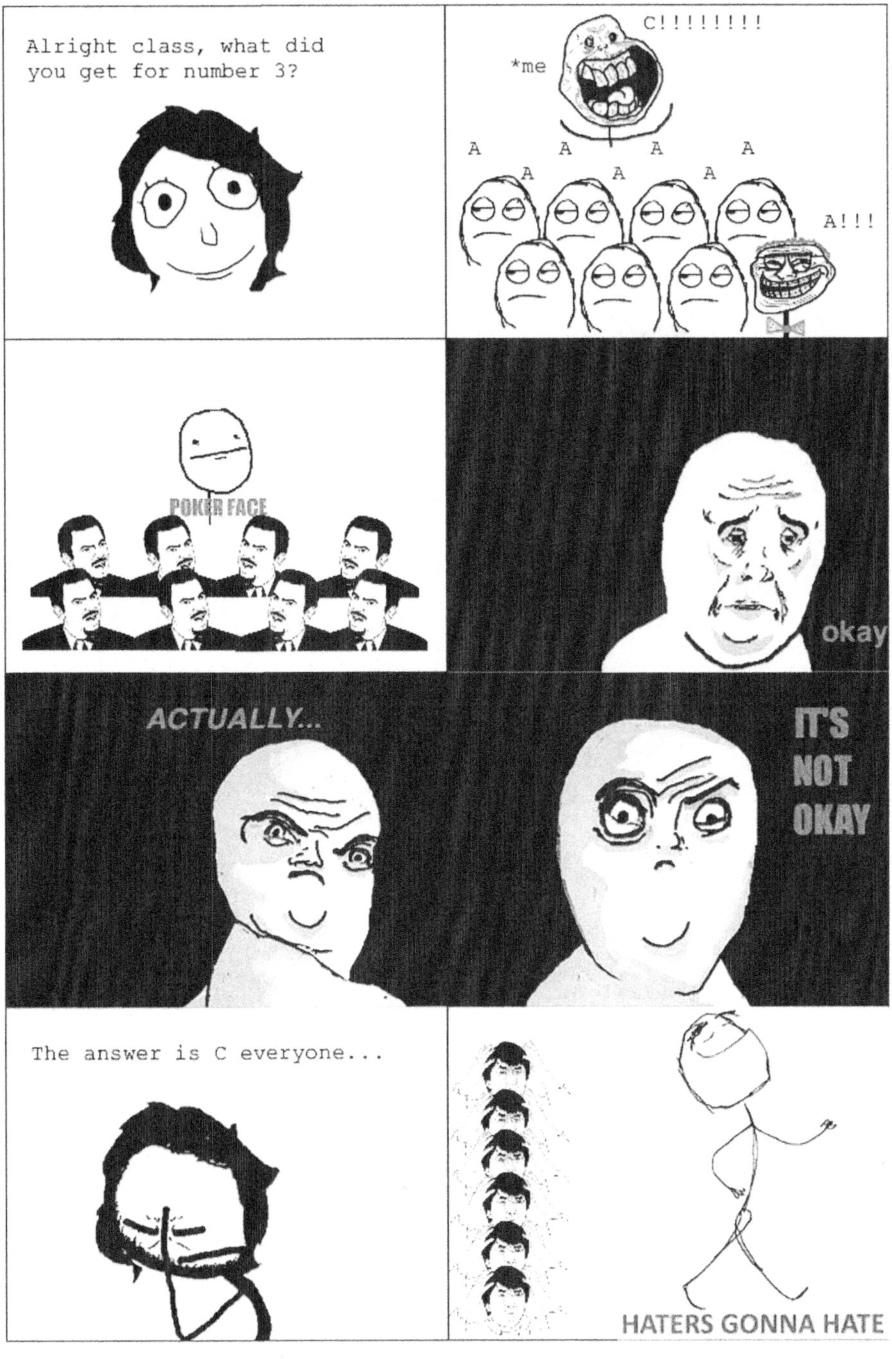

Alright class, what did you get for number 3?
*me
C!!!!!!!!
A A A A
A A A
A!!!
POKER FACE
okay
ACTUALLY...
IT'S NOT OKAY
The answer is C everyone...
HATERS GONNA HATE

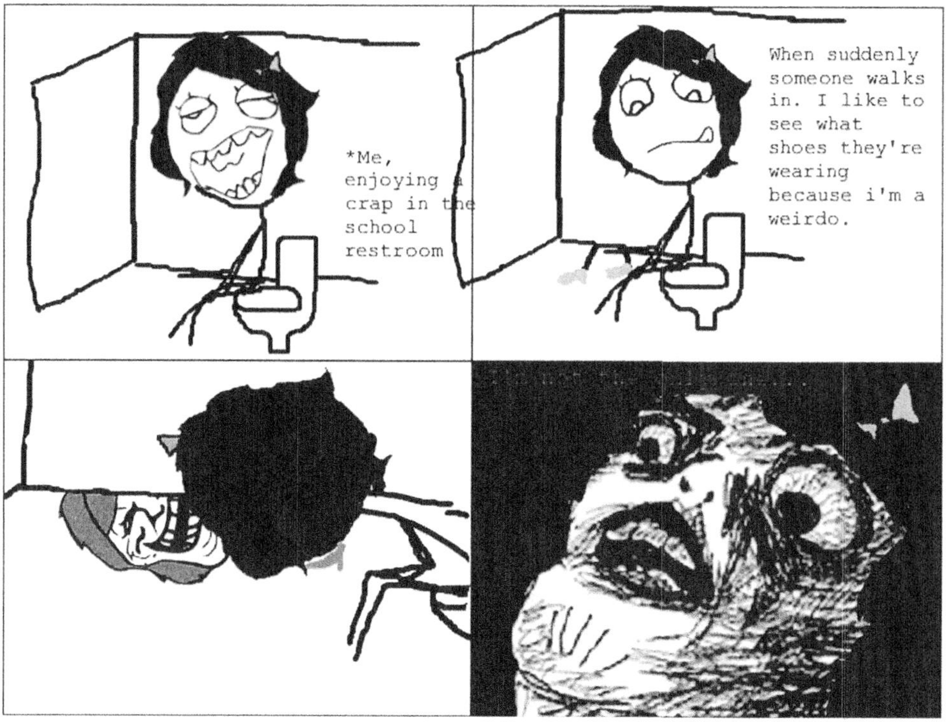
*Me, enjoying a crap in the school restroom
When suddenly someone walks in. I like to see what shoes they're wearing because i'm a weirdo.

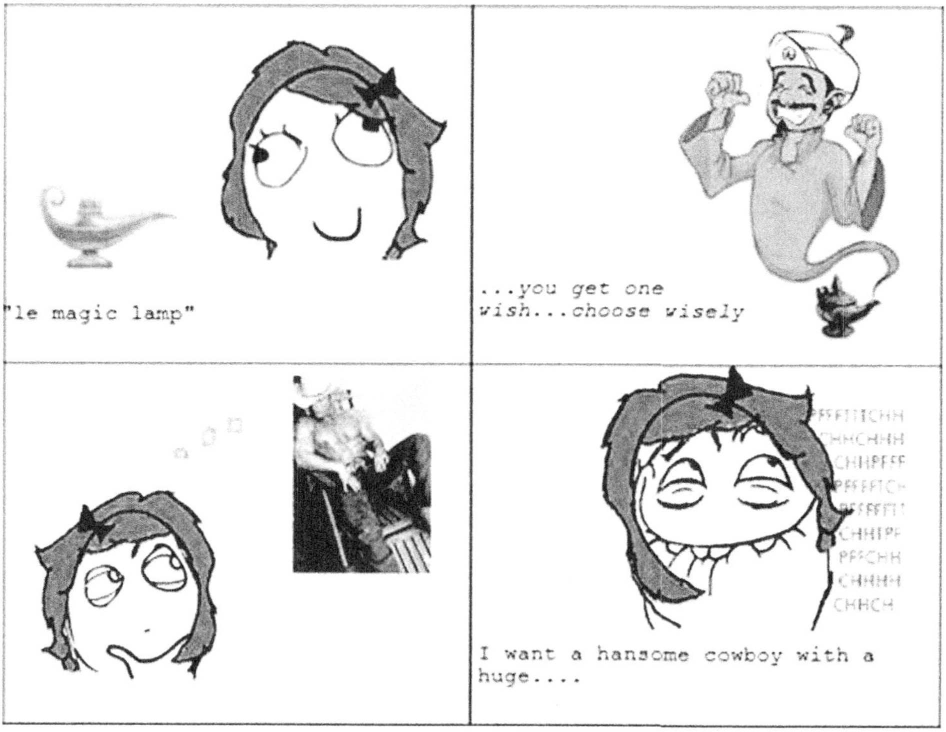
"le magic lamp"
...you get one wish...choose wisely
I want a hansome cowboy with a huge....

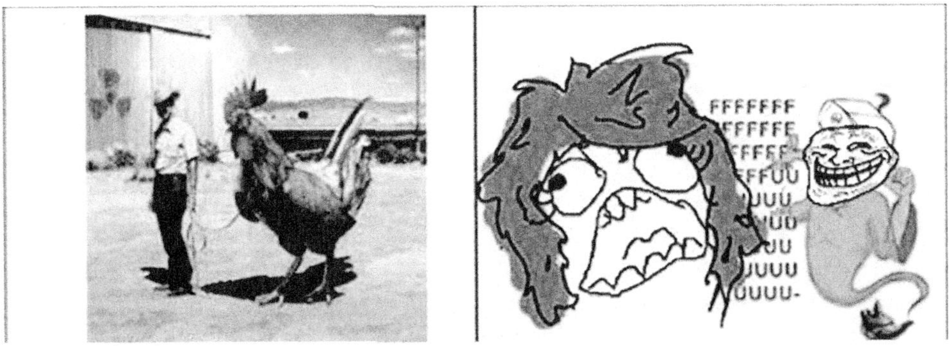
FFFFFFF
FFFFFF
FFFFF
FFUU
UUUU
UUUU
UUUU
UUUU
UUUU-

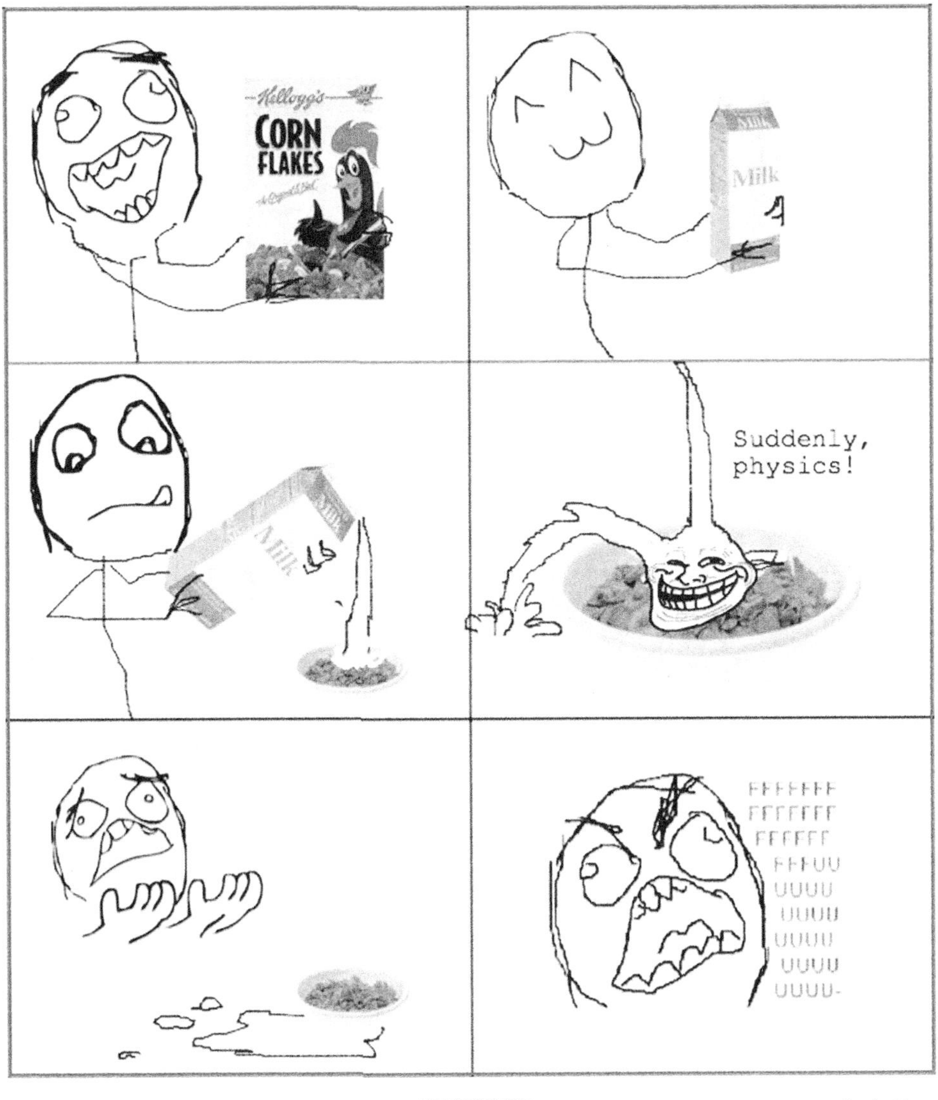
Kellogg's
CORN
FLAKES
Milk
Suddenly,
physics!
FFFFFFF
FFFFFFF
FFFFFF
FFFUU
UUUU
UUUU
UUUU
UUUU
UUUU-

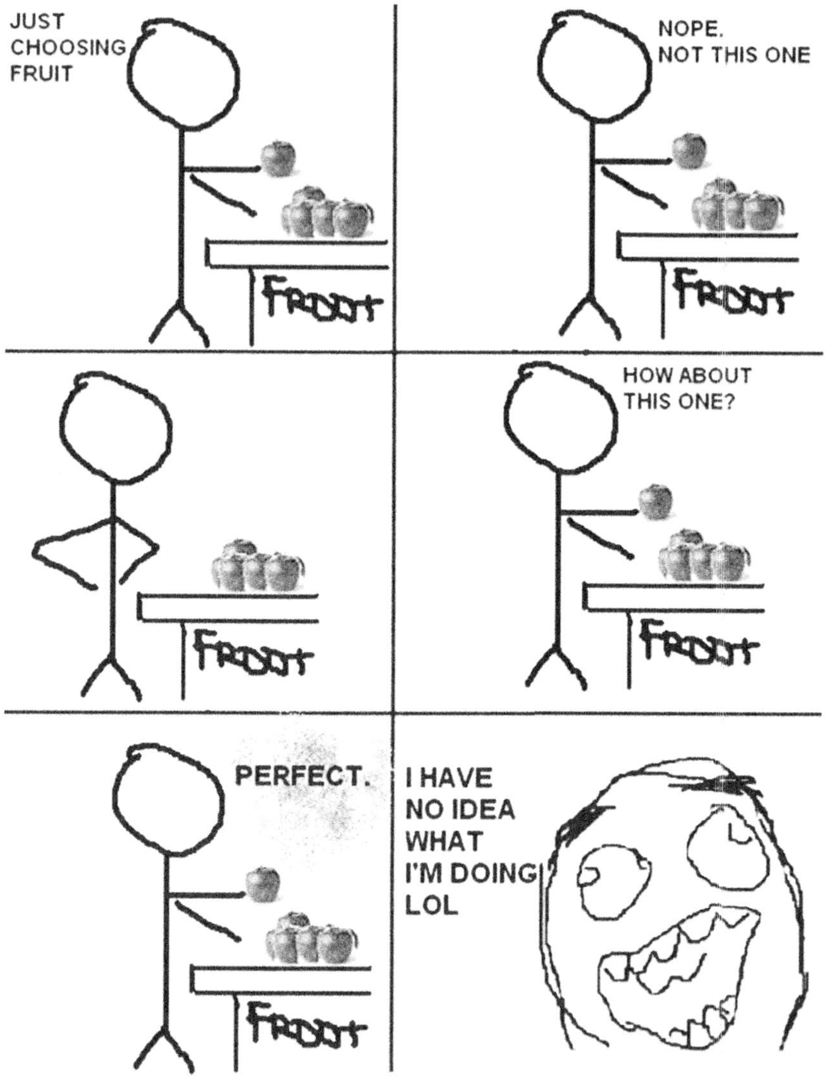
JUST CHOOSING FRUIT
FROOT
NOPE. NOT THIS ONE
FROOT
FROOT
HOW ABOUT THIS ONE?
FROOT
PERFECT.
FROOT
I HAVE NO IDEA WHAT I'M DOING LOL

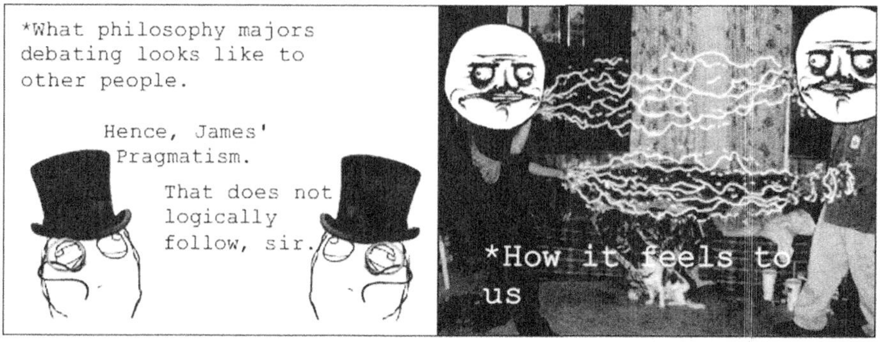
*What philosophy majors debating looks like to other people.
Hence, James' Pragmatism.
That does not logically follow, sir.
*How it feels to us

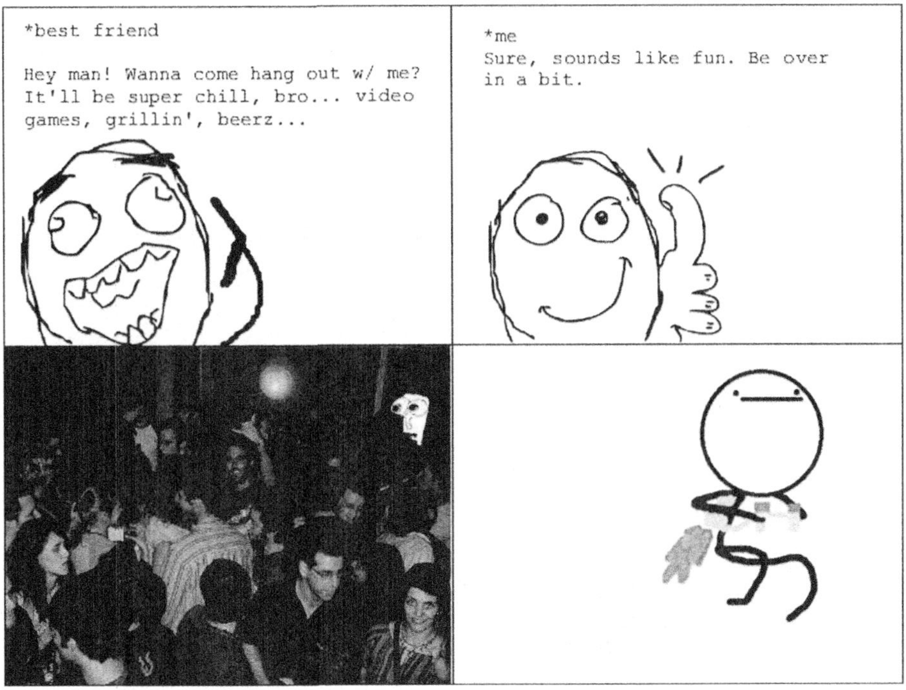
*best friend
Hey man! Wanna come hang out w/ me? It'll be super chill, bro... video games, grillin', beerz...
*me
Sure, sounds like fun. Be over in a bit.

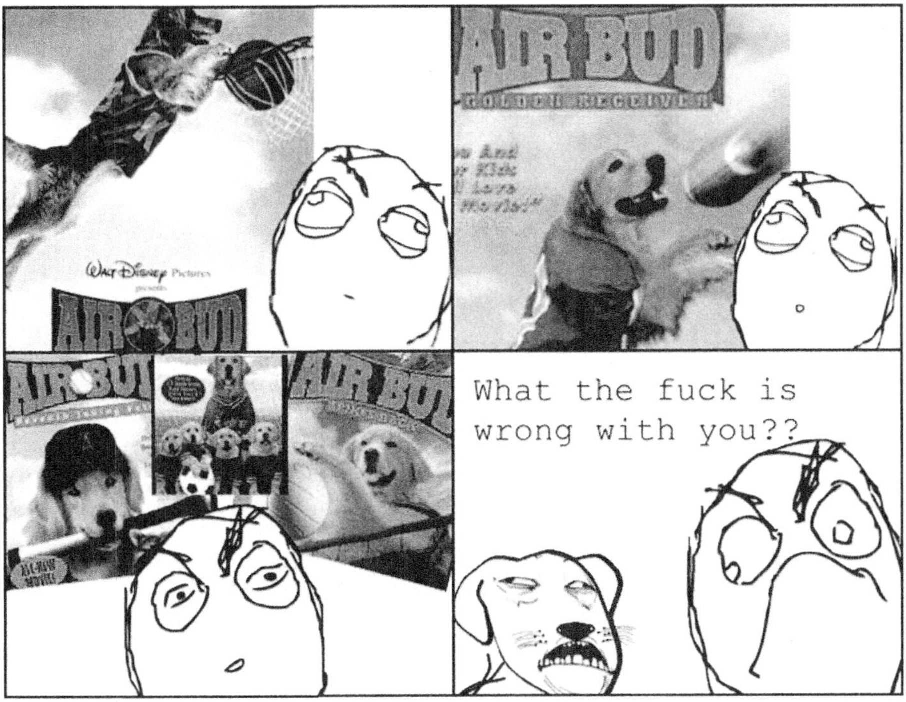
Walt Disney Pictures
AIR BUD
AIR BUD
What the fuck is wrong with you??

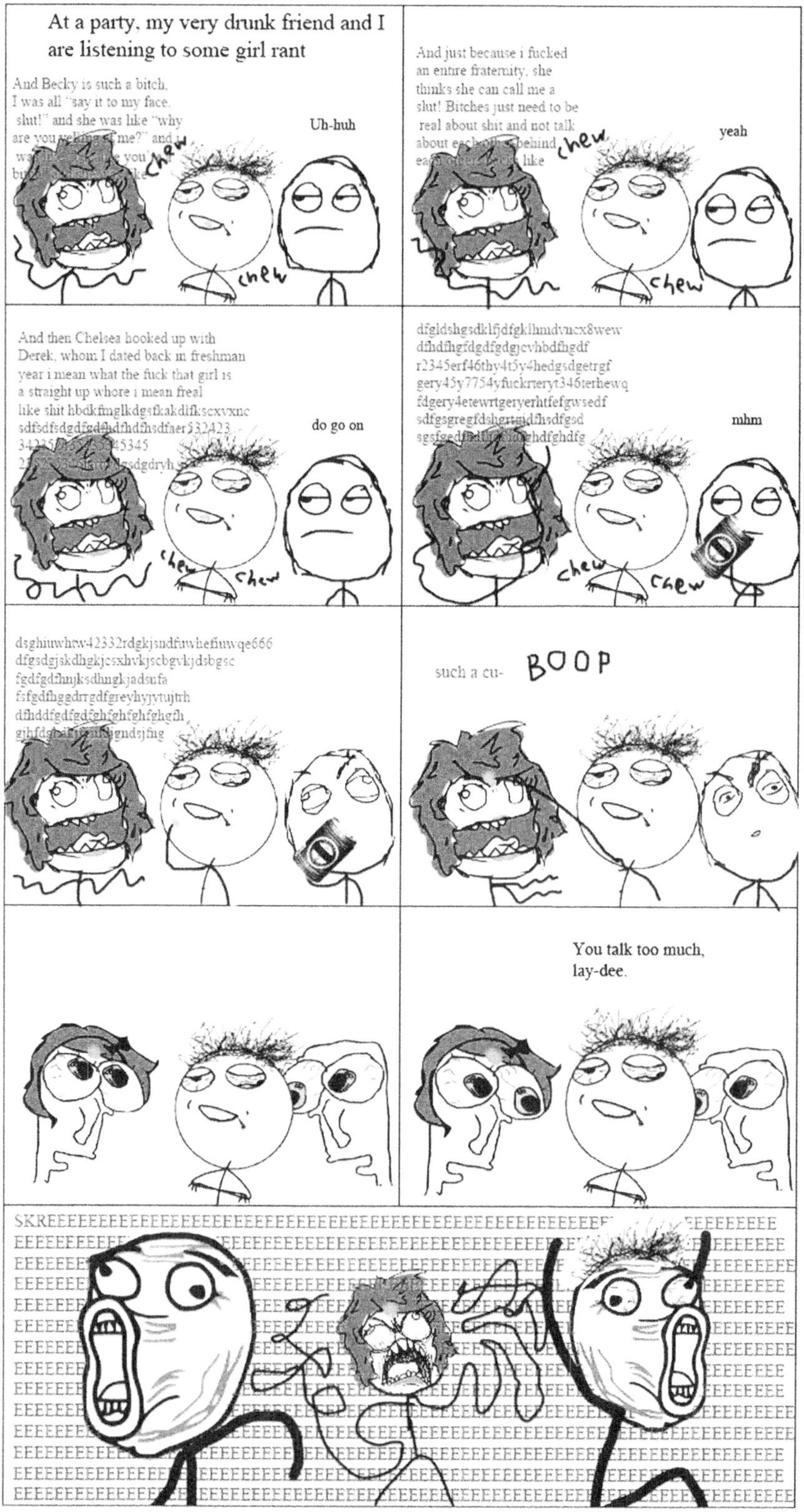

At a party, my very drunk friend and I are listening to some girl rant
And Becky is such a bitch, I was all "say it to my face, slut!" and she was like "why
chew
Uh-huh
chew
And just because i fucked an entire fraternity, she thinks she can call me a slut! Bitches just need to be real about shit and not talk
chew
yeah
chew
And then Chelsea hooked up with Derek, whom I dated back in freshman year i mean what the fuck that girl is a straight up whore i mean freal like shit hbdkfmglkdgsfkakdlfkscxvxnc
do go on
chew
chew
dfgldshgsdklfjdfgklhmdvncx8wew
dfhdfhgfdgdfgdgjcvhbdfhgdf
r2345erf46thy4t5y4hedgsdgetrgf
gery45y7754yfuckrteryt346terhewq
fdgery4etewrtgeryerhtfefgwsedf
mhm
chew
chew
dsghiuwhrw42332rdgkjsndfuwhefiuwqe666
dfgsdgjskdhgkjcsxhvkjscbgvkjdsbgsc
fgdfgdfhnjksdhngkjadsnfa
fsfgdfhggdrrgdfgreyhyjytujtrh
dfhddfgdfgdfghfghfghfghgfh
such a cu-
BOOP
You talk too much, lay-dee.
SKREEEEEEEEEEEEEEEEEEEEEEEEEEEEEEEEEEEEEEEEEEEEEEEEEEE

At the doctors office*

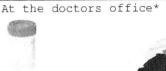

Nurse*

alright Mr derp, as a standard procedure we're going to need a urine sample from you

CHALLENGE ACCEPTED

In le bathroom*

FAP
FIP
FAP
FAP

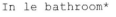

Here you go!

Mr Derp... I...I needed a urine sample...not a sample of your semen

Oh.. heh heh...

BAD POKER FACE

SHIT.

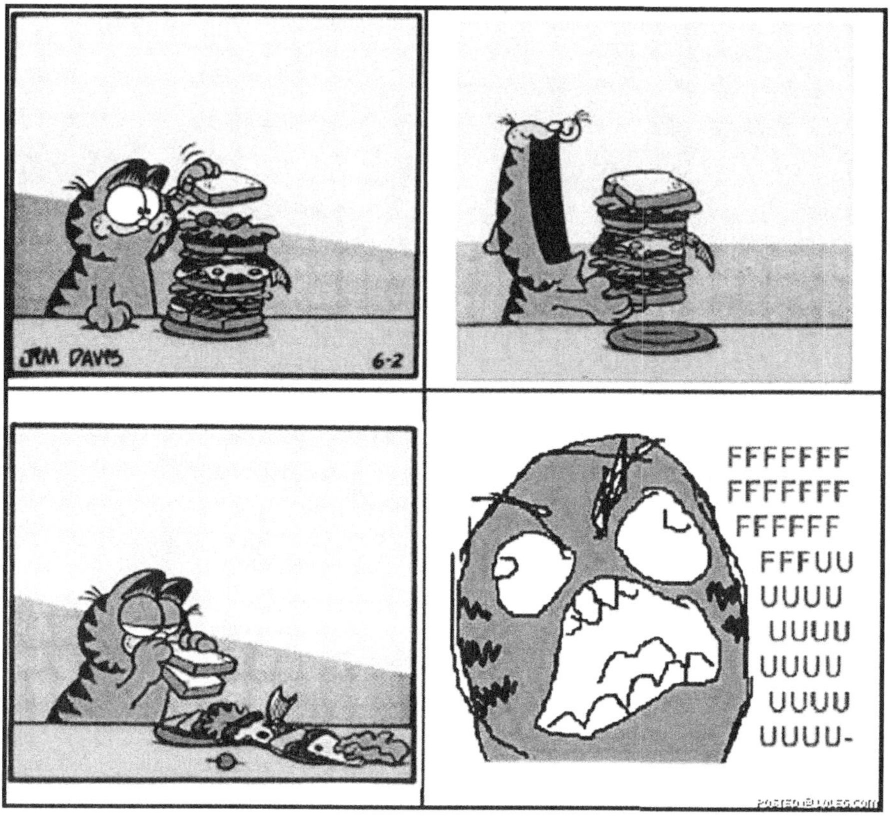
JIM DAVIS
6-2
FFFFFFF
FFFFFFF
FFFFFF
FFFUU
UUUU
UUUU
UUUU
UUUU
UUUU-

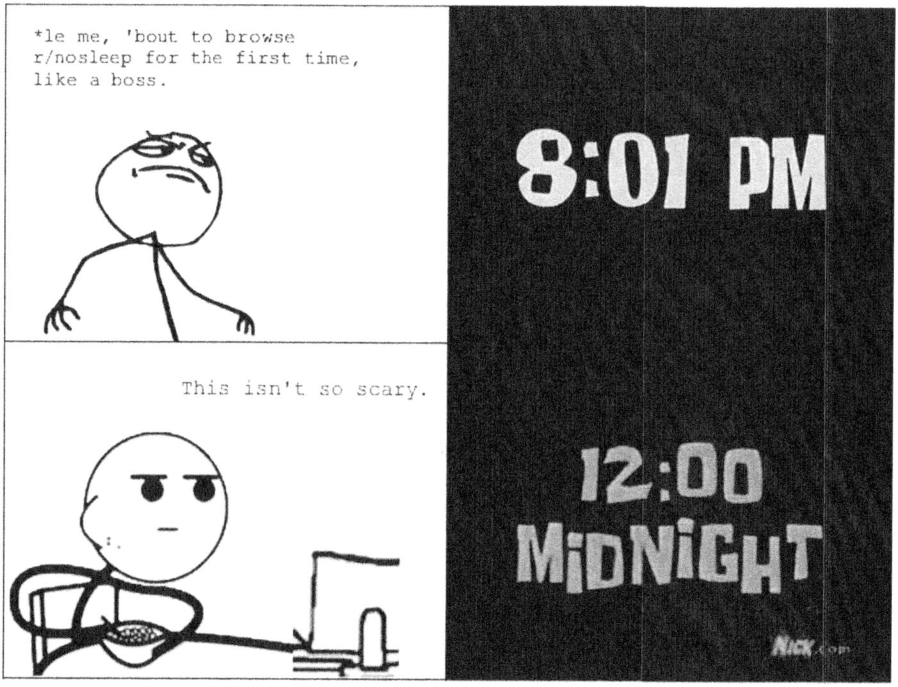
*le me, 'bout to browse r/nosleep for the first time, like a boss.
8:01 PM
This isn't so scary.
12:00 MIDNIGHT

→

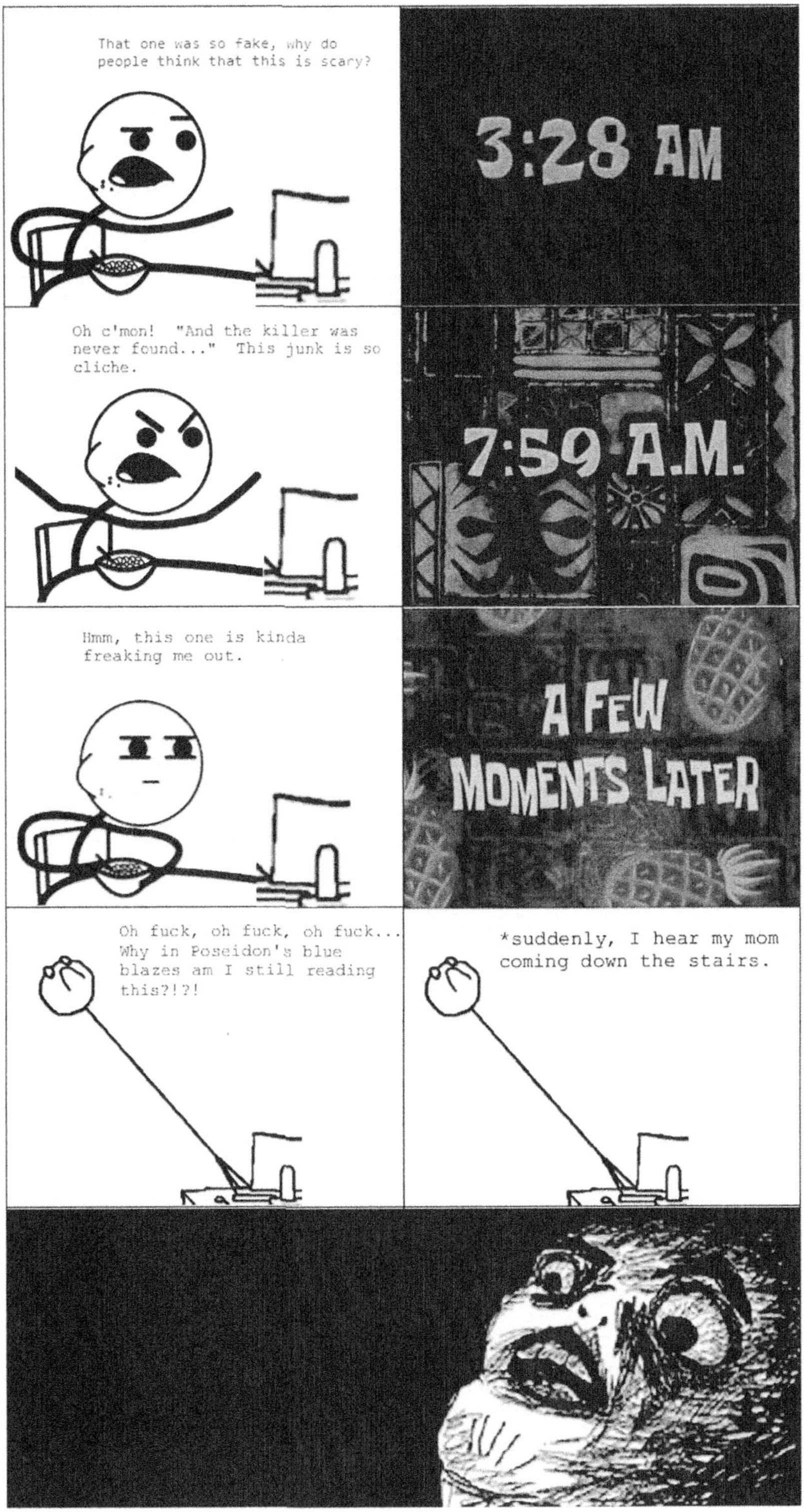
That one was so fake, why do people think that this is scary?
3:28 AM
Oh c'mon! "And the killer was never found..." This junk is so cliche.
7:59 A.M.
Hmm, this one is kinda freaking me out.
A FEW MOMENTS LATER
Oh fuck, oh fuck, oh fuck... Why in Poseidon's blue blazes am I still reading this?!?!
*suddenly, I hear my mom coming down the stairs.

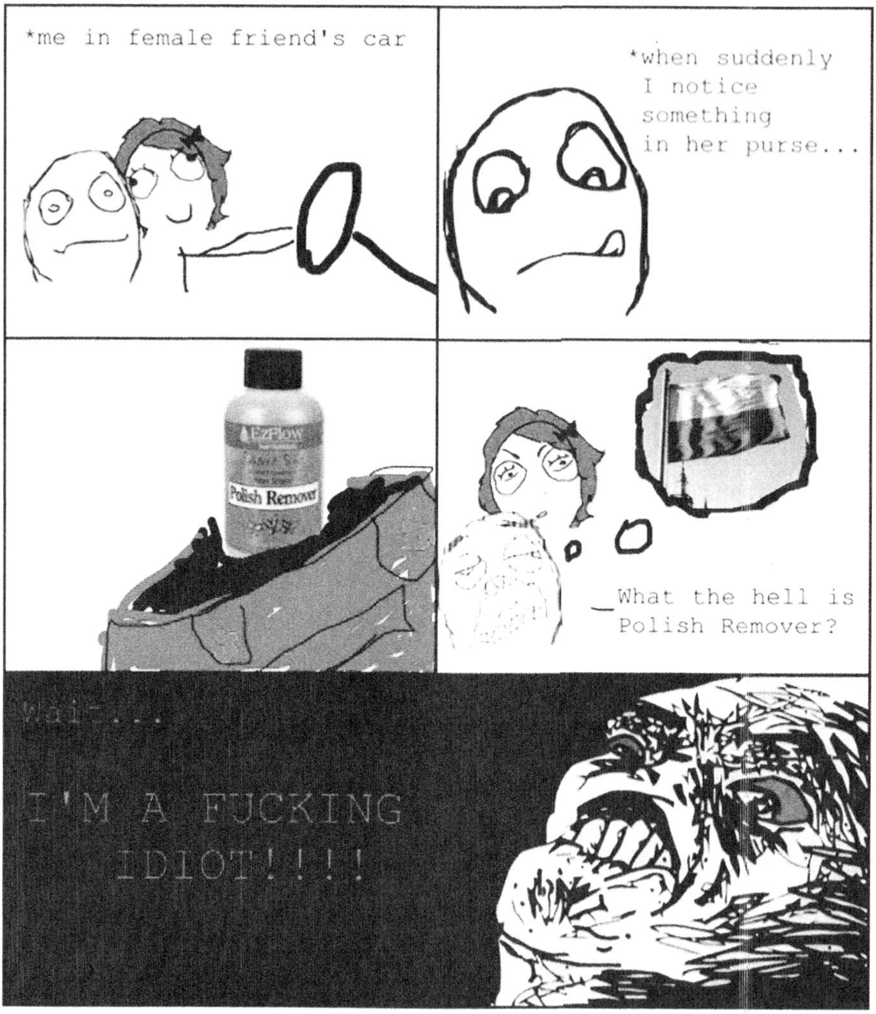
*me in female friend's car
*when suddenly I notice something in her purse...
Polish Remover
What the hell is Polish Remover?
I'M A FUCKING IDIOT!!!!

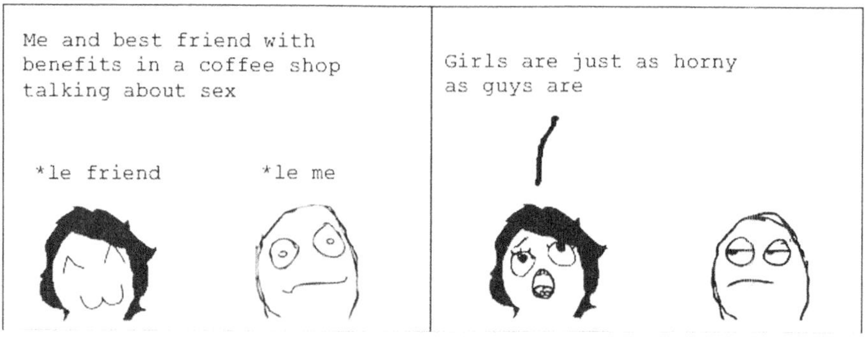
Me and best friend with benefits in a coffee shop talking about sex
*le friend
*le me
Girls are just as horny as guys are

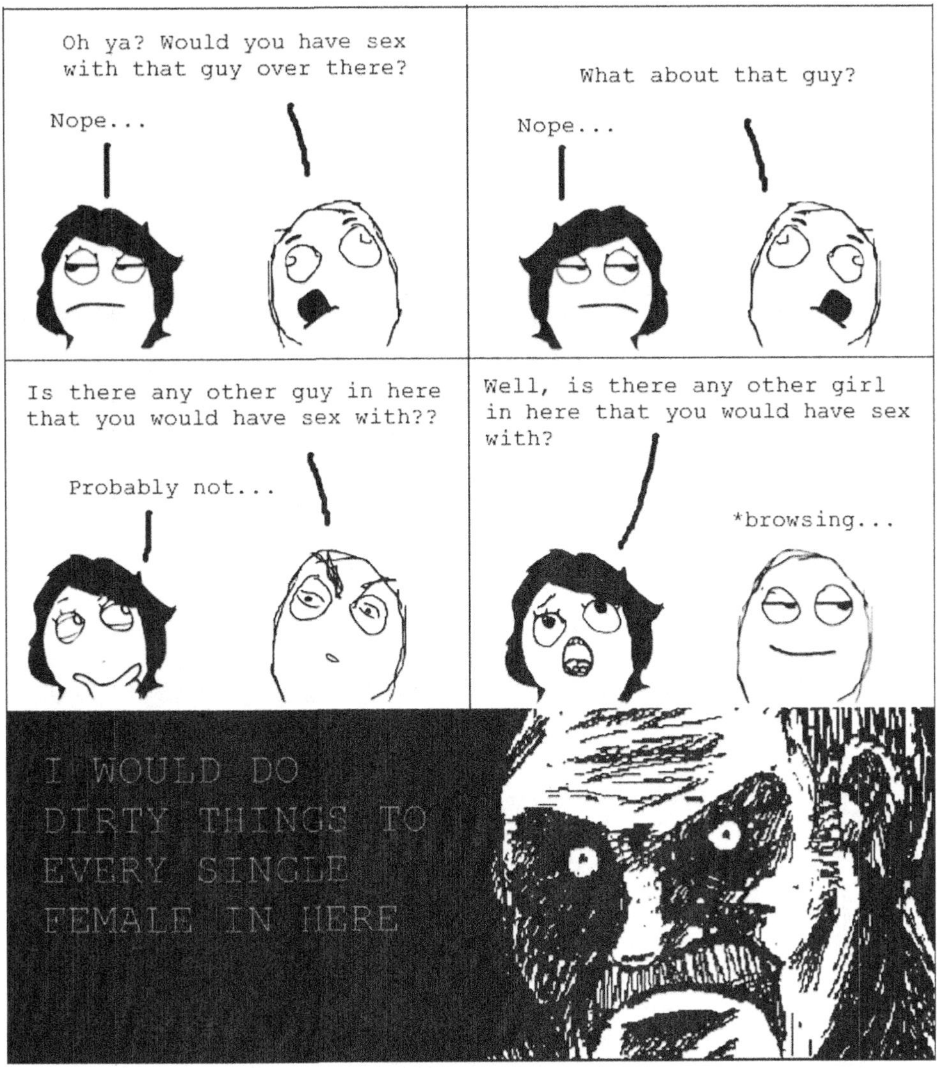
Oh ya? Would you have sex with that guy over there?
Nope...
What about that guy?
Nope...
Is there any other guy in here that you would have sex with??
Probably not...
Well, is there any other girl in here that you would have sex with?
*browsing...
I WOULD DO DIRTY THINGS TO EVERY SINGLE FEMALE IN HERE

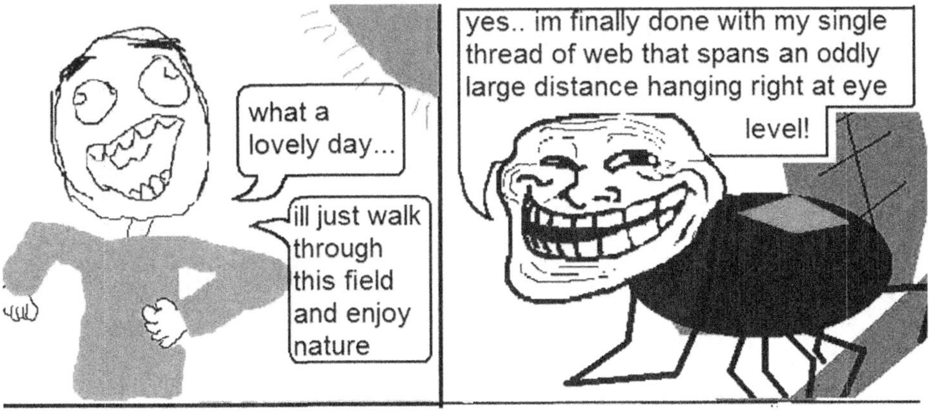
what a lovely day...
ill just walk through this field and enjoy nature
yes.. im finally done with my single thread of web that spans an oddly large distance hanging right at eye level!

→

FFFFFFF
FFFFFFF
FFFFFF
FFFUU
UUUU
UUUU
UUUU
UUUU
UUUU-

Okay class today we'll be watching a movie,

let's turn the lights off so you can see better!

alright! lights off!

maybe i can catch in some zz's

But professor!
I won't be able to write notes in the dark!

FUCKING MELVINA!

FFFFFF
FFFFFF
FFFFFF
FFFUU
UUUU
UUUU
UUUU
UUUU
UUUU-

September 21st, I'm chillin in class not really paying attention.

So class, does anyone know what today is?

128. ➔

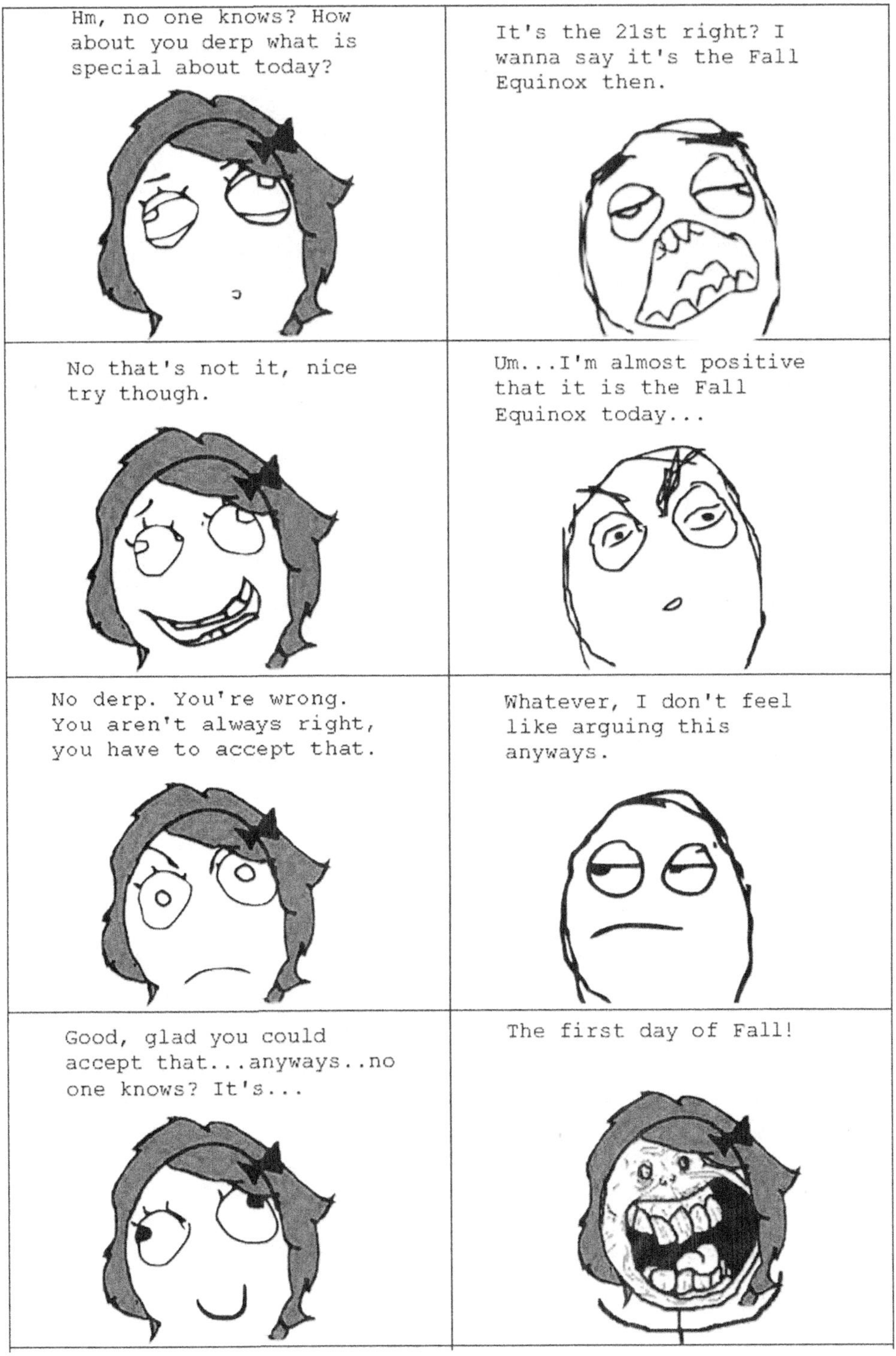

Hm, no one knows? How about you derp what is special about today?
It's the 21st right? I wanna say it's the Fall Equinox then.
No that's not it, nice try though.
Um...I'm almost positive that it is the Fall Equinox today...
No derp. You're wrong. You aren't always right, you have to accept that.
Whatever, I don't feel like arguing this anyways.
Good, glad you could accept that...anyways..no one knows? It's...
The first day of Fall!

→

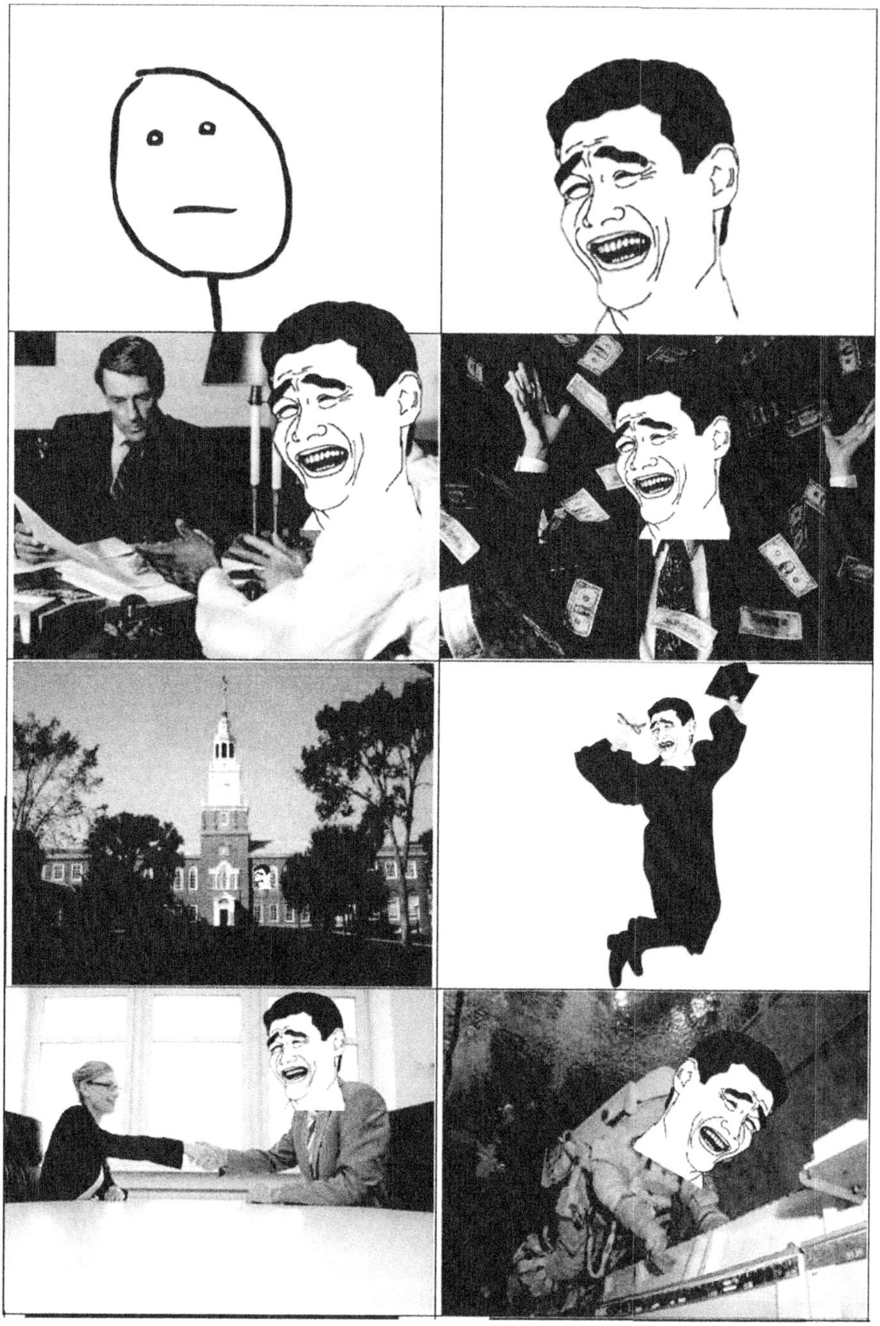

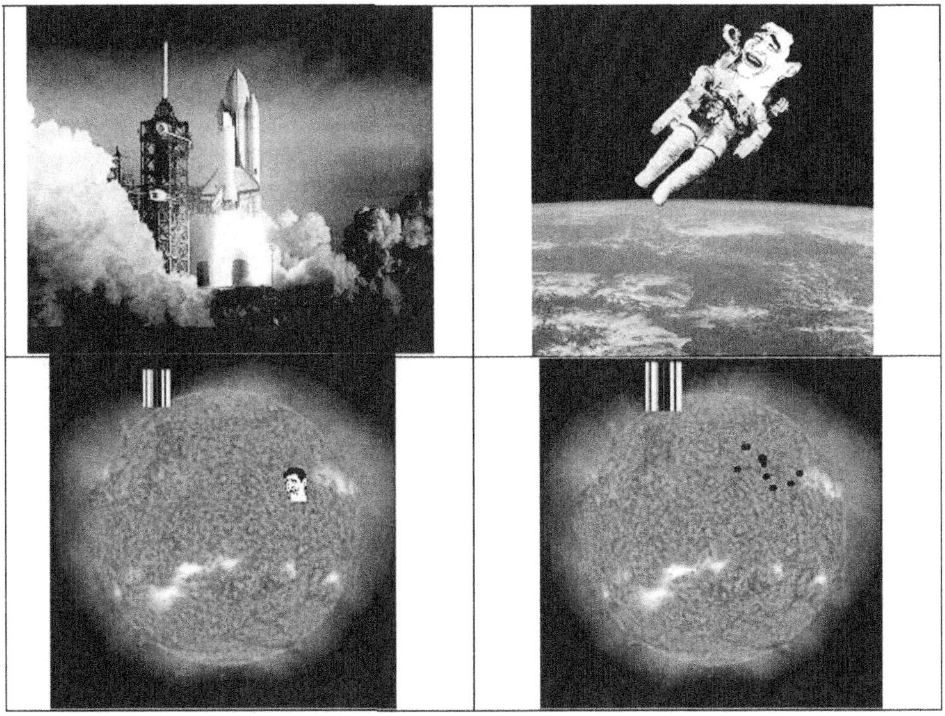

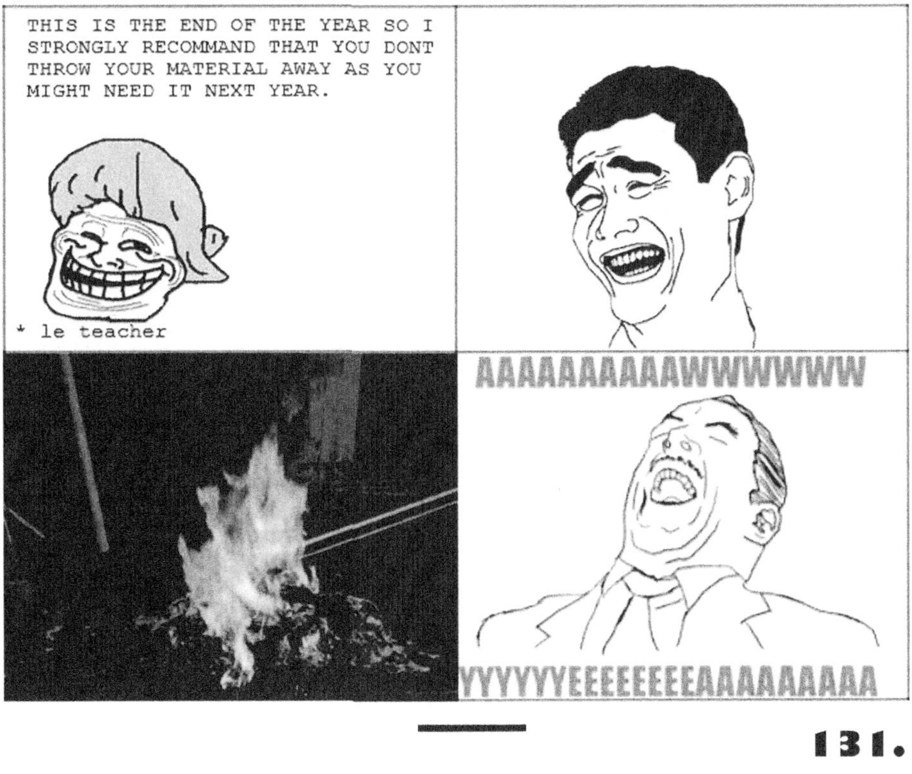
THIS IS THE END OF THE YEAR SO I STRONGLY RECOMMAND THAT YOU DONT THROW YOUR MATERIAL AWAY AS YOU MIGHT NEED IT NEXT YEAR.
* le teacher
AAAAAAAAAAWWWWWW
YYYYYYEEEEEEEEAAAAAAAAA

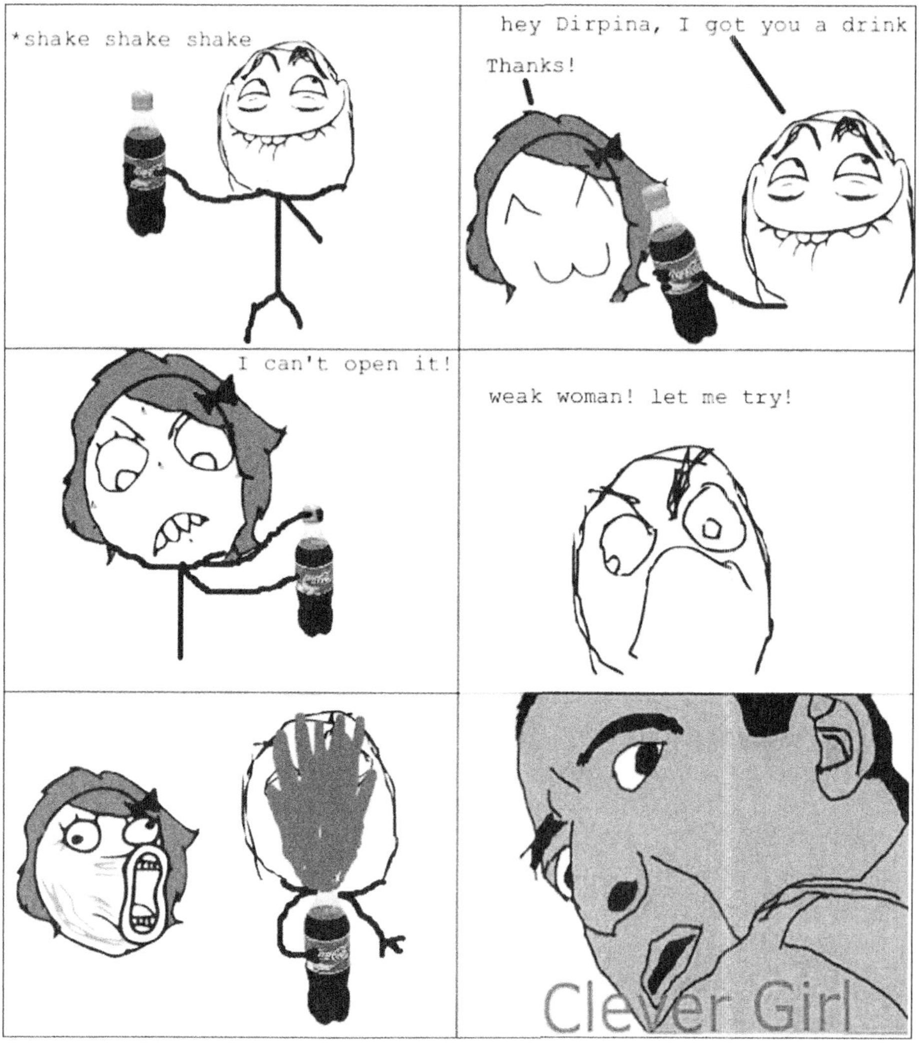
*shake shake shake
hey Dirpina, I got you a drink
Thanks!
I can't open it!
weak woman! let me try!
Clever Girl

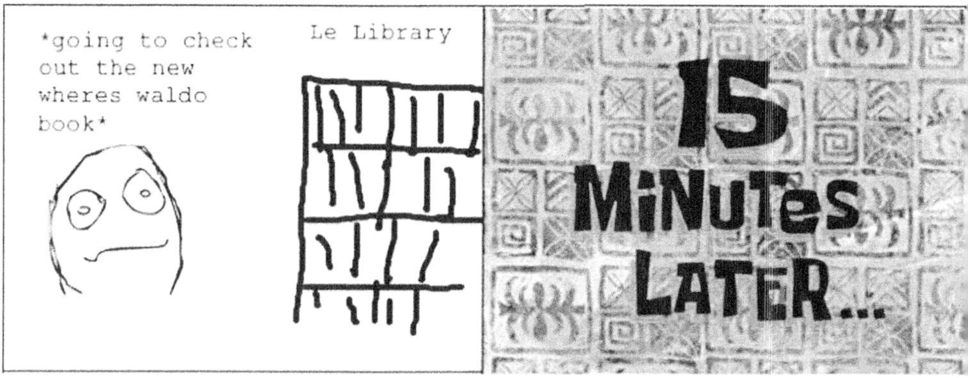
going to check out the new wheres waldo book
Le Library
15 MINUTES LATER...

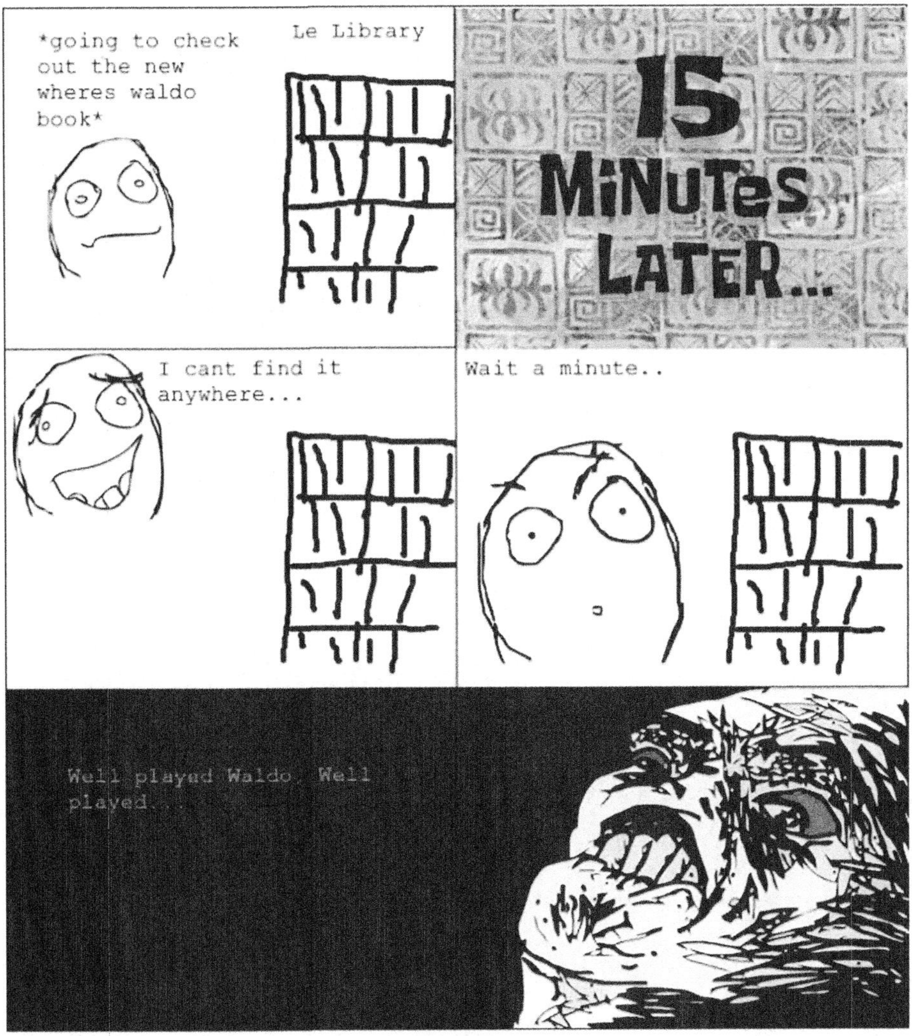

going to check out the new wheres waldo book
Le Library
15 MINUTES LATER...
I cant find it anywhere...
Wait a minute..
Well played Waldo. Well played...

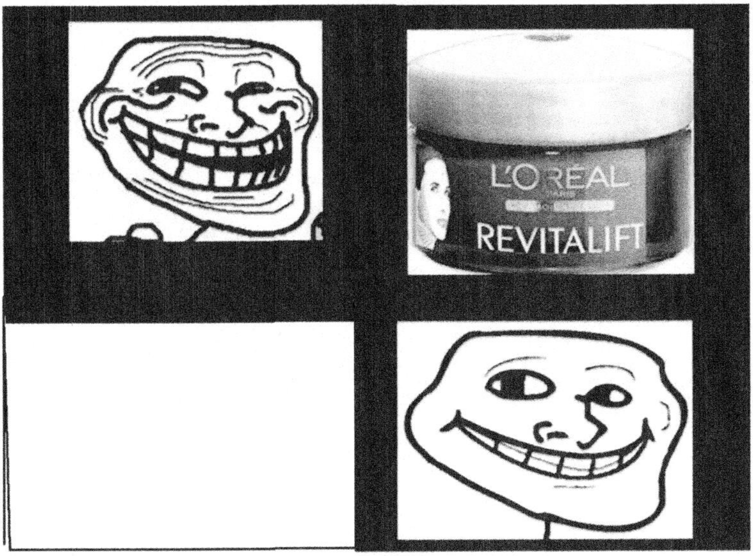

L'ORÉAL
REVITALIFT

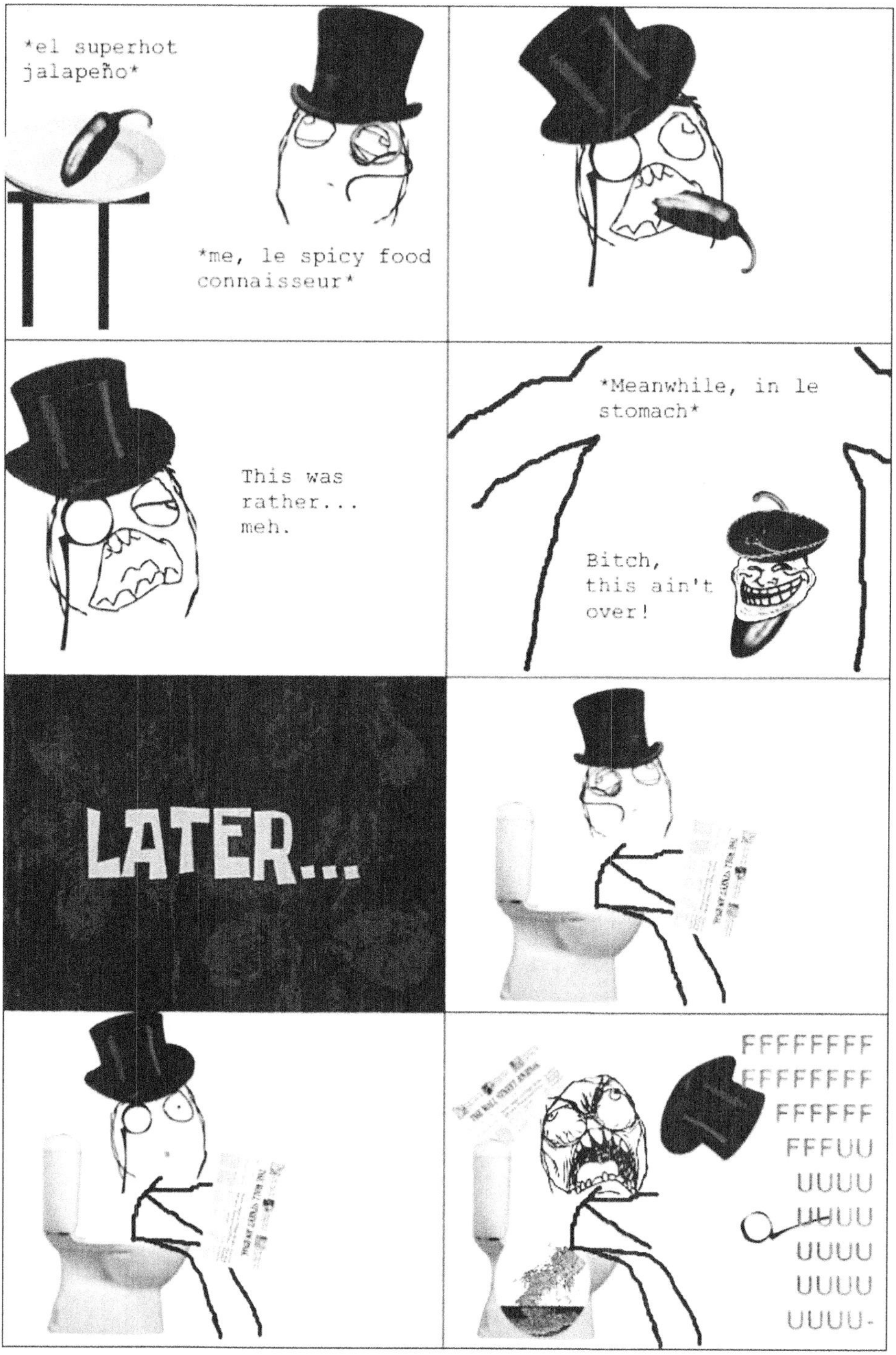
el superhot jalapeño
me, le spicy food connaisseur
This was rather... meh.
Meanwhile, in le stomach
Bitch, this ain't over!
LATER...
FFFFFFFF
FFFFFFFF
FFFFFF
FFFUU
UUUU
UUUU
UUUU
UUUU
UUUU-

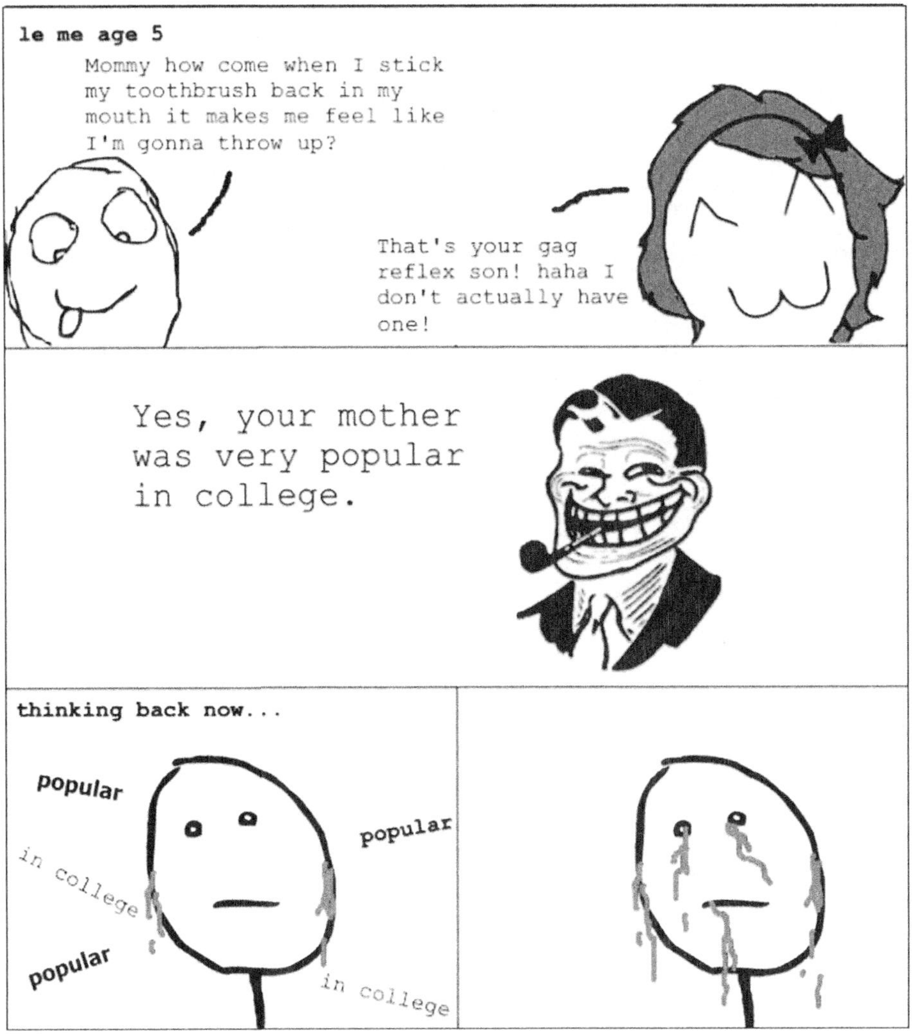

le me age 5
Mommy how come when I stick my toothbrush back in my mouth it makes me feel like I'm gonna throw up?
That's your gag reflex son! haha I don't actually have one!
Yes, your mother was very popular in college.
thinking back now...
popular
popular
in college
popular
in college

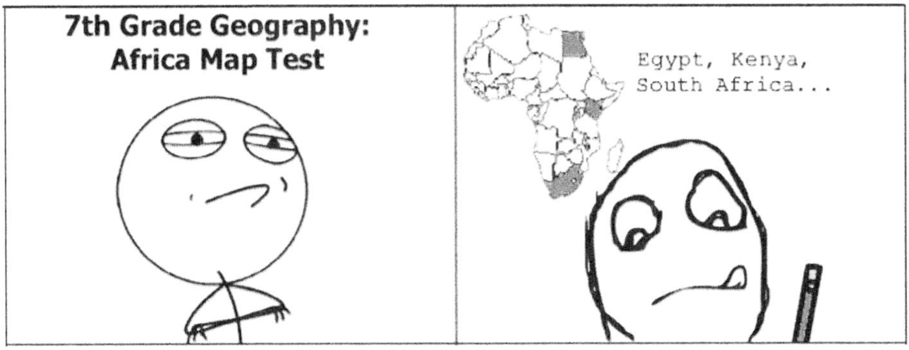

7th Grade Geography: Africa Map Test
Egypt, Kenya, South Africa...

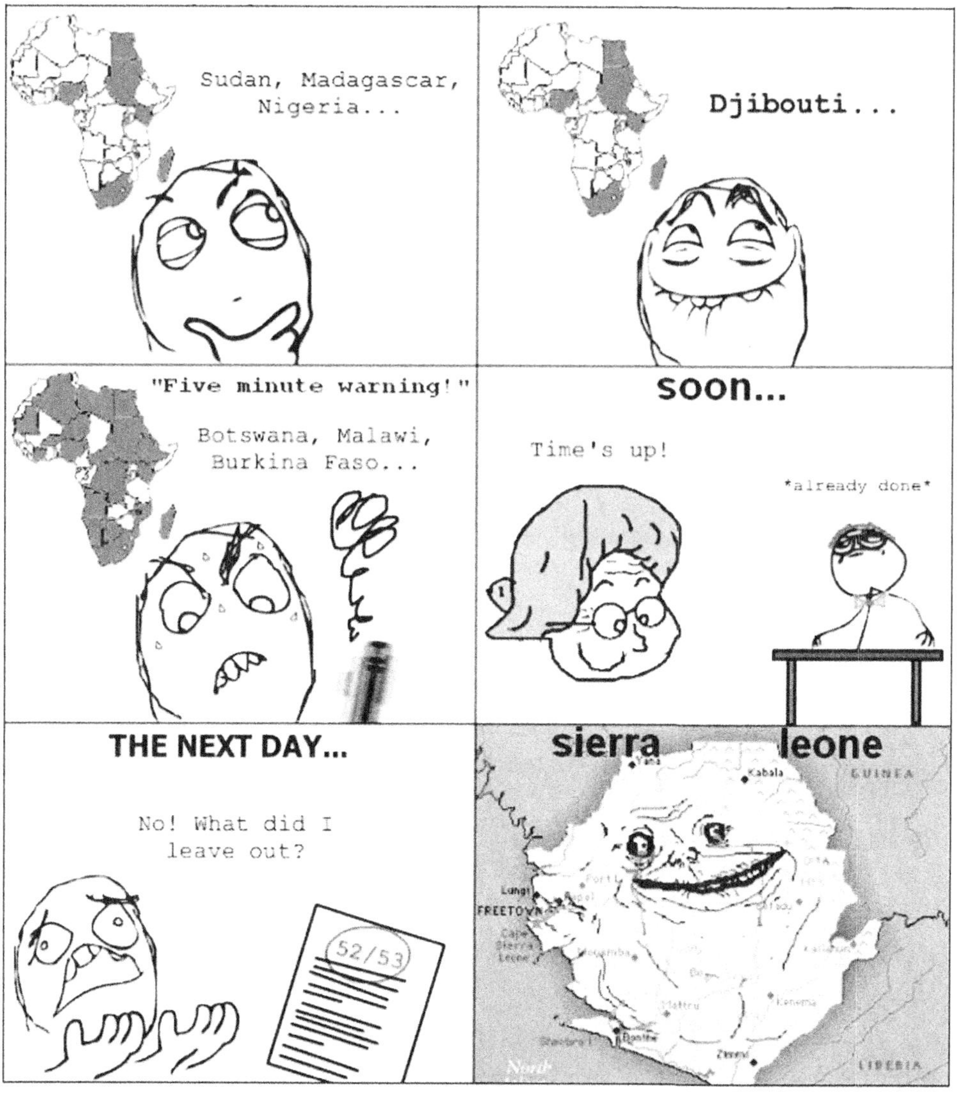
Sudan, Madagascar, Nigeria...
Djibouti...
"Five minute warning!"
Botswana, Malawi, Burkina Faso...
soon...
Time's up!
already done
THE NEXT DAY...
No! What did I leave out?
52/53
sierra leone

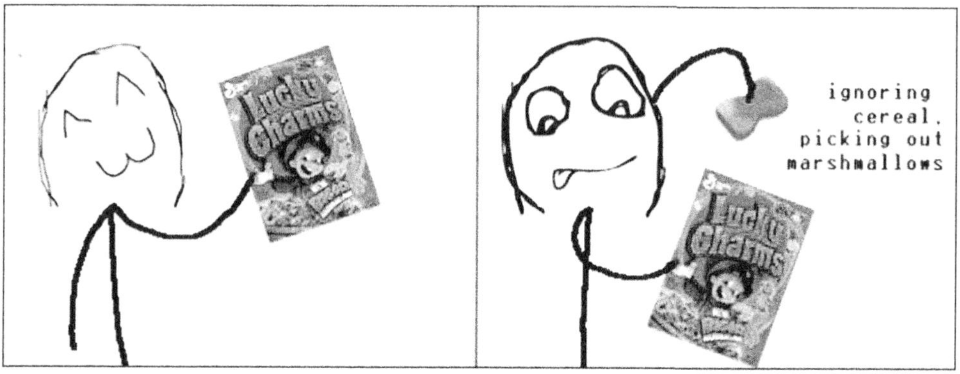
ignoring cereal, picking out marshmallows

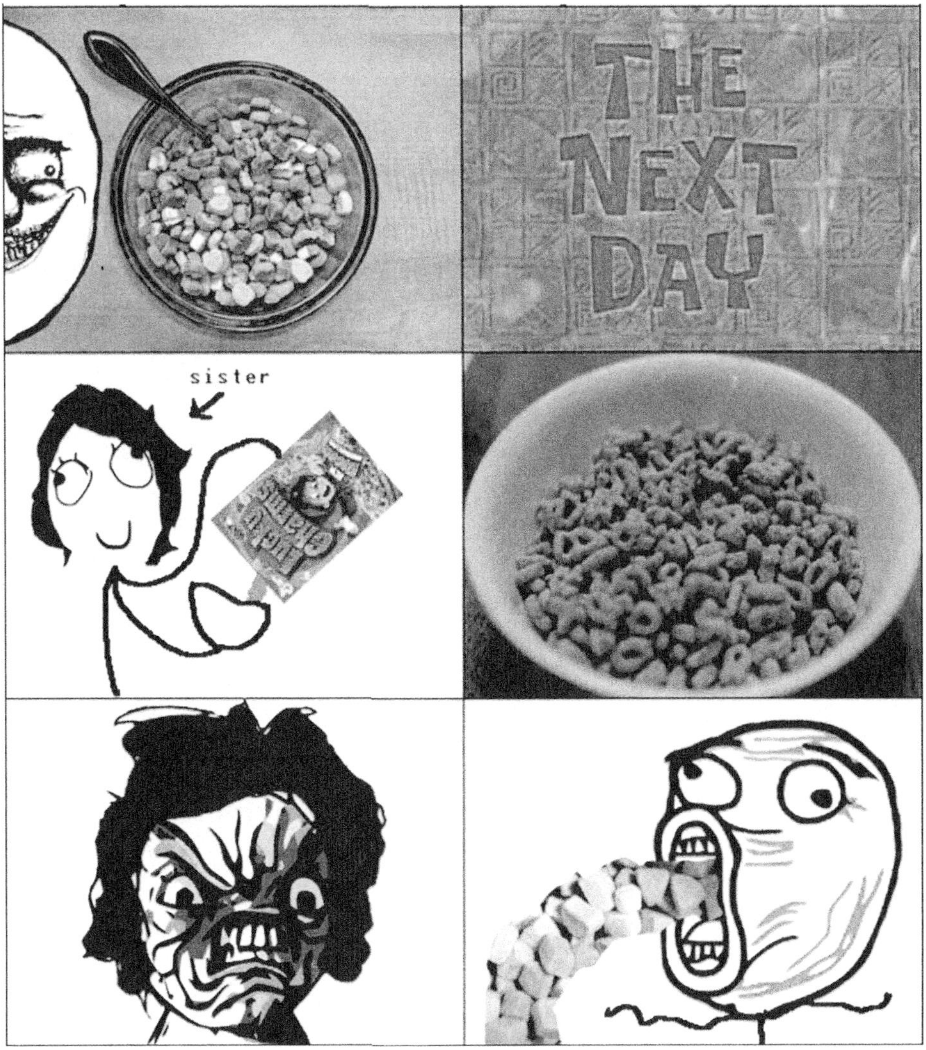
THE NEXT DAY
sister

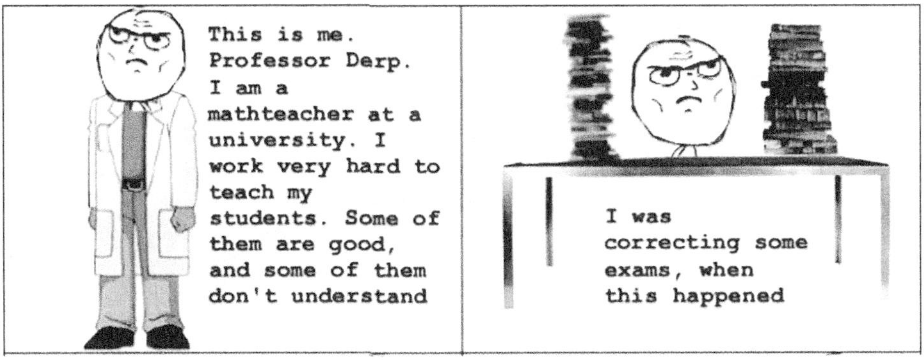
This is me. Professor Derp. I am a mathteacher at a university. I work very hard to teach my students. Some of them are good, and some of them don't understand
I was correcting some exams, when this happened

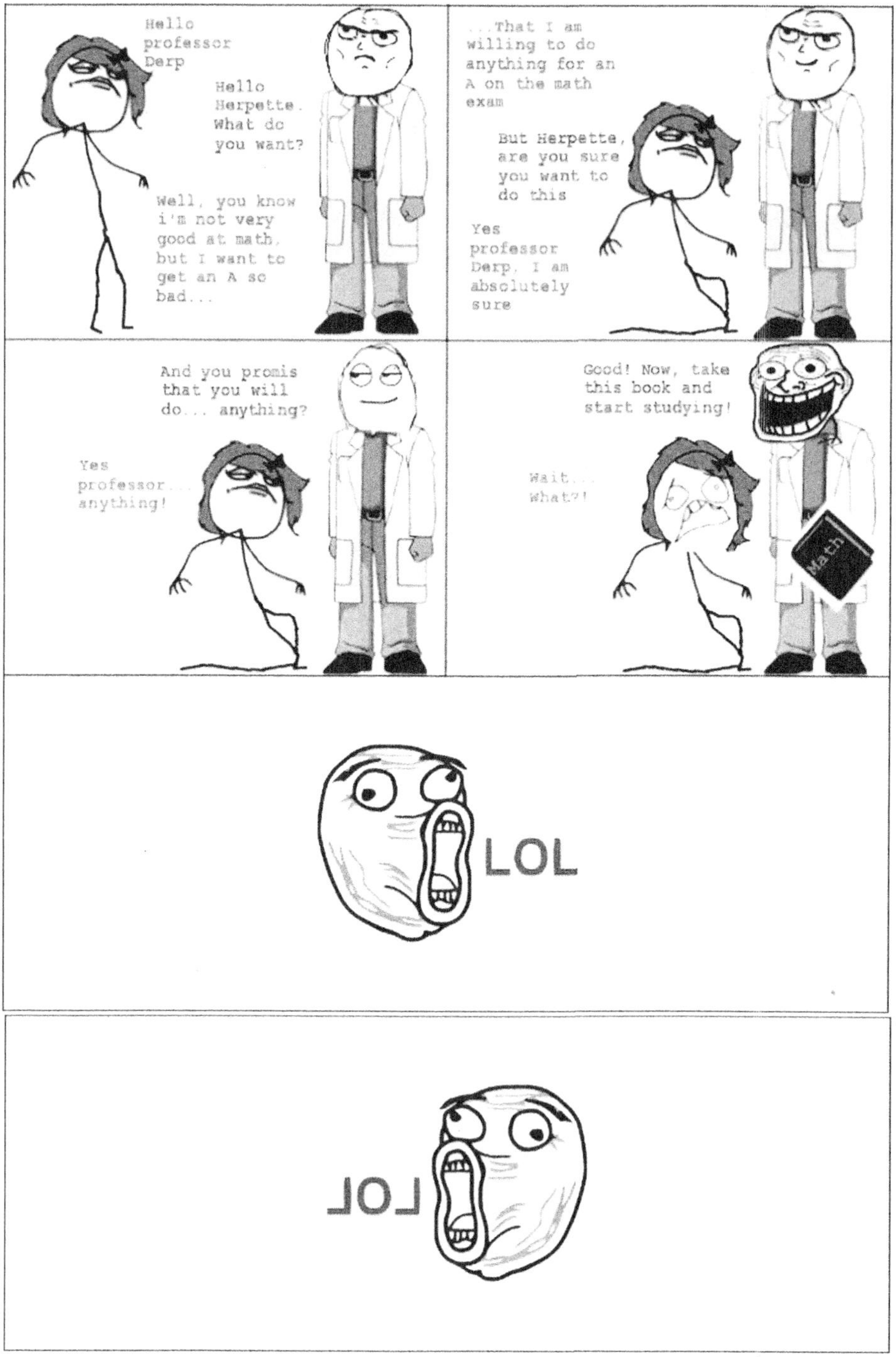
Hello professor Derp
Hello Herpette. What do you want?
Well, you know i'm not very good at math, but I want to get an A so bad...
...That I am willing to do anything for an A on the math exam
But Herpette, are you sure you want to do this
Yes professor Derp. I am absolutely sure
And you promis that you will do... anything?
Yes professor... anything!
Good! Now, take this book and start studying!
Wait... What?!
Math
LOL
LOL

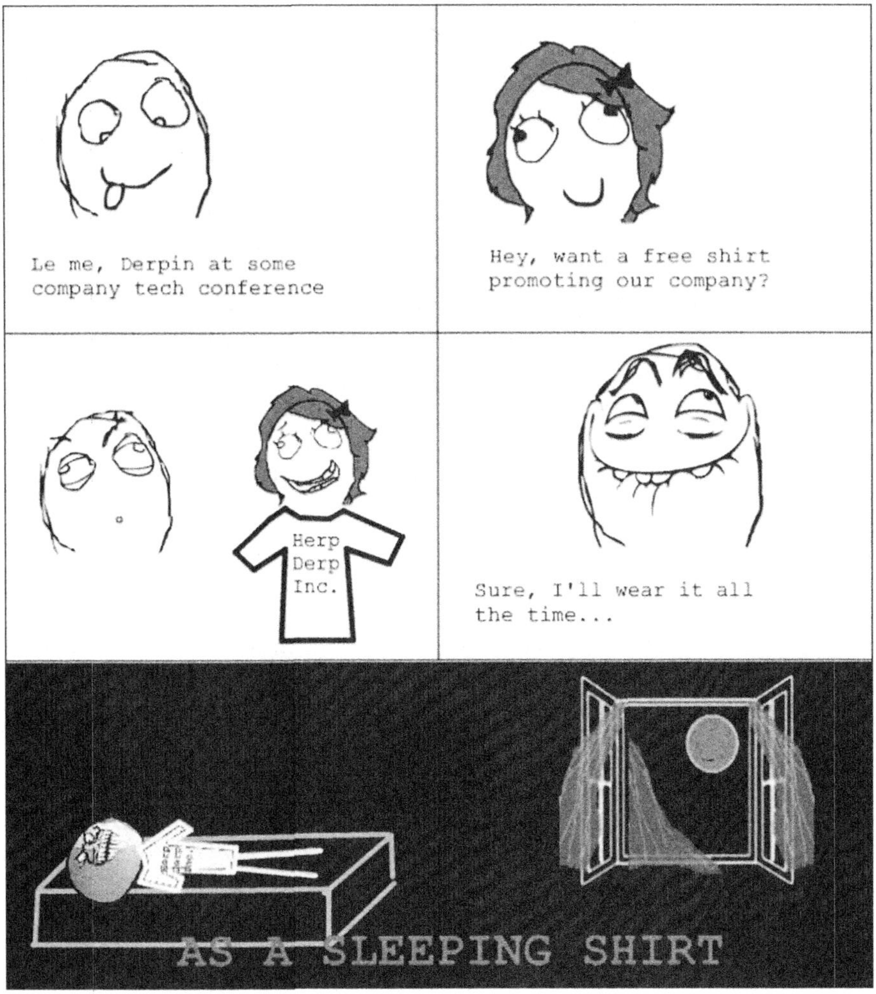
Le me, Derpin at some company tech conference
Hey, want a free shirt promoting our company?
Herp Derp Inc.
Sure, I'll wear it all the time...
AS A SLEEPING SHIRT

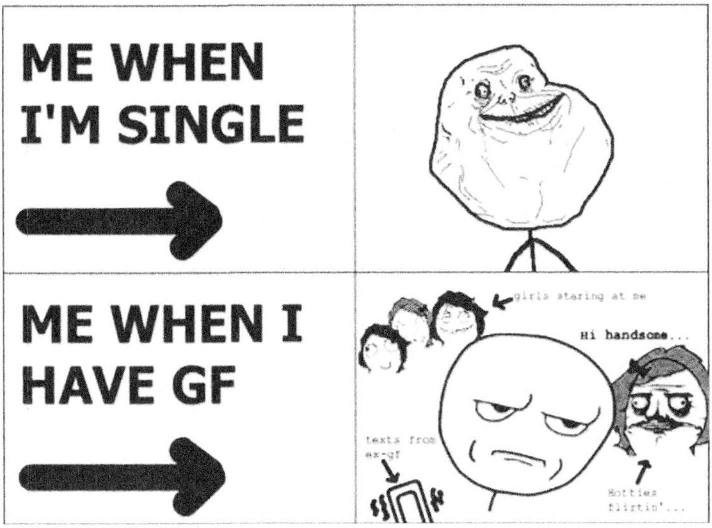
ME WHEN I'M SINGLE
ME WHEN I HAVE GF
girls staring at me
Hi handsome...
texts from ex-gf
Hotties flirtin'...

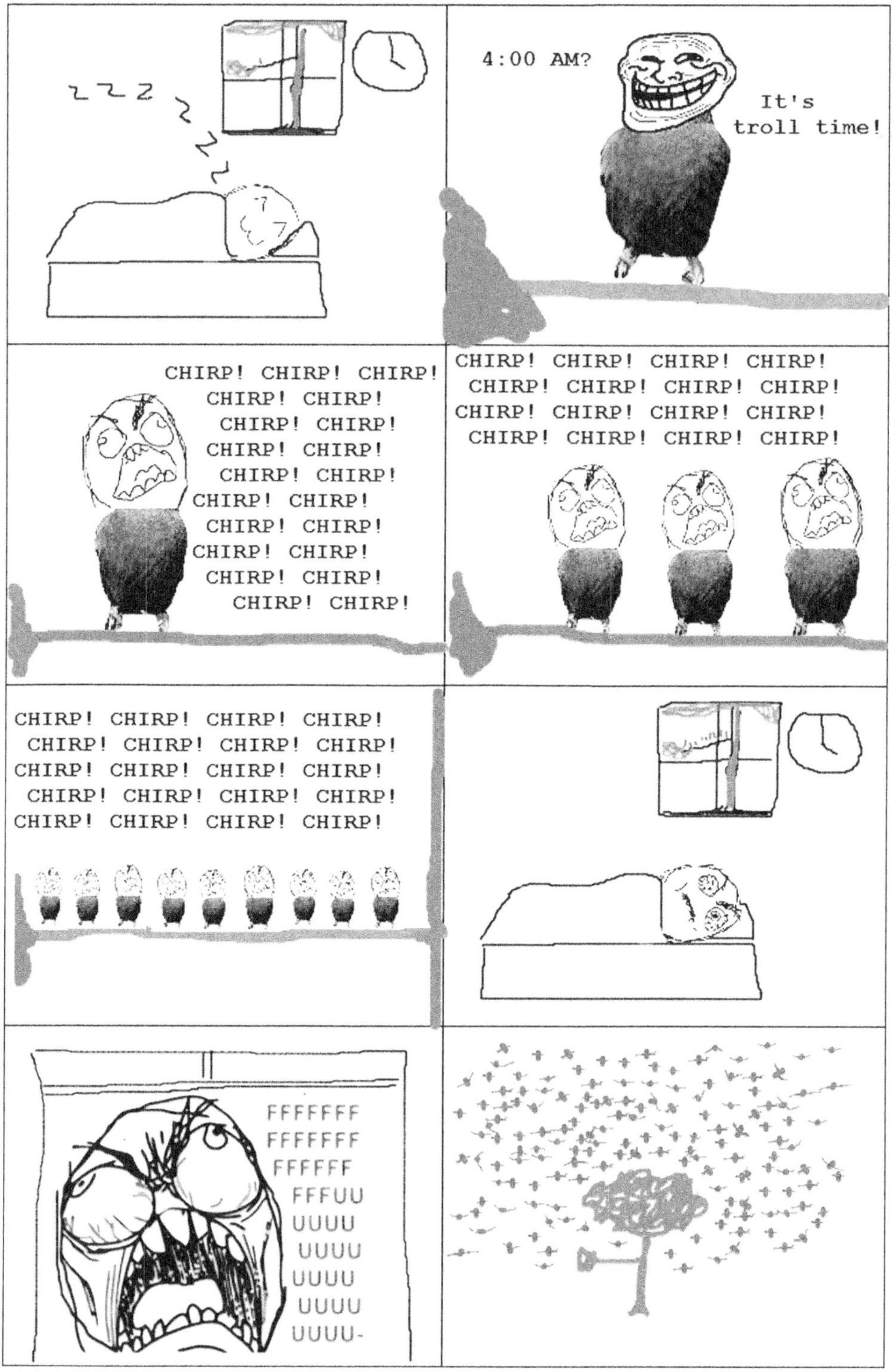
z z z
z z z
4:00 AM?
It's troll time!
CHIRP! CHIRP! CHIRP! CHIRP! CHIRP! CHIRP! CHIRP! CHIRP! CHIRP! CHIRP! CHIRP! CHIRP! CHIRP! CHIRP! CHIRP! CHIRP! CHIRP! CHIRP! CHIRP!
CHIRP! CHIRP! CHIRP! CHIRP! CHIRP! CHIRP! CHIRP! CHIRP! CHIRP! CHIRP! CHIRP! CHIRP! CHIRP! CHIRP! CHIRP! CHIRP!
CHIRP! CHIRP! CHIRP! CHIRP! CHIRP! CHIRP! CHIRP! CHIRP! CHIRP! CHIRP! CHIRP! CHIRP! CHIRP! CHIRP! CHIRP! CHIRP! CHIRP! CHIRP! CHIRP! CHIRP!
FFFFFFF FFFFFFF FFFFFF FFFUU UUUU UUUU UUUU UUUU UUUU-

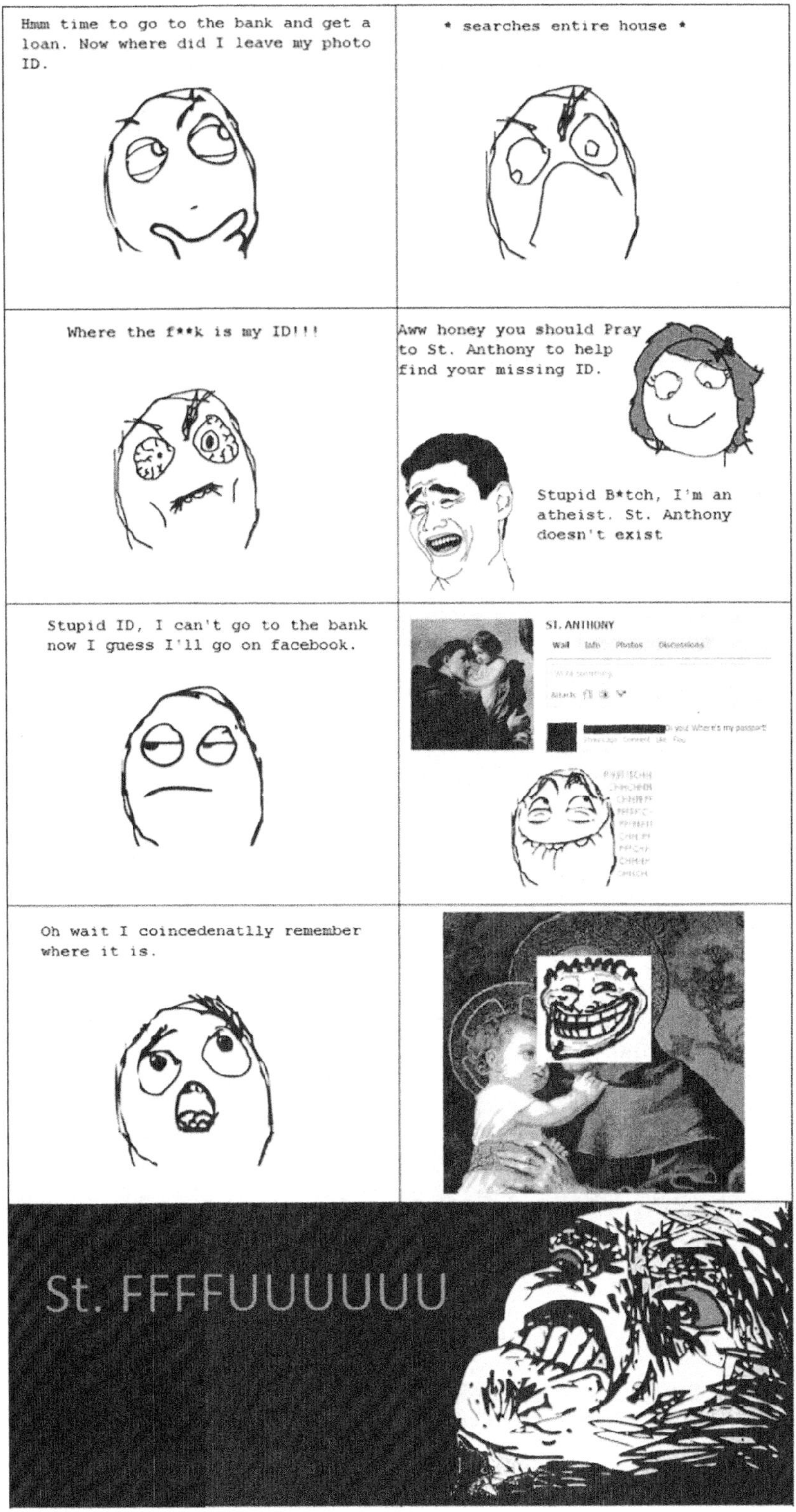

Hmm time to go to the bank and get a loan. Now where did I leave my photo ID.
* searches entire house *
Where the f**k is my ID!!!
Aww honey you should Pray to St. Anthony to help find your missing ID.
Stupid B*tch, I'm an atheist. St. Anthony doesn't exist
Stupid ID, I can't go to the bank now I guess I'll go on facebook.
ST. ANTHONY
Oh wait I coincedenatlly remember where it is.
St. FFFFUUUUUU

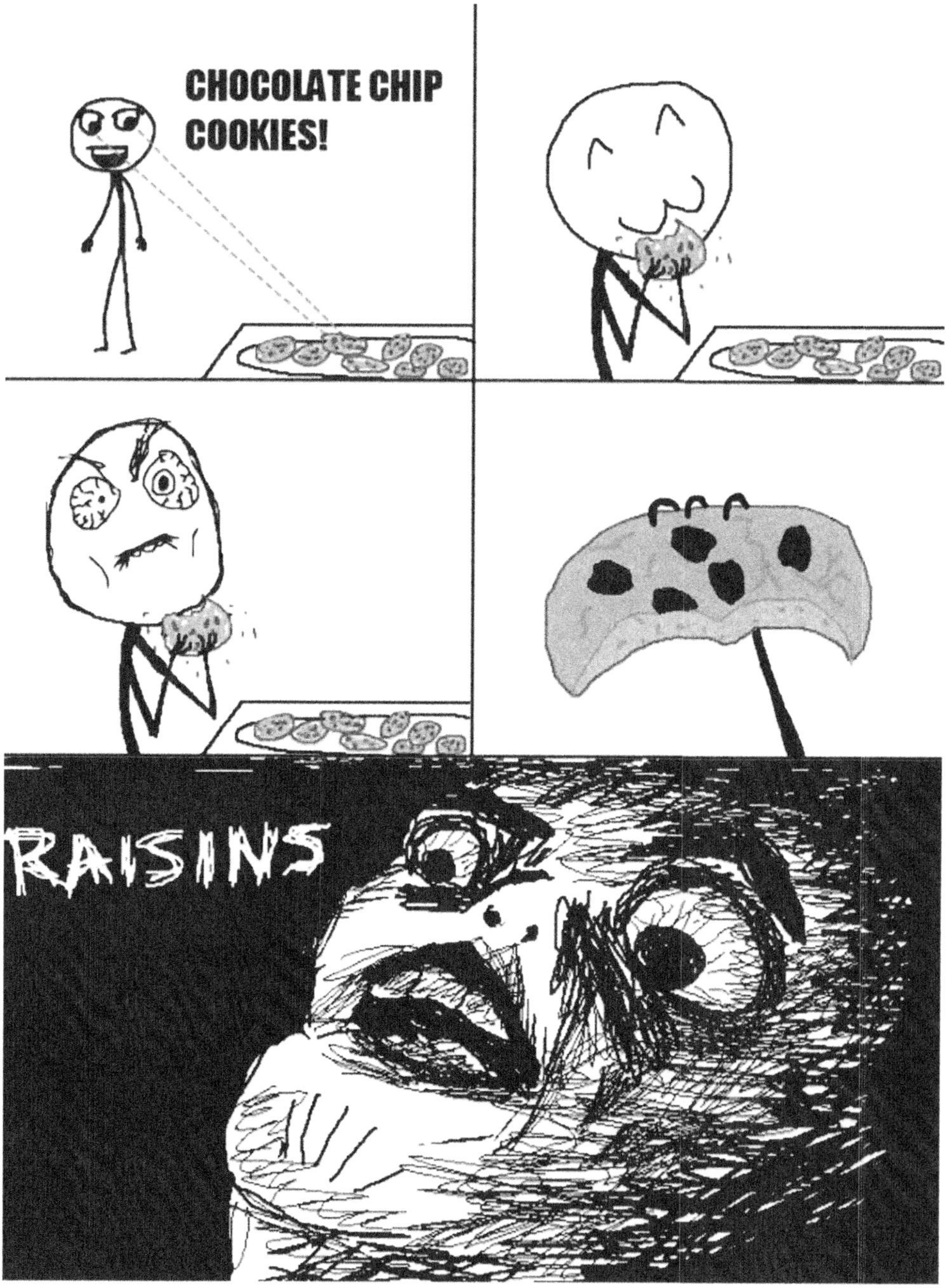
CHOCOLATE CHIP
COOKIES!
RAISINS

142.

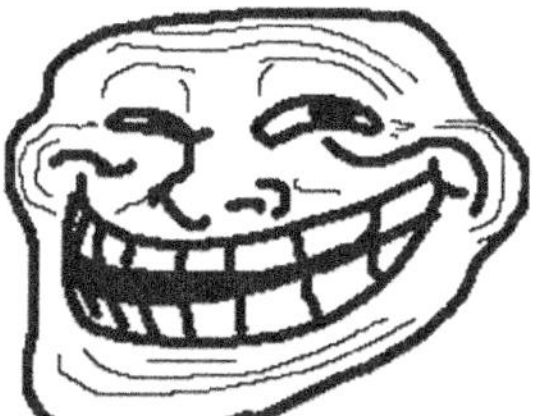

join the community!

reddit.com
rage-comics.net
leragecomics.com
ragecomicarchive.com
ragecollection.com
fffuuucomic.com

Printed in Great Britain
by Amazon

22353382R00086